THRESHOLD

Cambridge Pre-GED Program
in
Science

Donna Stelluto

CAMBRIDGE Adult Education
PRENTICE HALL CAREER & TECHNOLOGY
Englewood Cliffs, New Jersey 07632

Library of Congress Cataloging-in-Publication Data

Stelluto, Donna.
    Threshold : Cambridge pre-GED program in science / Donna Stelluto.
      p.   cm.
    ISBN 0-13-116419-8 (pbk.)
    1. Science—Problems, exercises, etc.   2. General educational
development tests—Study guides.   I. Title.
Q182.S89   1992
507.6—dc20   91–16685
                                                  CIP

Publisher: TINA B. CARVER
Executive Editor: JAMES W. BROWN
Editorial Supervisor: TIMOTHY A. FOOTE
Managing Editor: SYLVIA MOORE
Production Editor: JANET S. JOHNSTON
Pre-press Buyer: RAY KEATING
Manufacturing Buyer: LORI BULWIN
Scheduler: LESLIE COWARD
Interior designers: JANET SCHMID and JANET S. JOHNSTON
Cover coordinator: MARIANNE FRASCO
Cover designer: BRUCE KENSELAAR
Cover photo: JOHN PAUL ENDRESS / THE STOCK MARKET
Photo researcher: JULIE SCARDIGLIA
Permissions: ELLEN DIAMOND

 © 1992 by Prentice Hall Career & Technology
Prentice-Hall, Inc.
A Division of Simon & Schuster
Englewood Cliffs, New Jersey 07632

Printed in the United States of America

10   9   8   7   6

ISBN 0-13-116419-8

Prentice-Hall International (UK) Limited, *London*
Prentice-Hall of Australia Pty. Limited, *Sydney*
Prentice-Hall Canada, Inc., *Toronto*
Prentice-Hall Hispanoamericana, S.A., *Mexico*
Prentice-Hall of India Private Limited, *New Delhi*
Prentice-Hall of Japan, Inc., *Tokyo*
Simon & Schuster Asia Pte. Ltd., *Singapore*
Editora Prentice-Hall do Brasil, Ltda., *Rio de Janeiro*

CONTENTS

ACKNOWLEDGMENTS

CAMBRIDGE Adult Education thanks the men and women enrolled in ABE and Pre-GED courses who read parts of the *Threshold* manuscripts and offered valuable advice to the programs' authors and editors.

We also thank the following consultants for their many contributions throughout the preparation of the *Threshold* Pre-GED programs.

Cecily Kramer Bodnar
Consultant, Adult Learning
Adult Literacy Services
Central School District
Greece, New York

Pamela S. Buchanan
Instructor
Blue Ridge Job Corps Center
Marion, Virginia

Maureen Considine, M.A., M.S.
Learning Laboratory Supervisor   ABE/HSE Projects Coordinator
Great Neck Adult Learning Center   National Center for Disability Services
Great Neck, New York   Albertson, New York

Carole Deletiner
Instructor
Hunter College
New York, New York

Patricia Giglio
Remedial Reading Teacher
Johnstown ASACTC
Johnstown, New York

Diane Marinelli Hardison, M.S. Ed.
Mathematics Educator
San Diego, California

Margaret Banker Tinzmann, Ph. D.
Program Associate
The North Central Regional Educational Laboratory
Oak Brook, Illinois

INTRODUCTION

The *Threshold* Pre-GED Programs

Threshold provides a full-range entry-level course for adults whose goal is to earn a high school equivalency diploma. The men and women who use the six *Threshold* programs will learn—and profit from an abundance of sound practice in applying—the writing, problem-solving, and critical-reading and -thinking skills they'll need when they take the GED tests. They will gain a firm grounding in knowledge about social studies and science and will read many excellent selections from the best of classical and contemporary literature. In short, *Threshold* offers adults the skills, knowledge, and practice that will enable them to approach GED-level test preparation with well-deserved confidence and solid ability.

The *Threshold* Science Program

The instruction in *Threshold: Cambridge Pre-GED Program in Science* is organized by a hierarchy of critical-reading and -thinking skills. Units 1 and 2 cover *comprehension* of both verbal and graphic materials: Unit 1 concentrates on literal comprehension, and Unit 2 on comprehension that involves making inferrences. Unit 3 teaches *application*—using information from verbal and graphic materials in new situations and in different contexts. Unit 4 covers *analysis* and *evaluation*, the skills that make a reader one who thinks critically.

All of the reading passages in the book explore topics in and related to biology, earth science, chemistry, and physics. Many of the passages present basic concepts in science. Others discuss a variety of contemporary issues related to science—issues in conservation, energy, the environment, health, medicine, and nutrition, among others. In each unit and throughout the book, several "content themes" develop. Early reading passages lay foundations helpful in understanding later passages. For example, one of Unit 1's themes develops through passages that address the following topics in this order: the structure and function of cells (Lessons 7 and 8); how viruses enter and reproduce in cells (Lesson 11); what the immune system is and how it works (Lesson 11); and how HIV, a virus, causes AIDS by destroying cells in the immune system (Lesson 11). The knowledge base developed by that content theme is useful in understanding passages that appear later in the book: passages about immunity and allergies (GED Practice 1), a passage about vaccines (Posttest), and others.

The science program's two streams of organization—critical reading and -thinking skills in a hierarchy, and content by thematic development—are thoroughly integrated throughout the book. They make *Threshold: Cambridge Pre-GED Program in Science* an intelligent first course in preparation for the science test of the GED.

TO THE STUDENT

You will profit in several important ways by using this book as you begin to prepare for the science test of the GED:

- You will improve your reading skills.
- You will expand your knowledge about the four main branches of science.
- You will gain experience in answering questions like those on the GED.
- You will become more confident of your abilities.

To Find Out About Your Current Reading Skills and Science Knowledge . . .

Take the PRETEST. When you have finished, refer to the ANSWERS AND EXPLANATIONS at the back of this book to check your answers. Then look at the CHARTS that follow the Pretest. They'll give you an idea about which parts of this book you need to concentrate on most.

To Improve Your Reading Skills and Expand Your Science Knowledge . . .

Study the LESSONS. They present instruction about reading skills and give examples that show how the various skills can be applied to passages about science. Some of the examples—called TRY THIS and NOW TRY THIS—let you apply the reading skills. Each lesson has one or more EXERCISES for you to practice your reading skills. They have questions about science passages on various topics.

Study the readings in the SCIENCE READINGS sections, too. They come right after the lessons in each unit. Each reading is about a different topic in science. The questions in each set of readings give you more practice with all the reading skills you will have studied up to that point in this book.

To Gain Experience in Answering Questions Like Those on the GED . . .

Take the GED PRACTICE at the end of each unit. The GED Practices are made up of passages and questions like the ones on the science test of the GED. They offer test-taking experience that you will find useful when you take the GED.

Before you finish with this book, take the POSTTEST. Like the four GED Practices, it is similar to the GED science test. Look at the CHARTS that follow the Posttest. If you compare your Pretest and Posttest performances, you will probably find that your skills and knowledge have improved as you have worked through this book. The charts can give you an idea about which parts of this book you should review.

Pretest

The following Pretest is similar to the Science Test of the GED. Taking it will help you find out what you need to study most in this book.

The Pretest has 33 multiple-choice items—half as many as there are on the GED. About half of the items are based on readings in biology. The rest are based on readings in the physical sciences—earth science, chemistry, and physics. The questions test your understanding of the readings and your ability to apply information and to think critically.

To begin preparing for the Science Test of the GED, take this Pretest. Work through it at a pace that is comfortable for you. You don't need to study anything before you take the Pretest. The information you need to answer the questions is given in the readings.

The three states of water: liquid (the lake), solid (the snow), and gaseous (in the air). Jackson Lake, Grand Teton Mountains, Wyoming.

SCIENCE PRETEST

Directions: Choose the <u>one best answer</u> to each item.

<u>Items 1 and 2</u> are based on the following paragraph.

Earth, the fifth largest planet, is the only planet known to support life. It is the third planet from the sun and revolves around it at an average distance of 93 million miles. The earth has a single natural satellite—the moon. Earth is covered by a blanket of air that is 78% nitrogen, 21% oxygen, and 1% other gases. Viewed from space, the earth can be identified by its blue waters and white clouds. Although our planet seems big to us, it is only a tiny speck in the universe.

1. What is the paragraph mainly about?

    (1) the sun
    (2) the universe
    (3) the planets
    (4) the earth
    (5) the moon

2. Which of the following is true about the earth?

    (1) It is the fifth planet from the sun.
    (2) It is the only planet known to have life.
    (3) It is about 93,000 miles from the sun.
    (4) It is surrounded by air that contains 78% oxygen.
    (5) It is the largest planet.

<u>Items 3 and 4</u> are based on the following paragraph.

There are about 4000 species of mammals. Humans, elephants, whales, and bats are all mammals, for example. Despite their many differences, all mammals have certain things in common. They are all warm-blooded, which means their body temperature stays the same regardless of their surroundings. Mammals have hair, lungs, and a four-chambered heart. Mammals feed their young with milk from the female's mammary glands.

3. Which of the following sentences from the paragraph states the main idea?

    (1) There are about 4000 species of mammals.
    (2) Humans, elephants, whales, and bats are all mammals, for example.
    (3) Despite their many differences, all mammals have certain things in common.
    (4) Mammals have hair, lungs, and a four-chambered heart.
    (5) Mammals feed their young with milk from the female's mammary glands.

4. In the paragraph, the details are organized to

    (1) show the order of the stages of a mammal's development
    (2) compare humans to other mammals
    (3) explain what causes a mammal's body temperature to stay the same
    (4) describe different kinds of mammals
    (5) list the characteristics of mammals

Items 5 and 6 are based on the following paragraph.

　　　　Animals migrate for two reasons. They migrate when they need a place to breed or spawn. For example, salmon return to fresh water to deposit eggs. Animals also move when their food supplies diminish. When the northern part of the United States begins to turn cold in fall, for example, many birds fly south to look for food.

5. What does <u>migrate</u> mean?

　　(1) produce offspring
　　(2) swim
　　(3) look for food
　　(4) eat
　　(5) move from one place to another

6. What does <u>diminish</u> mean?

　　(1) decrease
　　(2) increase
　　(3) supply
　　(4) turn cold
　　(5) warm up

Item 7 is based on the following graph.

　　　　The following graph shows that the pressure of a gas on the walls of its container changes as the temperature of the gas changes.

GAS PRESSURE RELATED TO TEMPERATURE

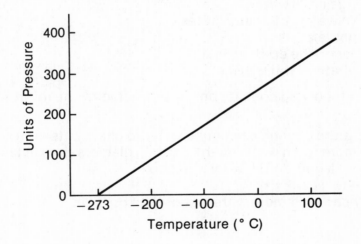

7. About how much pressure does a gas put on the walls of its container when the temperature of the gas is –100°C?

　　(1) 　0 units
　　(2) 100 units
　　(3) 175 units
　　(4) 250 units
　　(5) 350 units

Item 8 is based on the following passage.

The pupil is the black circle in the center of the iris, the colored part of the eye. Light enters the eye through the pupil. As light conditions change, muscles in the iris adjust the size of the pupil. In dim light, one set of muscles makes the pupil bigger. In bright light, another set of muscles makes the pupil smaller.

8. Why does the pupil become larger in dim light?

(1) to make the iris black
(2) to make the iris a circle
(3) to shut out all light
(4) to let in as much light as possible
(5) to let in as little light as possible

Items 9 and 10 are based on the following passage.

Most of the water on the earth is in the liquid state. All the large bodies of water on the planet—oceans, rivers, and lakes—are made of liquid water.

Water is ice, the solid state of water when its temperature is 32°F (0°C) or below. The large glaciers that cover part of the land on the earth are sheets of ice.

Water vapor in the atmosphere is water in its gaseous state. When water vaporizes, it leaves the liquid state and enters the atmosphere as a gas. Evaporation—one kind of vaporization—occurs on the surface of liquid water all the time. Another kind of vaporization occurs when water reaches its boiling point, 212°F (100°C).

9. The main idea of the passage is that

(1) living things need water
(2) the earth's water is in three states
(3) water vapor is a gas
(4) most water on the earth is liquid
(5) the solid state of water is ice

10. Which of the following conclusions is supported by the information in the passage?

(1) A temperature change can cause water to change its state.
(2) There is more fresh water on the earth in glaciers than in lakes and rivers.
(3) To become a gas, liquid water must boil.
(4) Ocean water is salty.
(5) Warm air can hold more water vapor than cold air.

Items 11 and 12 are based on the following paragraph.

Ultrasonic sound, which humans cannot hear, has many uses in medicine. It is used to create sonograms, which are pictures of the inside of the body. Doctors use sonograms to follow the growth of an unborn baby inside its mother's uterus and to detect deformities the baby may have. Sonograms are also used to detect tumors, gallstones, kidney stones, and heart disorders. Ultrasonic sound is also used in surgical procedures. It is used to operate on nerves and to shatter kidney stones. Ultrasonic sound is also used to clean instruments because it can kill bacteria.

11. What is the topic of the passage?

    (1) sound waves
    (2) sonograms
    (3) surgery
    (4) ultrasonic sound
    (5) kidney stones

12. Which of the following sentences from the paragraph states the main idea?

    (1) Ultrasonic sound, which humans cannot hear, has many uses in medicine.
    (2) It is used to create sonograms, which are pictures of the inside of the body.
    (3) Ultrasonic sound is also used in surgical procedures.
    (4) It is used to operate on nerves and to shatter kidney stones.
    (5) Ultrasonic sound is also used to clean instruments because it can kill bacteria.

Items 13 to 17 are based on the following paragraph and table.

    In a typical American's diet, about 40% of the calories come from fat. Experts believe this amount should be reduced to 30%. Men, who take in 2400 calories a day on the average, should restrict their fat intake to 80 grams. Women, who take in 1600 calories a day on the average, should restrict their fat intake to 53 grams. To lose weight, men should take in only 30 to 60 grams of fat daily; women, only 20 to 40 grams.

CALORIE AND FAT CONTENT OF CERTAIN FOODS

Food	Serving Size	Calories	Fat (in grams)
Butter	1 tablespoon	100	11
Chicken, light meat without skin	3 ounces	145	4
Cottage cheese, low-fat	½ cup	100	2
Cream cheese	1 ounce	100	10
Egg, hard-cooked	1 large	80	6
Frankfurter	2 ounces (1 frank)	145	13
Ground beef	3 ounces	245	18
Ice cream	½ cup	135	7.2
Margarine	1 tablespoon	100	11
Mayonnaise	1 tablespoon	100	11
Milk, skim	1 cup	90	Trace
Milk, whole	1 cup	150	8
Oil	1 tablespoon	125	14
Peanut butter	2 tablespoons	95	15.3
Peanuts, roasted, salted	½ cup	420	35
Popcorn, plain	1 cup	30	Trace
Potato chips	10 chips	105	8
Salad dressing, low-calorie	1 tablespoon	25	2
Salad dressing, regular	1 tablespoon	85	9
Shrimp, boiled	3 ounces	100	1
Shrimp, fried	3 ounces	200	10
Spareribs	3 ounces	340	26
Swiss cheese	1 ounce	105	8
Tuna, packed in oil, drained	3 ounces	165	7
Tuna, packed in water, drained	3 ounces	135	1
Turkey, light meat without skin	3 ounces	135	3
Yogurt, frozen	1 cup	190	3
Yogurt, plain, low-fat	1 cup	145	3.5

13. What is the maximum daily fat intake recommended for a woman who wants to lose weight?

    (1) 20 grams
    (2) 30 grams
    (3) 40 grams
    (4) 53 grams
    (5) 60 grams

14. How many grams of fat are there in 2 tablespoons of peanut butter?

    (1) 11
    (2) 15.3
    (3) 35
    (4) 95
    (5) 420

15. How many calories are there in 10 potato chips?

    (1) 8
    (2) 10
    (3) 25
    (4) 30
    (5) 105

16. Which of the following contains the most fat?

    (1) ½ cup of ice cream
    (2) ½ cup cottage cheese
    (3) ½ cup of peanuts roasted and salted
    (4) 3 ounces of ground beef
    (5) 3 ounces of tuna packed in water

17. Which of the following conclusions is supported by the information in the table?

    (1) Meat products contain more fat than vegetable products.
    (2) Foods that contain fat come only from animals.
    (3) Foods that contain fat come only from plants.
    (4) Foods that contain fat come from both plants and animals.
    (5) All foods contain fat.

Items 18 to 20 are based on the following paragraph.

    The bottom, thicker layer of the skin is the dermis. It contains such things as blood vessels and nerves. The thin upper layer of the skin is the epidermis. It contains melanin, which gives skin color. The epidermis also contains the unique patterns that make a person's fingerprints.

18. In the word epidermis, the root, derm, means "skin." The meaning of the prefix epi- is most likely

    (1) bottom
    (2) blood
    (3) thick
    (4) outer
    (5) nerve

19. Melanin is

(1) the top layer of the skin
(2) the bottom layer of the skin
(3) the pattern that makes a fingerprint
(4) the pigment that colors skin
(5) the part of the skin that contains blood vessels

20. The main idea of the paragraph is that

(1) the two layers of the skin are different
(2) the dermis is the more important layer of the skin
(3) the epidermis contains a person's fingerprints
(4) the dermis is the inner layer of the skin
(5) the epidermis protects the dermis

Items 21 and 22 are based on the following passage.

Radon is a radioactive gas that rises from the ground. You can't see it or smell it, but it causes lung cancer. The risk is highest for smokers, children, and people who sleep in basements.

Radon gets into some houses. It comes in through cracks and through the plumbing. For this reason, you should have your house or apartment tested for radon.

To find out more about radon, call the Environmental Protection Agency (EPA). The EPA is listed in the phone book under "U.S. Government."

21. You can't tell if there is radon in your home without a test because

(1) it is radioactive
(2) it rises from the ground
(3) you can't see it or smell it
(4) it causes lung cancer
(5) it gets into houses through cracks and through the plumbing

22. Which of the following sentences from the passage states an opinion rather than a fact?

(1) Radon is a radioactive gas that rises from the ground.
(2) You can't see it or smell it, but it causes lung cancer.
(3) Radon gets into some houses.
(4) For this reason, you should have your house or apartment tested for radon.
(5) The EPA is listed in the phone book under "U.S. Government."

Items 23 and 24 are based on the following passage.

Asbestos is the name for a variety of minerals that break into very tiny fibers. These fibers are odorless and very strong. They do not burn or conduct heat or electricity. These qualities once made asbestos useful in construction and industry.

Asbestos has not been widely used since its dangers were discovered. It tends to break down into a dust of tiny fibers that remain suspended in the air for long periods of time. These fibers can be inhaled easily and, because they are so strong, they remain in the body.

Asbestos can cause disease years after exposure. In general, asbestos-related conditions are latent for a long period of time. In fact, disease symptoms often do not appear for 20 to 40 years. Lung cancer is one disease that can be caused by inhaling asbestos. It is more likely to occur if the exposed person is a smoker. Asbestos also causes asbestosis, a lung disease that can lead to death by making breathing progressively more difficult.

23. The word <u>latent</u> in the last paragraph means

    (1) exposed
    (2) active
    (3) contagious
    (4) hidden
    (5) fatal

24. Before the dangers of asbestos were discovered, which of the following products was most likely made with asbestos?

    (1) electric wires
    (2) pots and pans
    (3) bathing suits
    (4) fire fighters' gloves
    (5) pillows

<u>Items 25 and 26</u> are based on the following passage.

Humidity is the moisture in the air. Unlike the amounts of nitrogen and oxygen in the air, the amount of water in the air is always changing.

Relative humidity is a comparison between the amount of water the air is holding and the amount it can hold. If the air is holding all the water it possibly can, the relative humidity is 100%. If the relative humidity is 75%, the air is holding three-quarters of the water that it can. Warm air can hold more moisture than cold air.

25. At 50% relative humidity, how much of the water that the air can hold is it holding?

    (1) all of it
    (2) three-quarters of it
    (3) half of it
    (4) one-quarter of it
    (5) none of it

26. There is the least moisture in the air when the relative humidity is 80% and the temperature is

    (1) 95°F
    (2) 80°F
    (3) 65°F
    (4) 32°F
    (5) 0°F

Items 27 and 28 are based on the following passage.

The color of an object is the color of the light it reflects. A red apple reflects red light and absorbs all other colors. Green leaves reflect green light and absorb all other colors.

If an object reflects all the colors of the spectrum and absorbs none, it appears white. White, therefore, is the combination of all colors. On the other hand, if an object absorbs all colors and reflects none, it appears black. Black is the absence of color.

27. A white dress

(1) reflects all colors
(2) absorbs all colors
(3) reflects white
(4) absorbs white
(5) reflects black

28. A blue balloon reflects

(1) all colors
(2) all colors except blue
(3) blue
(4) white
(5) no colors

Items 29 and 30 are based on the following passage.

MSG (monosodium glutamate) is a flavor enhancer widely used by restaurants and in prepared foods. Scientists are not sure exactly how MSG works, but they suspect that it increases the number of nerve impulses that allow us to taste things.

Several years ago, public pressure stopped manufacturers from using MSG in baby foods. Studies had shown that large amounts of MSG destroy brain cells in mice. Another food additive, Red Dye No. 40, may cause lymph tumors when fed in large amounts to mice.

After eating large amounts of MSG, some people get a burning sensation in the neck and forearms, tightness in the chest, and a headache. The government should ban the use of MSG.

29. Which of the following sentences from the passage expresses an opinion rather than a fact?

(1) MSG (monosodium glutamate) is a flavor enhancer widely used by restaurants and in prepared foods.
(2) Several years ago, public pressure stopped manufacturers from using MSG in baby foods.
(3) Studies had shown that large amounts of MSG destroy brain cells in mice.
(4) After eating large amounts of MSG, some people get a burning sensation in the neck and forearms, tightness in the chest, and a headache.
(5) The government should ban the use of MSG.

30. Which of the following sentences from the passage is irrelevant to the main idea of its paragraph?

(1) Scientists are not sure exactly how MSG works, but they suspect that it increases the number of nerve impulses that allow us to taste things.
(2) Studies had shown that large amounts of MSG destroy brain cells in mice.
(3) Another food additive, Red Dye No. 40, may cause lymph tumors when fed in large amounts to mice.
(4) After eating large amounts of MSG, some people get a burning sensation in the neck and forearms, tightness in the chest, and a headache.
(5) The government should ban the use of MSG.

Items 31 to 33 are based on the following passage and map.

As you know, a day on the earth is 24 hours long. During these 24 hours, the earth rotates 360°, or 15° every hour. People have divided the earth into 24 time zones that are each 15° wide. Local time throughout each time zone is the same.

The time zones in the continental United States are shown on the map. As you go east, it is 1 hour later in each time zone. For instance, when it is 3:00 A.M. in Dallas, it is 4:00 A.M. in the time zone that contains New York, Washington, and Miami. Notice that the boundaries of the time zones are jagged. This is to avoid splitting major cities and some states between two time zones.

TIME ZONES IN THE CONTINENTAL UNITED STATES

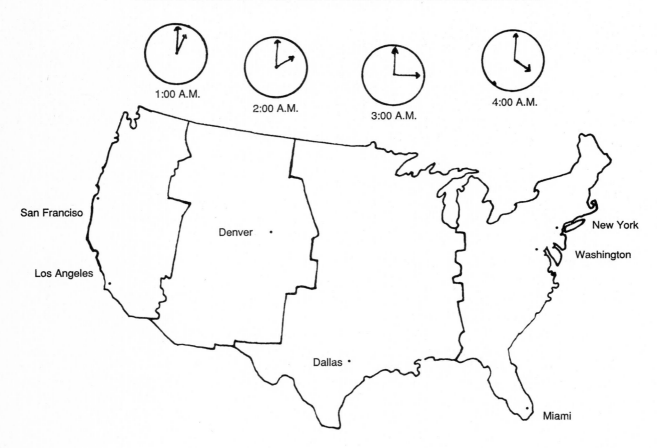

31. What time is it in Miami when it is 2:00 P.M. in Denver?

    (1) 12:00 noon
    (2) 1:00 P.M.
    (3) 2:00 P.M.
    (4) 3:00 P.M.
    (5) 4:00 P.M.

32. What time is it in Los Angeles when it is 5:00 P.M. in San Francisco?

    (1) 3:00 P.M.
    (2) 4:00 P.M.
    (3) 5:00 P.M.
    (4) 6:00 P.M.
    (5) 7:00 P.M.

33. When it is noon in Dallas, what time is it in Hawaii, which is four time zones to the west?

    (1) 2:00 A.M.
    (2) 8:00 A.M.
    (3) 4:00 P.M.
    (4) 8:00 P.M.
    (5) 12:00 noon

Check your answers on page 199.

SCIENCE PRETEST SKILLS CHART

To study the reading skills covered by the items in the Science Pretest, study the following parts of this book.

Unit 1	Comprehending What You Read	Item Number
Chapter 1	Prereading Strategies	1, 11
Chapter 2	Word Parts	18
Chapter 3	Details in Passages	2, 13, 19
Chapter 4	The Stated Main Idea	3, 12
Chapter 5	Patterns of Organization	4
Chapter 6	Tables and Graphs	7, 14, 15, 16

Unit 2	Inferring as You Read	
Chapter 1	Inferences	5, 6, 8, 21, 23
Chapter 2	The Implied Main Idea	9, 20

Unit 3	Applying Information You Read	24, 25, 26, 27, 28, 31, 32, 33

Unit 4	Analyzing and Evaluating What You Read	
Chapter 1	Relevant and Irrelevant Information	30
Chapter 2	Facts and Opinions	22, 29
Chapter 3	Conclusions and Supporting Information	10, 17

SCIENCE PRETEST CONTENT CHART

The following chart shows the type of content each item in the Science Pretest is based on.

Content	Item Number
Biology	3, 4, 5, 6, 8, 13, 14, 15, 16, 17, 18, 19, 20, 29, 30
Earth science	1, 2, 25, 26, 31, 32, 33
Chemistry	9, 10, 21, 22, 23, 24
Physics	7, 11, 12, 27, 28

UNIT 1

Comprehending What You Read

Skill at reading starts with comprehending, or understanding, what you read. The lessons in this unit will give you practice using strategies that can increase your reading comprehension. You will get that practice as you read about different topics in science, which will help you prepare for the GED.

A microbiologist studies microscopic animal and vegetable organisms such as bacteria and viruses.

Unit 1 Overview

Chapter 1   Prereading Strategies
Chapter 2   Word Parts
Chapter 3   Details in Passages
Chapter 4   The Stated Main Idea
Chapter 5   Patterns of Organization
Chapter 6   Tables and Graphs

Science Readings 1
GED Practice 1

Chapter

1 PREREADING STRATEGIES

When you are having guests for dinner, planning ahead can save you time and energy. A grocery list can save you a last-minute trip to the store. A time schedule can give you an idea of how long it will take to prepare the meal.

Just as you can prepare to cook a meal, you can prepare to read. One way to do this is to use **prereading strategies** that help you think about what you are going to read.

This chapter introduces three prereading strategies: **previewing**, **brainstorming**, and **setting a purpose**. You can use these strategies with many kinds of reading material. However, this chapter focuses on passages like the ones on the science test of the GED.

Lesson 1

Previewing Passages

To preview means "to see before." When you preview something, you take an advance look at it. You think about it a bit. For instance, you preview a movie when you watch the coming attractions in a theater. You preview a TV show when you see a few scenes from it in a TV ad.

In this lesson you will practice previewing passages to find their topics. A passage is a short reading. The topic of a passage is what the passage is about. Two steps are used to preview a passage.

How to Preview a Passage to Find Its Topic

STEP 1: Read the first sentence.
STEP 2: Scan the passage to see if a key word is repeated.

To see how previewing works, do the following example.

TRY THIS

Read the first sentence in the following paragraph and then answer the question below the paragraph. DO NOT READ THE WHOLE PARAGRAPH.

The fruit is the part of a plant that contains its seeds. The fruit protects the seeds while they are forming. When the seeds are ripe, the fruit helps to scatter them so that new plants will grow. Most people know that apples, pears, and cherries are fruit. Cucumbers, tomatoes, peas, and green beans are also fruit.

What is the first sentence of the paragraph about? _____

The first sentence is about fruit. There is a chance that the whole paragraph is about fruit. Step 2 will help you find out.

The second step in previewing requires scanning. When you scan a passage, you do not read every word. You move your eyes over the passage very quickly. It's the same thing you do when you look through a telephone book to find a name. When you scan a passage, you try to find out if an important word is used several times.

NOW TRY THIS

Look back at the paragraph whose first sentence is about fruit. Scan the paragraph to see if a key word is repeated. Then answer the following question.

What key word is repeated several times in the passage?

_____

The word *fruit* is repeated throughout the paragraph.

The topic of this passage is fruit. The first sentence is about fruit, and the word *fruit* appears several times in the passage.

EXERCISE 1

Three passages follow. Use the two-step strategy to preview them, but do not read them. Answer the question that follows each passage.

> ### How to Preview a Passage to Find Its Topic
> STEP 1: Read the first sentence.
> STEP 2: Scan the passage to see if a key word is repeated.

Question 1 is based on the following paragraph.

The human body contains about 206 bones of different sizes and shapes. Bones have many important functions in the body. Bones protect vital organs. For example, the skull protects the brain. Bones shape and support the body. Most bones are attached to muscles, such as those in the arms and legs. Working together, bones and muscles move the body. Blood cells are made in the long bones of the body. Bones also store important minerals, such as calcium and phosphorus.

1. What is the topic of the paragraph? _____

Question 2 is based on the following passage.

Fish live in water. Their smooth bodies are propelled through the water by their tail fins. Other fins help fish steer, stay upright, and stop.

Most fish have no lungs. Therefore, they cannot take oxygen from the air. Instead, they take oxygen from the water that passes through openings called gills.

Fish are cold-blooded. This means that their bodies have no heat of their own. Their body temperature is the same as the temperature of the water they swim in.

Fish are an important source of food and valuable oils for humans and other animals. Salmon, cod, halibut, tuna, and other fish provide many important proteins, vitamins, and minerals needed for good nutrition.

2. What is the topic of the passage? _____

Question 3 is based on the following passage.

Vitamins are essential to human life. They are needed for normal growth and repair of the body. *Vitamin* comes from the Latin root *vita*, which means "life."

Vitamins are either water-soluble or fat-soluble. B complex vitamins, vitamin C, and bioflavonoids are water-soluble. The body cannot store these vitamins. Vitamins A, D, E, and K are fat-soluble. The body stores these vitamins in its fatty tissue.

Each vitamin performs one or more special jobs in the body. Therefore, it's important to eat a well-balanced diet to supply the body with all the vitamins it needs. Some people take daily vitamin supplements to be on the safe side.

3. What is the topic of the passage? _____

Check your answers on page 201.

Check your answers on page 201.

Lesson 2

Brainstorming

When you read, you relate new information to things you already know. Therefore, what you already know about a topic can help you understand what you read. Brainstorming is a prereading strategy that can help you recall what you know about a topic before you begin reading about it.

To brainstorm a topic, you call to mind everything you know about it. You can keep a mental list of what you know or jot things down as they come to mind. Your goal is to recall things you already know about a topic before you start to read about it.

One reader previewed the paragraph about fruit on page 15 and wrote this list:

Topic: Fruit

sweet   *has seeds*
grows on trees   *many kinds*

Notice how brainstorming can increase reading comprehension. One of the things the reader already knows about fruit is that it *has seeds*. The reader can relate this knowledge to the information in the first sentence in the paragraph: *The fruit is the part of a plant that contains its seeds*. Then, the reader can more easily understand the other information about fruit in the paragraph.

When you brainstorm, you become more actively involved in what you are reading. Brainstorming in a group can be helpful. People often help each other remember things they know about a topic.

The topics of the three passages in Exercise 1 (pages 15–17) are listed below. Brainstorm these topics. Jot down at least two things you know about each one.

1. Topic: Bones

    _____

    _____

2. Topic: Fish

    _____

    _____

3. Topic: Vitamins

    _____

    _____

Check your answers on page 201.

Lesson 3

Setting a Purpose

Like previewing and brainstorming, setting a purpose is a helpful pre-reading strategy. You preview a passage to discover what topic you are going to read about. Then, you brainstorm the topic to recall what you already know about it. When you set a reading purpose, you determine <u>why</u> you are reading.

You may want to learn how to do something. You may want to increase your knowledge about a subject. You may want to find the answer to a question. Whatever your purpose, being aware of it will help you get more out of what you are reading.

When you take the GED science test, you will read passages so that you can answer questions. This lesson will give you practice in reading with that purpose.

TRY THIS

Read the following question. Then read the paragraph about fruit below to find the answer. Finally, answer the question.

What part of a plant protects its seeds? _____

> The fruit is the part of a plant that contains its seeds. The fruit protects the seeds while they are forming. When the seeds are ripe, the fruit helps to scatter them so that new plants will grow. Most people know that apples, pears, and cherries are fruit. Cucumbers, tomatoes, peas, and green beans are also fruit.

The answer to the question is in the second sentence. The fruit protects the seeds.

You probably found that when you read the paragraph with the question in mind, it was easy to find the answer.

Read each question. Then read the passage that follows it to find the answer. Finally, answer the question. (You previewed these passages in Exercise 1 and brainstormed their topics in Exercise 2.)

1. What are two minerals that are stored in bones? _____ and _____

The human body contains about 206 bones of different sizes and shapes. Bones have many important functions in the body. Bones protect vital organs. For example, the skull protects the brain. Bones shape and support the body. Most bones are attached to muscles, such as those in the arms and legs. Working together, bones and muscles move the body. Blood cells are made in the long bones of the body. Bones also store important minerals, such as calcium and phosphorus.

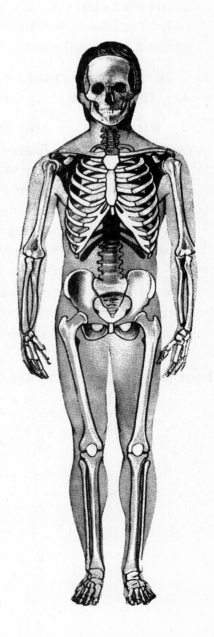

2. What helps fish swim?

    (1) gills   (2) fins   (3) lungs

    Fish live in water. Their smooth bodies are propelled through the water by their tail fins. Other fins help fish steer, stay upright, and stop.

    Most fish have no lungs. Therefore, they cannot take oxygen from the air. Instead, they take oxygen from the water that passes through openings called gills.

    Fish are cold-blooded. This means that their bodies have no heat of their own. Their body temperature is the same as the temperature of the water they swim in.

    Fish are an important source of food and valuable oils for humans and other animals. Salmon, cod, halibut, tuna, and other fish provide many important proteins, vitamins, and minerals needed for good nutrition.

3. Which kind of vitamins does the body store?

    (1) fat-soluble   (2) water-soluble   (3) B complex

    Vitamins are essential to human life. They are needed for normal growth and repair of the body. *Vitamin* comes from the Latin root *vita*, which means "life."

    Vitamins are either water-soluble or fat-soluble. B complex vitamins, vitamin C, and bioflavonoids are water-soluble. The body cannot store these vitamins. Vitamins A, D, E, and K are fat-soluble. The body stores these vitamins in its fatty tissue.

    Each vitamin performs one or more special jobs in the body. Therefore, it's important to eat a well-balanced diet to supply the body with all the vitamins it needs. Some people take daily vitamin supplements to be on the safe side.

Check your answers on page 201.

Chapter

2 WORD PARTS

Many words can be broken into smaller parts. There are three kinds of word parts: **roots**, **prefixes**, and **suffixes**. Each word part is a clue that can help you figure out a word's meaning. The more word part meanings you know, the more clues you will have to help you define words.

Lesson 4

Using Prefixes

The following example shows how the prefix *micro-* can be added to the word *biology* to make a new word.

First, the word *biology* means "study of life." It is made up of the root *bio* and the suffix *-ology*.

Root		Suffix		
BIO	+	OLOGY	=	BIOLOGY
↓		↓		↓
life	+	study of	=	study of life

Since *bio* ends in an *o*, the first *o* in the suffix *-ology* is omitted in *biology*.

A **prefix** is a word part that appears at the beginning of a word. *Micro-* is a prefix that means "small." When *micro-* is put in front of *biology*, the word means "study of small life (forms)."

Prefix		Root		Suffix		
MICRO	+	BIO	+	OLOGY	=	MICROBIOLOGY
↓		↓		↓		↓
small	+	life	+	study of	=	study of small life (forms)

The following table lists some common prefixes. The examples show that adding prefixes to words makes new words with new meanings.

TABLE OF PREFIXES

Prefix	Meaning	Example
anti-	against	antifreeze: against freezing
auto-	by oneself, by itself	automobile: moving by itself
epi-	above, outer	epicenter: above the center
hyper-	over	hyperactive: overactive
hypo-	under, below	hypocenter: below the center
micro-	small	microphone: small sound
pre-	before	preheat: heat before
re-	again, back	reread: read again
trans-	across, change	transform: change form
mono-, uni-	one	monotone: one tone unicycle: one wheel
bi-, di-	two	bicycle: two wheels dioxide: two oxygen (molecules)
tri-	three	tricycle: three wheels
multi-, poly-	many	multivitamin: many vitamins polysyllable: many syllables
un-, dis-, il-, im-, in-, ir-, non-	not	unhealthy: not healthy immature: not mature

EXERCISE 4

Part A. Use the Table of Prefixes to help you define the following words.

Example: transatlantic _across the Atlantic_

1. pretest _____
2. reproduce _____
3. microwave _____
4. antiwar _____
5. dishonest _____
6. monorail _____
7. insane _____
8. nonviolent _____
9. multicolored _____
10. triangle _____

Part B. Use the Table of Prefixes to help you complete each of the following statements.

1. There are two kinds of muscles in the human body. Voluntary muscles are those that we can control. Involuntary muscles are those that we _____.

2. Animals fall into two large groups. Vertebrates are animals with backbones, like humans and dogs. Invertebrates, like worms and jellyfish, are animals _____.

3. Multicelled animals are animals with two or more cells. Unicelled animals are animals with only _____.

4. Mollusks are animals with soft, fleshy bodies usually covered by a hard shell. One-shelled mollusks, like conchs, are called univalves. _____ mollusks, like clams, are called bivalves.

5. Carbon monoxide is a poisonous gas. It is made up of one carbon atom and one oxygen atom. Carbon dioxide is part of the air we breathe. It also has one carbon atom, but it has _____ oxygen atoms.

6. Hypotension is abnormally low blood pressure. Hypertension is abnormally _____ blood pressure.

Part C. Use the Table of Prefixes to help you match the words in Column A with their definitions in Column B.

Column A	Column B
____ 1. trimester	(a) an abnormally low amount of sugar in the blood
____ 2. polygon	(b) a figure with more than one side
____ 3. autotroph	(c) being married to one person
____ 4. hypoglycemia	(d) a plant that makes its own food
____ 5. monogamy	(e) a period of 3 months

Check your answers on page 201.

Lesson 5

Using Roots

A **root** is a word part that gives a word its basic meaning. Unlike a prefix, which comes at the beginning of a word, a root can appear anywhere in a word. A single word may contain more than one root.

As you know, the root *bio* means "life." Knowing the meaning of a single root, such as *bio*, can help you figure out the meanings of many words. The following table gives the meanings of a few words that contain the root *bio*.

WORDS WITH THE ROOT *BIO*

Word	Meaning
biology	the study of life
biochemistry	the branch of chemistry that deals with living things and their life processes
biography	a written account of a person's life
biome	a community of living things

Notice that each definition relates to the meaning of *bio*. That is, each definition contains the word *life* or *living*.

The following table lists some common roots. Many of them are used in biology.

TABLE OF ROOTS

Root	Meaning	Example
bio	life	biosphere: the zone of the earth that contains living things
cardi	heart	cardiovascular: relating to the heart and blood vessels
chlor	green	chlorine: greenish-yellow gas
derm, dermat	skin	dermatologist: person who studies the skin
graph, gram	write, draw, describe, record	phonograph: record of sound
hydr	water	dehydration: loss of water from the body
neur	nerve	neuron: nerve cell
path	feeling, disease	apathy: without feeling
psych	mind	psychic: relating to the mind
scope	look at	telescope: instrument used to look at something far away
tox, toxic	poison	intoxicate: to put poison in

EXERCISE 5a

Use the Table of Roots to help you match the words in Column A with their definitions in Column B.

Column A	Column B
_____ 1. chlorophyll	(a) a record of the heart's activity
_____ 2. neuralgia	(b) the use of water to treat certain diseases
_____ 3. hydrotherapy	(c) nerve pain
_____ 4. cardiogram	(d) something that causes a disease
_____ 5. pathogen	(e) green pigment

Check your answers on page 201.

By putting the meanings of both a prefix and a root together, you can usually get a good idea of the meaning of a word. Using the following four steps can help you define a word when you know the meanings of its parts.

How to Use Word Part Meanings to Define Words
STEP 1: Divide the word into its parts.
STEP 2: Write the meaning of each word part.
STEP 3: Combine the word part meanings.
STEP 4: Check your definition in a dictionary.

The following example shows you how to define *microscope* by using these four steps.

STEP 1: Divide the word into its parts.

MICRO + SCOPE

Two word parts make up the word *microscope*, the prefix *micro-* and the root *scope*.

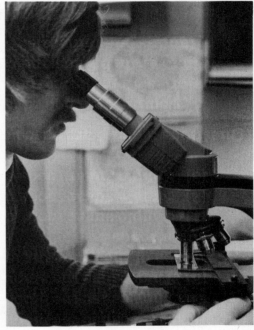

STEP 2: Write the meaning of each word part.

MICRO + SCOPE
↓ ↓
small + look at

STEP 3: Combine the word part meanings.

MICRO + SCOPE = MICROSCOPE
↓ ↓ ↓
small + look at = look at small (things)

Keep in mind that word parts are clues. The combination usually adds up to a rather rough definition. You may be able to guess what the polished definition is, but if you can't, go to the next step.

STEP 4: Check your definition in a dictionary.

The dictionary definition of *microscope* is *an instrument that makes small things look larger*. It is much smoother than *look at small (things)*, but the definition based on word parts is quite close.

Use the Table of Prefixes (page 22) and the Table of Roots (page 24) to help you write definitions for the words that follow. Use the four-step strategy.

How to Use Word Part Meanings to Define Words

STEP 1: Divide the word into its parts.
STEP 2: Write the meaning of each word part.
STEP 3: Combine the word part meanings.
STEP 4: Check your definition in a dictionary.

---

1. epidermis

   Step 1: _____

   Step 2: _____

   Step 3: _____

   Step 4: _____

2. hypodermic

   Step 1: _____

   Step 2: _____

   Step 3: _____

   Step 4: _____

3. antitoxin

   Step 1: _____

   Step 2: _____

   Step 3: _____

   Step 4: _____

4. polygraph

   Step 1: _____

   Step 2: _____

   Step 3: _____

   Step 4: _____

5. psychopath

   Step 1: _____

   Step 2: _____

   Step 3: _____

   Step 4: _____

Check your answers on page 202.

Lesson 6

Using Suffixes

A **suffix** is a word part that comes at the end of a word. In the table below, different suffixes are added to the root *zo*, which means "animal," to form three different words.

WORDS WITH A SUFFIX ADDED TO *ZO*

Word	Meaning
zoology	the study of animals
zoologist	a person who studies animals
zoophobia	an abnormal fear of animals

Sea lions at the Bronx Zoo.

The following table lists some common suffixes.

TABLE OF SUFFIXES

Suffix	Meaning	Example
-er, -or	a person or thing that does something	gardener: a person who gardens
-ist	a person who does something	therapist: a person who gives therapy
-itis	inflammation	tonsillitis: inflammation of the tonsils
-ize	to make	Americanize: to make American
-ologist	a person who studies	ecologist: a person who studies the environment
-ology	study of	ecology: study of the environment
-phobia	abnormal fear of	claustrophobia: abnormal fear of enclosed spaces

EXERCISE 6

Part A. Use the Table of Suffixes to help you match the words in Column A with their definitions in Column B.

Column A	Column B
____ 1. acrophobia	(a) an inflammation of the larynx
____ 2. laryngitis	(b) the study of ancient peoples
____ 3. botanist	(c) to make fertile
____ 4. archaeology	(d) an abnormal fear of heights
____ 5. fertilize	(e) a person who specializes in plants

Part B. Use the Table of Prefixes (page 22), the Table of Roots (page 24), and the Table of Suffixes (page 27) to help you write definitions for the words that follow. Use the four-step strategy.

How to Use Word Part Meanings to Define Words

STEP 1: Divide the word into its parts.
STEP 2: Write the meaning of each word part.
STEP 3: Combine the word part meanings.
STEP 4: Check your definition in a dictionary.

---

1. autobiographer

   Step 1: _____

   Step 2: _____

   Step 3: _____

   Step 4: _____

2. carditis

   Step 1: _____

   Step 2: _____

   Step 3: _____

   Step 4: _____

3. pathology

   Step 1: _____

   Step 2: _____

   Step 3: _____

   Step 4: _____

4. psychologist

   Step 1: _____

   Step 2: _____

   Step 3: _____

   Step 4: _____

5. hydrophobia

   Step 1: _____

   Step 2: _____

   Step 3: _____

   Step 4: _____

Check your answers on page 202.

Chapter

3 DETAILS IN PASSAGES

In a paragraph or a longer passage, there are usually many **details** about the topic. To find particular details, it is helpful to have questions in mind as you read. On tests, questions often ask about details by **restating** information—that is, by saying something in a different way. To answer such questions, it is useful to notice **key words** in the passage and in the question.

Lesson 7

Finding Details in Paragraphs

Look at this party invitation:

Come to a Surprise Birthday Party!

For: Jennifer Ashley
Date: March 22
Time: 8:00 p.m.
Place: 2400 Homestead Avenue, Spring Lake Heights
Given by: Phyllis + Jim

The invitation is filled with **details**. It tells **why** and for **whom** the party is being given, **when** and **where** the party will be, and **who** is giving the party.

When you read to find specific information, you are reading for details. You probably use this reading skill many times a day. For example, you read for details when you look in a newspaper to find out where and when a movie is playing. When you take the GED, you will read to find details that help you answer questions. As you found in Lesson 3, when you read, it's best to have the question in mind that you want to answer.

TRY THIS

Preview the following paragraph. Then, read the questions that come after the paragraph. Finally, read the paragraph to find the details you need to answer the questions.

All living things are made of cells. Most cells are so small that they can be seen only with a powerful microscope. Some living things are made up of one cell. However, a human body is made up of more than 100 trillion cells.

What are living things made of? _____

About how many cells are there in a human body? _____

Living things are made of cells. This detail is in the first sentence of the paragraph. The human body contains about 100 trillion cells. That detail is in the last sentence.

Whenever you are reading for details, it's a good idea to read the questions before you read the passage, as you just did in the example.

EXERCISE 7

Preview each paragraph and read the questions that come after it. Then, read the paragraph to find the details the questions ask about. Finally, answer the questions.

Questions 1 to 4 are based on the following paragraph.

Plant and animal cells have several parts. The **nucleus** is the "brain" of the cell. It controls everything the cell does. A **nuclear membrane** separates the nucleus from the rest of the cell. Outside the nucleus, the cell is filled with **cytoplasm**, a clear, jelly-like fluid. Cytoplasm contains organelles. **Organelles** are small structures that do special jobs. For example, **mitochondria** supply most of the cell's energy by breaking down sugar. Finally, the **cell membrane** is a thin, flexible cover for the cell. It protects the cell and separates one cell from another.

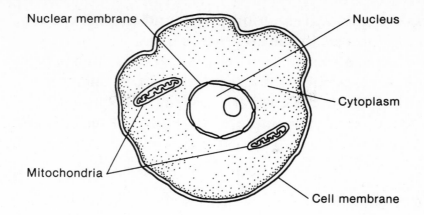

Nuclear membrane

Nucleus

Cytoplasm

Mitochondria

Cell membrane

1. Which part of a cell is in charge of the whole cell? _____

2. What kind of substance is cytoplasm? _____

3. How do mitochondria provide a cell with energy? _____

4. What cell part separates cells from each other? _____

Questions 5 to 8 are based on the following paragraph.

Plant cells have two important parts that animal cells do not have. An animal cell's only protection is its cell membrane. However, a plant cell is protected by both a cell membrane and a cell wall. The **cell wall** is strong and stiff. Cell walls provide support for cells so that plants can stand upright. Plant cells also have **chloroplasts**, small structures that contain chlorophyll. **Chlorophyll** is a green chemical that gives plants their color. Plants use chlorophyll to make their own food.

CHLOR(O) + PLAST	CHLOR(O) + PHYLL
↓ ↓	↓ ↓
green + form	green + leaf

5. Besides the cell membrane, what protects a plant cell?

    _____

6. What gives a plant's cells the support that allows it to stand?

    _____

7. What makes plants green? _____

8. What parts of a plant contain its chlorophyll? _____

Questions 9 to 14 are based on the following paragraph.

Green plants make their own food by a process called **photosynthesis**. A plant needs four ingredients to make food:

PHOTO +	SYN +	THE(SIS)
↓	↓	↓
light +	together +	put
(to) put together (with) light		

carbon dioxide, water, chlorophyll, and sunlight. **Carbon dioxide**, a gas present in the air, enters a plant through tiny openings in its leaves. **Water** from the soil enters through the plant's roots. The **chlorophyll** in the plant absorbs energy from the rays of the sun. The **sun's energy** enables the carbon dioxide to combine with the water to make a food called **glucose**, a simple sugar.

PHOTOSYNTHESIS

carbon dioxide + water + chlorophyll + sun's energy → glucose

---

9. What is the name of the process by which plants make their own food? _____

10. What are the four ingredients a plant uses to make its food?

   _____ _____ _____ _____

11. Where does carbon dioxide come from? _____

12. How does water get inside a plant? _____

13. Which ingredient enables a plant to obtain energy from sunlight?

   _____

14. What is the name of the food plants make? _____

Check your answers on page 202.

Lesson 8

Restating Information

Read these sentences:

    Sunday is the first day of the week.
    The week begins on Sunday.

The sentences above are two ways to say the same thing. The second sentence **restates** the idea in the first sentence. It states the idea in a different way.

When you understand what is stated in a passage, you are able to identify the same information when it is stated differently. In multiple-choice questions, looking for key words and synonyms can help you find restated information.

TRY THIS

Read the following sentence in which the key words are in dark type. Answer the question that follows it. Key words from the first sentence and synonyms for them are in dark type in the choices.

Each year plants **make** about **300 billion tons of food** in the form of **simple sugars**.

Which of the following sentences has the same meaning as the above sentence?
   (1) Plants need light to make **simple sugars**.
   (2) **Three hundred billion tons** of **sugar** are sold **each year**.
   (3) **Three hundred billion tons** of **simple sugars are produced** by plants **annually**.

All three choices mention *sugar* or *simple sugars*. However, only Choices (2) and (3) mention *three hundred billion tons*. So, Choice (1) can be eliminated. Choice (2) has the words *are sold*. The original has no words meaning *are sold*. This rules out Choice (2). Choice (3) has the words *are produced by plants*. This is another way of saying *plants make*, as in the original sentence. Also, the word *annually* in Choice (3) has the same meaning as *each year* in the original sentence. Therefore, Choice (3) restates the information in the sentence.

NOW TRY THIS

Read the following paragraph and answer the question that follows it.

   (1) Each year **plants** make about 300 billion tons of **food** in the form of simple sugars. (2) Only about 40 billion tons of this **food** are made by **land plants**. (3) **Marine plants** produce the largest supply of **food**.

Which sentence in the paragraph has the same meaning as the following sentence: **Sea plants** make the most **food**?
   (1) Sentence 1   (2) Sentence 2   (3) Sentence 3

All three of the sentences contain the key words *plants* and *food*. However, only Sentence (3) talks about *sea plants*. *Marine* means "of the sea." Also, *produce the largest supply* in Sentence (3) is another way of saying *make the most*, which is in the restatement.

Read the following passages and answer the questions.

Questions 1 and 2 are based on the following paragraph.

(1) All living things need food to stay alive. (2) Green plants make their own food. (3) Unlike green plants, animals cannot make their own food. (4) Animals must eat plants and other animals to survive.

1. Which sentence in the paragraph has the same meaning as the following sentence? Plants and animals would die without food.
   (1) Sentence 1   (2) Sentence 2   (3) Sentence 3
2. Which of the following sentences has the same meaning as Sentence 4 in the paragraph?
   (1) Animals stay alive by eating other living things.
   (2) Animals eat other animals to stay alive.
   (3) Some animals eat only plants.

Questions 3 and 4 are based on the following paragraph.

(1) Food keeps the human body alive. (2) However, in order for the body to use food, the energy in the food must be released. (3) When food is combined with oxygen, the food's energy is released. (4) During this process, called **cellular respiration**, food is burned for energy just as wood is burned for heat.

3. Which sentence in the paragraph has the same meaning as the following sentence? The body cannot use food until the food's energy is let out.
   (1) Sentence 1   (2) Sentence 2   (3) Sentence 4
4. Which of the following sentences has the same meaning as Sentence 3 in the paragraph?
   (1) The body takes in oxygen from the air.
   (2) Energy is produced when food and oxygen are mixed.
   (3) The body needs food.

Questions 5 and 6 are based on the following passage.

(1) The amount of energy in food is measured in calories. (2) A calorie is a unit of heat energy. (3) One calorie is the amount of heat needed to raise the temperature of one kilogram of water one degree Celsius.

(4) Some foods contain more calories than others—and thus supply more energy. (5) Fats contain 9 calories per gram. (6) Carbohydrates and proteins contain 4 calories per gram. (7) High-calorie foods produce a great amount of energy, while low-calorie foods produce less energy.

(8) Whenever the body takes in more calories than it uses, the extra calories are stored as fat. (9) Too much body fat causes overweight and obesity. (10) To lose weight and get rid of stored fat, people need to burn more energy than they take in.

5. Which of the following sentences has the same meaning as Sentence 4?
   (1) Some foods have no calories.
   (2) All foods have the same number of calories.
   (3) Foods have different numbers of calories.
6. Which sentence in the last paragraph has about the same meaning as the following sentence? Weight loss occurs when people eat less and use fat deposits in the body for energy.
   (1) Sentence 8   (2) Sentence 9   (3) Sentence 10

Check your answers on page 203.

On the GED, the answers to some questions are restatements of information in passages. The following exercise will give you practice in answering such questions.

EXERCISE 8b

Read the following passages and answer the questions.

Questions 1 and 2 are based on the following passage.

Carbohydrates are the body's chief source of energy. Anyone with a "sweet tooth" has craved simple carbohydrates, or simple sugars. Simple sugars include white refined sugar, brown sugar, honey, and maple syrup.

In their natural state and in cookies, cakes, and candy, simple sugar foods give the body a quick fix of energy. This is because they cause a sudden rise in the amount of sugar in the blood. However, the blood sugar level drops fast. When this happens, a person craves more sweets and may get a headache and feel dizzy, tired, depressed, and nervous.

Not only do simple sugars create a vicious cycle of highs and lows, but they also contain mostly empty calories. That is, they contain few of the nutrients the body needs. Even worse, simple sugar foods are often high in calories. Therefore, a diet rich in simple sugar foods can lead to obesity. A diet high in sugar also promotes tooth decay. In short, simple sugar foods are poor food choices.

1. How do simple sugar foods give the body quick energy?
   (1) They cause the blood sugar level to increase sharply.
   (2) They cause the blood sugar level to decrease sharply.
   (3) They cause the amount of blood sugar to level off.
2. Which of the following is NOT a true statement about simple sugar foods?
   (1) Simple sugar foods cause cavities.
   (2) Simple sugar foods deprive the body of calories.
   (3) Simple sugar foods can cause people to gain weight.

Questions 3 and 4 are based on the following passage.

Complex carbohydrates give you a lot of nutrition for your calories. Complex carbohydrates are foods such as vegetables, whole-grain breads and cereals, and brown rice. They are rich in vitamins and minerals. They also break down very slowly and

give the body a steady supply of energy instead of a quick fix. Experts recommend that 50% to 60% of one's total daily calories come from complex carbohydrates. A diet rich in these foods helps a person maintain a stable energy level.

Instead of eating complex carbohydrates, many people eat processed or refined grains and cereals. Processed carbohydrates are "simpler" forms of the original grains. Therefore, eating them can create many of the same effects as eating simple sugars. For example, they give the body a surge of energy instead of a steady flow.

Polished rice and products made from white flour, such as white bread, rolls, and crackers, are examples of processed foods. Unfortunately, the processes that polish rice and make flour white also remove most of their nutrients. For example, when white flour is made from wheat, the most nutritious parts of the wheat, the germ and the bran, are removed.

3. According to nutritionists, what portion of the calories in a person's daily diet should come from complex carbohydrates?
   (1) all   (2) half or more   (3) less than half
4. When complex carbohydrates are refined
   (1) they give the body a steady supply of energy
   (2) they remain in their natural state
   (3) many of their vitamins and minerals are removed

Check your answers on page 203.

Chapter 4

THE STATED MAIN IDEA

The **main idea** is the main point a writer makes about a topic. It is often stated in one of the sentences in a paragraph or a passage. The other sentences in the paragraph are **supporting sentences**. They contain details that explain, prove, or give examples of the main idea.

If friends of yours told you that they were getting married, that would be the "big news," or the main idea. Specific information about the wedding—its date, time, and place—would be the supporting details.

Lesson 9

Finding the Heading for a Word List

Finding the main idea of a paragraph, which you will do in the next lesson, is similar to finding the heading for a word list. The main idea controls a paragraph, just as the heading controls a list. The supporting details in a paragraph are like the items on a list.

The term that controls the following list is checked:

- ____ cell membranes
- ✓ cell parts
- ____ cytoplasm
- ____ mitochondria
- ____ nuclear membranes
- ____ nuclei
- ____ organelles

When this term is written as the heading, the list looks like this:

Cell Parts

cell membranes
cytoplasm
mitochondria
nuclear membranes
nuclei
organelles

Find the heading for this list.

_____ fish
_____ frogs
_____ animals
_____ lions
_____ humans

Animals is the term that controls the list, so it should be the heading. It is the only word that is broad enough to cover the whole list. All the other words in the list are names of animals.

EXERCISE 9

Part A. Find the heading for each list.

1. _____ bushes
   _____ flowers
   _____ grass
   _____ plants
   _____ trees

2. _____ ants
   _____ bees
   _____ beetles
   _____ insects
   _____ mosquitoes

3. _____ daisies
   _____ flowers
   _____ lilies
   _____ roses
   _____ tulips

4. _____ bears
   _____ dogs
   _____ mammals
   _____ tigers
   _____ whales

Part B. The heading is at the top of each of the following lists. Add two or more words to each list.

1. **Organs**
   liver
   heart
   _____
   _____

2. **Fish**
   trout
   _____
   _____

Part C. Write lists with four or more words under each of the following headings.

1. **Birds** _____

_____

_____

_____

_____

2. **Trees** _____

_____

_____

_____

_____

Part D. Choose two headings and write your own word lists, each with four words or more.

1. _____

_____

_____

_____

_____

2. _____

_____

_____

_____

_____

Check your answers on page 203.

Lesson 10

Finding the Main Idea of a Paragraph

Topics and Main Ideas

Writers present ideas in groups of sentences called paragraphs. As Lesson 1 showed, each paragraph has a topic. The topic is what the paragraph is about. It is usually possible to state the topic of a paragraph in a word or a phrase, such as "sharks" or "the animal kingdom."

A paragraph also has a **main idea**. A paragraph's main idea is the most important and/or general statement it makes about its topic. A main idea is always stated in a complete sentence.

The following is an example of a topic and a main idea:

Topic	Main Idea
Birds	Birds help humans by eating many harmful insects.

Notice that the topic, *birds*, is stated in a single word, while the main idea about birds is stated in a complete sentence.

A topic is much broader than a main idea. Countless main ideas can be written about one topic. Here are three different main ideas written about one topic.

Topic	Main Ideas
Plants	Plants make their own food.
	Plants cleanse the air.
	Plants are used to decorate homes.

TRY THIS

Write three main ideas about the topic "dogs."

Topic	Main Ideas
Dogs	_____
	_____
	_____

There are many main ideas that you could have written about the topic. Here are three examples:

Dogs make good pets.

Dogs, such as German shepherds and bloodhounds, help solve crimes.

There are many different breeds of dogs.

Main Ideas and Supporting Details

Like the heading of a list, the main idea of a paragraph is the broadest idea in the paragraph. It is the most important and/or general idea in the paragraph. It covers the other ideas in the paragraph.

Like the items on a list, a paragraph's supporting details are more specific than its main idea. They explain, prove, or give examples of the main idea.

Three steps can help you find the stated main idea of a paragraph.

> **How to Find the Stated Main Idea of a Paragraph**
>
> STEP 1: Find the topic of the paragraph.
> STEP 2: Find the most important and/or most general statement about the topic.
> STEP 3: Test to prove that the statement is the main idea by making sure the other sentences support it.

The following example shows how these three steps are used to find the main idea of this paragraph:

> The world is filled with **living and nonliving things**. Plants and animals are **living things**. Land, water, and air are **nonliving things**.

STEP 1:   Find the topic of the paragraph.

"Living and nonliving things" is the topic. *Living and nonliving things* is a phrase in the first sentence. *Living things* is repeated in the second sentence. *Nonliving things* is repeated in the last sentence.

STEPS 2 and 3:   Find the most important and/or most general statement about the topic. Test to prove that the statement is the main idea by making sure the other sentences support it.

The first sentence in the paragraph is the main idea. It is broad enough to cover the other sentences. It mentions both living and nonliving things. The other sentences are the supporting details. They are more specific than the main idea. The second sentence gives examples of living things. The third sentence gives examples of nonliving things.

Steps 2 and 3 in finding a stated main idea are really two parts of the same thought process. To be sure which sentence states the main idea, you need to look at each one in relation to the others. A main idea and its supporting details go hand in hand. You can't have one without the other.

The following shows how a topic and a main idea are related, and how supporting sentences relate to the main idea.

The **topic** is a word or phrase.	**Living and nonliving things**
The **main idea** is a sentence **about** the topic.	The world is filled with **living and nonliving things**.
The **supporting ideas** relate to the main idea.	Plants and animals are **living things**. Land, water, and air are **nonliving things**.

The first or last sentence of a paragraph usually states the main idea. However, the main idea can be stated in any sentence.

In the following paragraphs, the main ideas are in different positions. When the main idea is the last sentence, it usually sums up the ideas in the paragraph:

Plants and animals are **living things**. Land, water, and air are **nonliving things**. <u>The world is filled with both **living and non-living things**</u>.

In the next paragraph, the main idea is the second sentence:

Many different kinds of things fill the world. <u>Everything in the world is either a **living thing** or a **nonliving thing**</u>. Plants and animals are **living things**. Land, water, and air are **nonliving things**.

No matter where the main idea sentence is, it still has the same relationship to the supporting details.

EXERCISE 10

Use the three-step strategy to find the main idea of each paragraph below.

How to Find the Stated Main Idea of a Paragraph

STEP 1: Find the topic of the paragraph.

STEP 2: Find the most important and/or most general statement about the topic.

STEP 3: Test to prove that the statement is the main idea by making sure the other sentences support it.

Questions 1 and 2 are based on the following paragraph.

Unlike nonliving things, living things carry on four life processes. One, living things use energy. Two, living things grow. Three, living things respond to their surroundings. Four, living things reproduce.

1. What is the topic of the paragraph? _____
2. Which sentence states the main idea? _____

Questions 3 and 4 are based on the following paragraph.

Plants are grouped according to the number of growing seasons they live. A growing season is the part of the year when the climate in an area supports plant growth. Annuals are plants that complete their life cycle in one growing season. Grains, peas, and beans are annuals. Biennials take two growing seasons to complete their life cycles. Cabbage, turnips, and carrots are biennials. Perennials, such as trees and shrubs, live for more than two growing seasons.

3. What is the topic of the paragraph? _____
4. Which sentence states the main idea? _____

Questions 5 and 6 are based on the following paragraph.

Some trees shed all their leaves in the fall. Others stay green all year because they shed only a few leaves at a time. The way they shed their leaves divides trees into two groups. Trees that are bare in winter are called deciduous. Trees that keep their leaves in winter are called evergreen.

5. What is the topic of the paragraph? _____
6. Which sentence states the main idea? _____

Questions 7 and 8 are based on the following paragraph.

Vertebrates are animals that have a spine. Humans, frogs, and birds are examples of vertebrates. In contrast, invertebrates are animals that do not have a spine. Shellfish, jellyfish, and insects are invertebrates. All animals are either vertebrates or invertebrates.

7. What is the topic of the paragraph? _____
8. Which sentence states the main idea? _____

Questions 9 and 10 are based on the following paragraph.

Like other amphibians, frogs live part of their lives in water and part on dry land. Frogs lay their eggs and hatch their young in water. After young frogs mature, they move onto the land.

9. What is the topic of the paragraph? _____

10. Which sentence states the main idea? _____

Questions 11 and 12 are based on the following paragraph.

Roots hold a plant in the ground, take in water and minerals from the soil, and store food. A plant's stem holds the leaves and flowers up. The stem also carries substances from the roots to the top of the plant and stores food. The leaves absorb carbon dioxide and sunlight and release oxygen during photosynthesis. The flowers contain a plant's reproductive organs. Each part of a plant does a special job that helps it to stay alive and grow.

11. What is the topic of the paragraph? _____

12. Which sentence states the main idea? _____

Check your answers on page 204.

Lesson 11

Finding the Main Idea of a Passage

Although passages are often made up of more than one paragraph, they still have a single main idea. In this lesson, a four-step process for finding the main idea of a passage is modeled. It is similar to the three-step process you used in Lesson 10.

> **How to Find the Stated Main Idea of a Passage**
>
> STEP 1: Find the topic of the passage.
> STEP 2: Find the main idea of each paragraph.
> STEP 3: Decide which main idea is the most important and/or general.
> STEP 4: Test the main idea of the passage by making sure the main ideas of the other paragraphs support it.

The following example shows how these four steps are used to find the main idea of this passage:

Viruses are one of the most serious threats to human life. A **virus** is a small piece of genetic material covered with protein. The body mistakes a virus for something good and pulls it into a cell. Inside the cell, the **virus** multiplies. When this happens, the **virus** can cause a disease. What makes matters worse is that a **virus** cannot be killed by medicine.

Viruses can reproduce only by taking over living cells. A **virus** is not alive. It is simply a package of genes, or a set of instructions that tell a cell what to do. However, when a **virus** enters a living cell, it "comes alive." The normal functions of the cell stop because the **virus** takes over. Following directions from the **virus**, the cell makes hundreds of copies of the **virus**. Eventually, the cell bursts open, and the **virus** invades other cells. This invasion is known as a **viral** infection.

Viruses cause many human diseases. **Viruses** cause such childhood diseases as mumps, measles, and chicken pox. They also cause some infections of the respiratory system, such as influenza (the flu) and the common cold. AIDS is caused by a **virus** known as HIV.

> HIV stands for Human Immunodeficiency Virus.

There is no cure for a disease caused by a **virus**. Therefore, when you are ill with a **virus**, such as when you have a cold, you simply have to allow the **virus** to run its course. Luckily, people recover from most diseases caused by **viruses**. This is because the body's immune system fights a **virus** until the **virus** stops reproducing. However, some diseases caused by **viruses** can be fatal.

STEP 1: Find the topic of the passage.

"Viruses" is the topic. The word *viruses* appears in the first sentence of the passage, and *virus*, *viruses*, and *viral* are repeated throughout the passage.

STEP 2: Find the main idea of each paragraph.

The main ideas are underlined in each paragraph in the example.

STEP 3: Decide which main idea is the most important and/or general.

The main idea of the first paragraph is the most important and most general statement about viruses. Therefore, it is the main idea of the passage.

STEP 4: Test the main idea of the passage by making sure the main ideas of the other paragraphs support it.

Just as the main idea of a paragraph needs support, so does the main idea of a passage. In order to test a statement you think is a main idea, look at the main ideas of each of the other paragraphs. They do the same job that supporting details do in a single paragraph.

In the example, the main ideas of the second, third, and fourth paragraphs each support the main idea of the passage in a different way. The main idea of the second paragraph tells **how** viruses threaten human life: they take over living cells. The main idea of the third paragraph tells **what kind of** threat viruses are: they cause diseases. The main idea of the fourth paragraph tells **how serious** a threat viruses are: there is no cure for a disease caused by a virus.

The following table shows how a passage's topic and main idea are related and how the main idea is related to the other paragraphs' main ideas.

The **topic** is a word or phrase.	**Viruses**
The **main idea of a passage** is the most important and/or general main idea in the passage.	**Viruses** are one of the most serious threats to human life.
The main ideas of the other paragraphs **support** the main idea of the passage.	Viruses can reproduce only **by taking over living cells.** Viruses **cause** many human **diseases.** There is **no cure** for a disease caused by a virus.

Use the four-step strategy to find the main idea of each passage.

> **How to Find the Stated Main Idea of a Passage**
> STEP 1: Find the topic of the passage.
> STEP 2: Find the main idea of each paragraph.
> STEP 3: Decide which main idea is the most important and/or general.
> STEP 4: Test the main idea of the passage by making sure the main ideas of the other paragraphs support it.

Questions 1 to 3 are based on the following passage.

Soldiers attack foreign invaders who threaten to destroy their country. The immune system does the same job in the body. The **immune system** is a network of special cells and organs that defend the body against old and new enemies. It fights off harmful invaders such as viruses.

The immune system knows the difference between what belongs in the body and what does not. Every cell carries molecules that identify it. When an invader such as a flu virus gets inside the body, the immune system finds it and tries to destroy it.

The immune system also remembers past invaders. For instance, once you have had a certain disease, such as chicken pox or measles, your immune system will prevent you from being infected again. When you can no longer get a disease, you are immune to it.

1. What is the topic of the passage? _____
2. Find the main idea of each paragraph.

   Paragraph 1: _____
   Paragraph 2: _____
   Paragraph 3: _____
3. Which paragraph's main idea is the main idea of the passage?

   _____

Questions 4 to 6 are based on the following passage.

AIDS is one of the most serious worldwide health problems that has ever existed. AIDS is contagious, incurable, and fatal.

The body cannot fight AIDS the way it can fight other serious conditions.

AIDS stands for Acquired Immune Deficiency Syndrome.

AIDS is caused by a virus, called HIV, that attacks the body's main weapon against disease. It attacks the immune system, itself. The virus usually lives in the body for years before a person gets sick. It slowly destroys white blood cells that fight infection.

Without a healthy immune system, people with AIDS are defenseless against many diseases. They cannot fight infections that would not bother them if their immune system were healthy. Although many different life-threatening infections are associated with AIDS, the most common is a form of pneumonia. The virus that causes AIDS is not what kills people. People with AIDS die of diseases caused by other infections their weakened immune systems cannot fight.

AIDS is contagious. The virus is spread by the exchange of body fluids. It is spread most often during sex and when people share a hypodermic needle to inject drugs. The virus can also be passed from a mother to her child during breast feeding. According to a 1988 report, sexual contact accounts for about 75% of AIDS cases, and needle sharing accounts for about 20%.

There is no cure for AIDS, but drugs called AZT and ddI have been approved for its treatment. They slow the destruction of the immune system. However, since both drugs have dangerous side effects, some people are unable to handle them. Other less damaging drugs are being tested for use in treating AIDS.

4. What is the topic of the passage? _____
5. Find the main idea of each paragraph.

   Paragraph 1: _____

   Paragraph 2: _____

   Paragraph 3: _____

   Paragraph 4: _____

   Paragraph 5: _____
6. Which paragraph's main idea is the main idea of the passage?

   _____

Check your answers on page 204.

PATTERNS OF ORGANIZATION

This chapter explores four ways that writers organize details in paragraphs and passages: by **list structure**, in **time order**, by **cause and effect**, and to show **comparison**. Recognizing these patterns as you read can increase your comprehension.

The following table gives examples of the patterns of organization.

PATTERNS OF ORGANIZATION

List Structure	Parts of the Circulatory System
	heart
	arteries
	veins
	capillaries
Time Order	First, oxygen-poor blood enters the heart. Then, the pulmonary artery carries it to the lungs.
Cause and Effect	A clogged artery can cause a heart attack.
Comparison	
Likeness	Arteries and veins are both blood vessels.
Difference	Arteries carry blood away from the heart; veins bring blood back to the heart.

Lesson 12

Identifying List Structure

People often organize their ideas by making lists. When planning a party, for instance, you may make lists of the people you want to invite, the food you want to serve, and the things you need to buy. By making lists like the one that follows, you organize your ideas about the party.

Things to Buy for the Party

invitations
paper dishes and cups
balloons and other decorations

One way that writers organize their ideas is to use **list structure**. They use list structure when they want to list several details that have the same relationship to the main idea.

As in the list of things to buy for the party, all the items in the following list have the same relationship to its heading.

Parts of the Circulatory System

> heart
> arteries
> veins
> capillaries

The heading serves the list in the same way a main idea serves a paragraph. The items on the list are its details. They are the names of individual parts of the circulatory system.

Here is the same information in paragraph form:

There are four main **parts of the circulatory system.** One, the **heart** pumps the blood. Two, **arteries** carry blood away from the heart. Three, **veins** bring blood back to the heart. Four, **capillaries** connect the veins and the arteries.

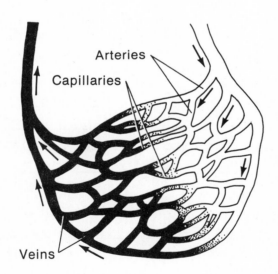

The preceding paragraph is organized by list structure. Its main idea is underlined. The other sentences support the main idea by listing the parts of the circulatory system (in dark print) and describing their functions.

The words *one*, *two*, *three*, and *four* are circled. They are called **signal words**. They give the reader a signal, or clue, that the details are in a list structure.

The following words often signal a list structure. If you see one or more of these words in a paragraph, the paragraph may be organized by list structure. To make sure, you need to think about the relationship between the main idea and its supporting details.

List Structure: Signal Words

also	finally
and	in addition
another	one, two, three, etc.
besides	other

TRY THIS

The following paragraph has a list structure. Read it and answer the questions that follow it.

> There are several symptoms of a heart attack. Most people have severe chest pain, which sometimes spreads to the neck, jaw, or left arm. People having a heart attack also experience weakness, shortness of breath, or nausea. In addition, heart attack victims often become pale and break into a cold sweat.

What is the main idea of the paragraph?

_____

What are the six items listed in the paragraph to support the main idea?

_____   _____

_____   _____

_____   _____

What two signal words are used in the paragraph?

_____   _____

The main idea of the paragraph is stated in the first sentence: *There are several symptoms of a heart attack.*

The following six items listed in the paragraph support the main idea: *chest pain, weakness, shortness of breath, nausea, become pale,* and *break into a cold sweat.* Notice that the number of items listed in each sentence differs. For instance, the second sentence mentions only one item, *chest pain.* However, the third sentence mentions three items: *weakness, shortness of breath,* and *nausea.* The last sentence mentions two items: *become pale* and *break into a cold sweat.*

The two signal words used in the paragraph are *also* (in the third sentence) and *in addition* (in the last sentence).

The paragraphs in this exercise are organized by list structure. Read each paragraph and answer the questions that follow it.

Questions 1 to 3 are based on the following paragraph.

Heart attack risk factors are traits and habits that increase a person's chances of having a heart attack. Three risk factors that cannot be changed are age, sex, and family history. Another three risk factors are ones that can be changed: cigarette smoking, high blood pressure, and high blood cholesterol. In addition, there are three less important risk factors: obesity, diabetes, and lack of exercise.

1. What is the main idea of the paragraph?

   _____

2. What are the nine items listed in the paragraph to support the main idea?

   _____   _____   _____

   _____   _____   _____

   _____   _____   _____

3. What two signal words are used in the paragraph?

   _____   _____

Questions 4 to 6 are based on the following paragraph.

Blood has four main parts. One, plasma is the straw-colored liquid part of blood. It is made mostly of water. In the plasma, digested food, enzymes, and wastes are carried through the body. Two, red blood cells are flexible red disks. Red blood cells carry oxygen to all the cells in the body. Three, white blood cells are colorless. They fight tiny invaders, such as bacteria and viruses, that threaten the well-being of the body. Four, platelets are tiny

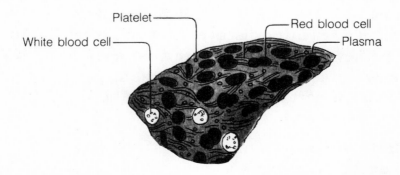

Platelet — Red blood cell

White blood cell — Plasma

bits of cells. They help form clots that stop a blood vessel from bleeding.

4. What is the main idea of the paragraph?

   _____

5. What are the four items listed in the paragraph to support the main idea?

   _____   _____

   _____   _____

6. What four signal words are used in the paragraph?

   _____   _____

   _____   _____

Check your answers on page 204.

Lesson 13

Identifying Time Order

Just as people make lists to organize their lives, they make time schedules. A time schedule is a list of things that is put in time order. For instance, on a day you are having a party, you may make a list like the following to be sure you have time to get everything done.

Things to Do

9:00–12:00 Clean house
1:00– 2:30 Go shopping for food
3:00– 5:30 Prepare food
5:30– 7:00 Set the table and decorate

The list tells you what has to be done for the party. It lists the things to do in time order.

Writers organize details by time order when it's important to know the order in which things happen in time. For example, when they write about a scientific discovery, writers often put the details in time order. They also use time order when they describe how a system of the body works or when they give the steps in an experiment.

The following is part of an explanation of how the circulatory system works:

First, oxygen-poor blood enters the heart.
Then, the pulmonary artery carries it to the lungs.

The signal words *first* and *then* make the time order clear.

The following paragraph is organized by time order. It explains how the circulatory system works:

The circulatory system carries oxygen to all the body's cells and removes carbon dioxide. First, oxygen-poor blood enters the heart. Then, the pulmonary artery carries it to the lungs. While in the lungs, the blood gets rid of carbon dioxide and picks up oxygen. Next, the pulmonary vein carries the oxygen-rich blood back to the heart. The blood is then pumped through arteries to all parts of the body.

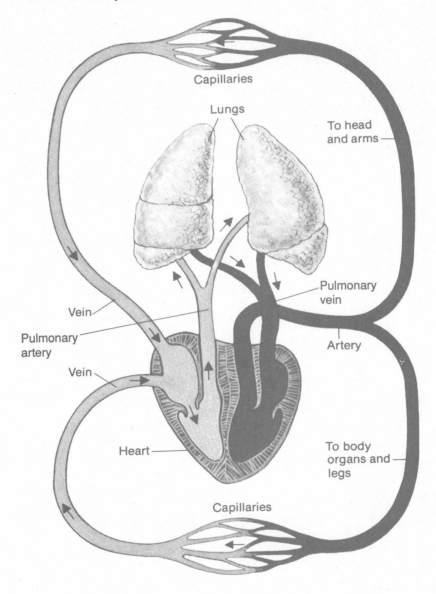

Capillaries

Lungs

To head and arms

Pulmonary vein

Vein

Pulmonary artery

Artery

Vein

To body organs and legs

Heart

Capillaries

The main idea of the paragraph is underlined. The other sentences support the main idea by explaining how the circulatory system works. They list the steps of the process in time order. The words in the paragraph that signal time order are circled. The signal words link the sentences together and make the time order of the details clear.

The following words are often used to signal time order. When you see one or more of these words in a paragraph, the details may be organized by time order.

Time Order: Signal Words

after	next
before	now
during	since
finally	then
first, second, third, etc.	when
later	while

The hour (for example, 1:00 A.M.), the date (for example, September 30, 1952), and other references to time are also used to signal time order. Using time order signal words can often help you find the answer to a question.

TRY THIS

Look back at the paragraph about the circulatory system and answer the following question.

What does the blood do while it is in the lungs?

_____
_____

The blood gets rid of carbon dioxide and picks up oxygen. The signal word *while* in the fourth sentence may have helped you find the answer.

EXERCISE 13

The paragraphs in this exercise are organized by time order. Read each paragraph and answer the questions.

Question 1 is based on the following paragraph.

Your pulse rate is the number of times your heart beats in a minute. Follow these steps to take your pulse. First, place one or more fingers on either side of your Adam's apple or inside your wrist below your thumb. Next, use a watch or clock with a second hand to keep time as you count how many times your heart beats in 6 seconds. Then, add a zero to that number. If your heart beats 7 times in 6 seconds, it beats 70 times in a minute.

1. The steps for taking your pulse are listed below in a mixed up order. Number the steps in the order in which the paragraph says to do them.

   _____ Look at a clock.

   _____ Find your pulse.

   _____ Add a zero to the number you get.

   _____ Count your pulse rate for 6 seconds.

Questions 2 and 3 are based on the following paragraph.

On December 3, 1967, a human heart was transplanted for the first time. The operation was performed by a team of surgeons headed by Christiaan Barnard of South Africa. The surgeons removed the healthy heart of a 25-year-old woman who had died after an automobile accident. They placed the heart in the chest of 55-year-old Louis Washkansky, whose own heart was damaged. Washkansky died of a lung infection 18 days after the operation.

2. In what year was the first human heart transplanted? _____

3. How long after the transplant did Washkansky die? _____

Check your answers on page 204.

Lesson 14

Identifying Cause and Effect

It is human nature to want to know why things happen. You probably question the causes of many things each day. For example, why won't your car start? Is it out of gas? Is there a problem with the starter? Is your battery dead? The reason your car won't start is the **cause**, and having a disabled vehicle is the **effect**, or result.

Science is based on the assumption that every natural event has a natural cause. Therefore, an important part of a scientist's job is to understand cause-and-effect relationships. For example, after scientists determine the cause of a disease such as cancer, they can work on finding a cure.

Writers organize details by cause and effect when they want to explain how one thing causes another thing to happen. The information in the following sentence has a cause-and-effect relationship:

A clogged heart artery can **cause** a heart attack.

Cause: clogged heart artery
Effect: heart attack

The following paragraph is organized by cause and effect. It explains how eating too much fatty food can lead to a heart attack:

Eating too much fatty food can cause a heart attack. Fat deposits from food can cause arteries to become clogged. As a result, arteries become narrow and allow less oxygen-rich blood to flow through them. When too little blood and oxygen reach the heart, the result is a heart attack.

The main idea of the paragraph is underlined. The other sentences support the main idea by describing the chain of causes and effects that lead to a heart attack. The words that help you understand the cause-and-effect relationships in the paragraph are circled.

The following diagram illustrates this chain. Notice how each effect becomes a cause of something else.

How Eating Fatty Food Causes a Heart Attack

Fatty food → Fat deposits → Clogged arteries →
Narrow arteries → Less oxygen-rich blood flows →
Too little blood and oxygen reach heart → Heart attack

The following words are often used to signal a cause-and-effect pattern of organization.

Cause and Effect: Signal Words

as a result	reason
because	result
cause	since
consequently	so
effect	therefore
on account of	thus

Part A. Find the causes and effects in the following descriptions.

1. Heart disease has been the number one cause of death in the United States since 1910.

   Cause: _____

   Effect: _____

2. When you exercise, tiny new blood vessels develop to feed the heart with blood.

   Cause: _____

   Effect: _____

3. Cigarette smoking shrinks arteries, releases carbon monoxide, a poisonous gas, into the blood instead of oxygen, and reduces lung capacity. (Note: One cause produces three effects.)

   Cause: _____

   Effects: _____

   _____

   _____

4. After you eat a large meal, the intestines take more oxygen from the blood to digest food. As a result, less oxygen reaches the brain and you feel tired. (Note: Show the chain of causes and effects in the description. One part of the chain is completed for you.)

   _____ → _____ →

   Less oxygen reaches the brain. → _____

Part B. The following paragraphs are organized by cause and effect. Read each paragraph and answer the questions that follow it.

Questions 1 and 2 are based on the following paragraph.

     The heart pumps blood through the arteries to all the organs and tissues. As it flows through the body, blood puts pressure on artery walls. If the blood has trouble circulating through the arteries, the heart has to pump harder. This results in high blood pressure. Besides being the leading cause of strokes, high blood pressure increases the risk of heart attack and kidney failure.

1. On what part of the body does blood put pressure? _____
2. What are the three possible effects of high blood pressure mentioned in the paragraph?

   _____ _____ _____

Questions 3 and 4 are based on the following paragraph.

A cut in a blood vessel causes platelets in the blood to surround the cut. They release a chemical called fibrin. Fibrin weaves tiny fibers across the cut. As a result, plasma and blood cells are trapped behind a net of fibrin. More and more cells pile up against the fibrin and form a clot. If the blood clot is on the surface of the skin, a scab develops.

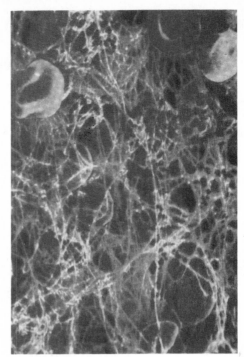

When you cut yourself, a network of fibrin threads forms over the injured area.

3. What is the name of the chemical in blood platelets that stops a cut from bleeding? _____

4. When does a blood clot form a scab? _____

Check your answers on page 204.

Lesson 15

Identifying Comparison

People naturally compare things. When you compare things, you note their likenesses and/or differences. You can increase your understanding of something new by comparing it to something with which you are familiar.

Scientists often make comparisons. Comparing such things as plants, animals, and diseases helps scientists understand them and describe them to others. For example, by comparing the traits and habits of heart attack victims to those of the general public, scientists have been able to identify heart attack risk factors.

Writers sometimes organize details by **comparison**. They are able to describe things very effectively by pointing out the likenesses and differences between two or more things.

Read the following sentence:

Arteries and veins are **both** blood vessels.

This sentence points out an important likeness between arteries and veins: They are both blood vessels. In contrast, the following sentence points out an important difference between arteries and veins:

Arteries carry blood away from the heart, **while** veins bring blood back to the heart.

The following paragraph is organized by comparison. It describes how arteries and veins are alike and how they are different.

Arteries and veins are both blood vessels. Arteries carry blood away from the heart, while veins bring blood back to the heart. Arteries are much smaller than veins. Arteries have thick, elastic walls that can stand the pressure put on them by the heart's pumping. However, veins do not have thick walls. They have tiny one-way valves that keep the blood flowing in the right direction—toward the heart.

The main idea of the paragraph is underlined. The other sentences support the main idea by describing arteries and veins. The words that signal comparisons are circled.

The following table shows the comparisons made in the paragraph.

THINGS COMPARED: ARTERIES AND VEINS

	Arteries	Veins
Likeness:	blood vessels	blood vessels
Differences:	carry blood away from heart	carry blood to heart
	smaller than veins	(larger than arteries)
	thick-walled and elastic	not thick-walled, but with one-way valves

The following words are often used to signal a comparison:

Comparison: Signal Words

Likeness	Difference	
also	although	on the contrary
both	but	on the other hand
likewise	however	unlike
similarly	in contrast	whereas
too	nevertheless	yet

Part A. Find the likenesses and differences described in the following items.

1. Both high blood pressure and high blood cholesterol can often be controlled by reducing the amount of dietary fat.

   Things compared: _____ and _____
   Likeness: _____   _____

2. Most plant products (fruits and vegetables) are low in fat, while most animal products (meats and dairy products) are high in fat.

   Things compared: _____ and _____
   Difference: _____   _____

3. Both strokes and heart attacks occur when major arteries are clogged. A stroke occurs when the brain does not get enough blood, while a heart attack occurs when the heart does not get enough blood.

   Things compared: _____ and _____
   Likeness: _____   _____
   Difference: _____   _____

4. Like running, swimming is aerobic exercise. Unlike running, swimming does not put pressure on the joints.

   Things compared: _____ and _____
   Likeness: _____   _____
   Difference: _____   _____

Part B. The following paragraphs are organized by comparison. Read each paragraph and answer the questions that follow it.

Questions 1 and 2 are based on the following paragraph.

   The blood in veins is not the same color as the blood in arteries. The blood in veins looks dull red or blue because it has released its oxygen into the cells and has picked up wastes. On the other hand, the blood in arteries is bright red because it is free of wastes and full of oxygen.

1. What two things are compared? _____
2. What difference between these two things is explained?

_____

Questions 3 to 5 are based on the following paragraph.

There are four chambers of the heart: two atria and two ventricles. The atria are the upper chambers, and the ventricles are the lower chambers. The atria receive blood from the veins as it returns from other parts of the body. In contrast, the ventricles are the pumping chambers. They force blood out of the heart into the arteries.

> The sound of a heartbeat is made when the ventricles contract to pump blood out of the heart.

3. What two things are compared? _____
4. What is similar about the two things? _____
5. What is different about the two things? _____

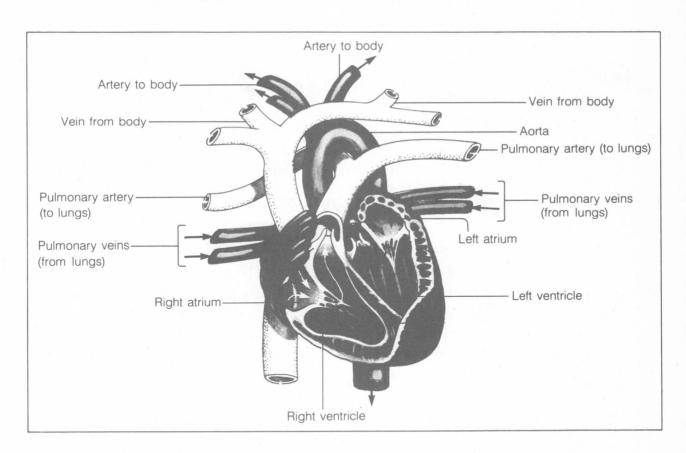

Check your answers on page 205.

Reviewing the Four Patterns
of Organization

In this chapter, you studied four ways writers organize details: list structure, time order, cause and effect, and comparison.

When you see how the details are organized in a passage you are reading, you can comprehend the passage better. For instance, you might be reading a passage about exercise and notice words that signal a comparison. This could lead you to realize that the passage describes how two types of exercise are alike or different. However, if the passage contains words that signal cause-and-effect organization, you might realize that the passage is about the effects of exercising.

In the following exercise, concentrate on finding the pattern of organization in the passages.

EXERCISE 16

Read each paragraph and answer the question that follows it.

Question 1 is based on the following paragraph.

Aerobic exercise increases your body's need for oxygen. In

Aerobic means "with oxygen."

order for your heart to send more oxygen to working muscles, it must work harder to pump blood throughout your body. When your heart does this regularly, it becomes stronger. Many experts feel that aerobic exercise is the most important part of a physical fitness program.

1. How are the details in the paragraph organized?
   (1) by cause and effect   (2) by comparison
   (3) by list structure   (4) by time order

Question 2 is based on the following paragraph.

Bypass surgery repairs blocked arteries that feed the heart with oxygen-rich blood. First, part of a large vein is removed from the leg. Then, one end is sewn to the aorta, the artery that sends oxygen-rich blood to both the heart and other parts of the body. Next, the other end is connected to the coronary artery past the blockage. The damaged part of the artery is bypassed. The new artery now carries the blood to the heart.

2. How are the details in the paragraph organized?
   (1) by cause and effect   (2) by comparison
   (3) by list structure   (4) by time order

Question 3 is based on the following paragraph.

The American Heart Association recommends the following dietary guidelines. Following these guidelines can reduce your risk of heart disease by lowering your blood pressure and blood cholesterol. One, eat fewer fats. No more than 30% of your total daily calories should come from fat. Two, cut the amount of saturated fat to 10% of your total daily calorie intake. Three, eat a diet that consists of 50% to 60% complex carbohydrates—fruits, vegetables, and grains. Four, get 15% of your calories from protein sources such as beans, fish, skinless poultry, and lean meats (broiled or baked because frying adds too much fat). Five, eat no more than two eggs per week. Six, limit your intake of sodium, including salt, to 3000 milligrams a day.

> Most table salt is 40% sodium. A teaspoon of salt contains about 2000 milligrams of sodium.

3. How are the details in the paragraph organized?
   (1) by cause and effect   (2) by comparison
   (3) by list structure   (4) by time order

Question 4 is based on the following paragraph.

Red blood cells and white blood cells are two parts of the blood. Unlike red blood cells, white blood cells have a nucleus

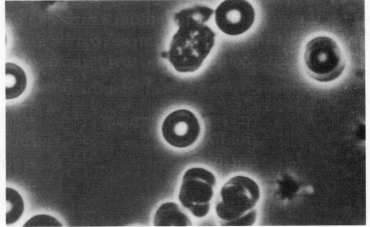

Human blood as seen through a microscope. The red blood cells have circular centers; a white blood cell is in the middle of the photograph.

Walter Dawn

and are able to reproduce. Red blood cells outnumber white blood cells by about 700 to 1 when a person is healthy. White blood cells are usually bigger and live longer than red blood cells. Red blood cells live only 120 days, but some white blood cells live for years.

4. How are the details in the paragraph organized?
   (1) by cause and effect   (2) by comparison
   (3) by list structure   (4) by time order

Question 5 is based on the following paragraph.

Since the first human heart was transplanted in 1967, there have been other major advances in the field of cardiology. A permanent artificial heart was implanted in 1982. The patient, Barney Clark, lived for 112 days after the operation. In 1984, the heart of a baboon was transplanted into the body of a human infant. The patient, a 12-day-old girl known as Baby Fae, died 21 days later. However, she lived longer than any of the four persons who had previously received animal hearts.

5. How are the details in the paragraph organized?
   (1) by cause and effect   (2) by comparison
   (3) by list structure   (4) by time order

Check your answers on page 205.

6 TABLES AND GRAPHS

In Chapter 5 you studied some of the ways writers organize information in paragraphs. Writers also organize information so that they can present it in tables and graphs, which show information visually. In this chapter you will study **tables**, **circle graphs**, **bar graphs**, and **line graphs**.

Lesson 17

Reading Tables

Read the following paragraph:

The National Cancer Institute recommends that people eat between 20 and 30 grams of fiber each day. Here are some low-calorie foods that contain fiber. One medium-sized apple has 80 calories and 3.5 grams of fiber. One-half cup of corn has 85 calories and 2.9 grams of fiber. One-half cup of green peas has 60 calories and 3.6 grams of fiber. One-half cup of kidney beans has 110 calories and 7.3 grams of fiber. One-half cup of lima beans has 65 calories and 4.5 grams of fiber. Three-quarters of a cup of oatmeal has 110 calories and 1.6 grams of fiber.

The above paragraph is one way to communicate information about the calorie and fiber content of foods. It is not the best way, however. Many words and phrases are repeated, such as *one-half cup*, *calories*, and *grams of fiber*. Reading the same words over and over again is boring. In addition, information about a specific food is hard to find because it is buried in the paragraph. Look at the same information in a table:

CALORIE AND FIBER CONTENT OF FOODS

Food	Serving Size	Calories*	Fiber[†] (in grams)
Apples	1 medium	80	3.5
Corn	½ cup	85	2.9
Green peas	½ cup	60	3.6
Kidney beans	½ cup	110	7.3
Lima beans	½ cup	65	4.5
Oatmeal	¾ cup	110	1.6

*Rounded to the nearest 5.
[†] Fiber includes the fiber in vegetable and fruit skins that can be eaten.
Source: U.S. Department of Health and Human Services

The table does a better job of organizing the information than the paragraph. The information in the table is organized in **columns**—lists that run vertically (top to bottom)—and in **rows**—lists that run horizontally (left to right).

In this table, there are four column headings: *Food, Serving Size, Calories*, and *Fiber*. The row headings are the names of various foods. A person reading the table can quickly find out how many grams of fiber there are in a specific food and make comparisons between foods.

Scientists use tables when they want to show a lot of information—especially information that can be compared. There are three steps in reading a table.

How to Read a Table

STEP 1: Read the title.
STEP 2: Read the column and row headings.
STEP 3: Read the table to find details.

The following example shows how to use these three steps to read the table shown above.

STEP 1: Read the title.

The title of the table is *Calorie and Fiber Content of Foods*. It lets you know what kind of information the table contains.

STEP 2: Read the column and row headings.

The column headings let you know what information is listed in each column. The row headings are the foods listed in the first column.

STEP 3: Read the table to find details.

Just as you read passages to find details, you can read tables to find details. When you know how a table is organized, you can easily find the details you are looking for. All the information in a row applies to the item named in its heading. For instance, the first item in the first column, *Apples*, is the heading of the first row. All the information in this row is about apples. It shows that one medium-sized apple supplies 80 calories and 3.5 grams of fiber.

When you are reading a table, it may help you to put a piece of paper under the row you are reading.

EXERCISE 17

Questions 1 to 5 are based on the following table, which is an extended version of the table you have already studied.

CALORIE AND FIBER CONTENT OF FOODS

Food	Serving Size	Calories*	Fiber[†] (in grams)
Apples	1 medium	80	3.5
Corn	½ cup	85	2.9
Green peas	½ cup	60	3.6
Kidney beans	½ cup	110	7.3
Lima beans	½ cup	65	4.5
Oatmeal	¾ cup	110	1.6
Pears	½ large	60	3.1
Potatoes	1 medium	105	2.5
Raisins	¼ cup	110	3.1
Spinach, cooked	½ cup	20	2.1
Strawberries	1 cup	45	3.0
Whole wheat bread	1 slice	60	1.4
Whole wheat pasta	1 cup	155	3.9

*Rounded to the nearest 5.
[†]Fiber includes the fiber in vegetable and fruit skins that can be eaten.

1. How many grams of fiber are there in ¼ cup of raisins?

   _____

2. How many calories are there in 1 cup of whole wheat pasta?

   _____

3. How many grams of fiber are there in ½ cup of corn? _____

4. Which serving of food listed in the table contains the most fiber?

   _____

5. Which of these servings of food has the fewest calories and the most fiber?

   (1) ¾ cup oatmeal   (2) ½ cup lima beans   (3) 1 medium potato

Questions 6 to 12 are based on the following two tables.

DESIRABLE WEIGHTS FOR MEN AGED 25 AND OVER (in pounds)				DESIRABLE WEIGHTS FOR WOMEN AGED 25 AND OVER (in pounds)			
Height	Small Frame	Medium Frame	Large Frame	Height	Small Frame	Medium Frame	Large Frame
5′ 1″	112–120	118–129	126–141	4′ 8″	92– 96	96–107	104–119
5′ 2″	115–123	121–133	129–144	4′ 9″	94–101	98–110	106–122
5′ 3″	118–126	124–136	132–148	4′ 10″	96–104	101–113	109–125
5′ 4″	121–129	127–139	135–152	4′ 11″	99–107	104–116	112–128
5′ 5″	124–133	130–143	138–156	5′ 0″	102–110	107–119	115–131
5′ 6″	128–137	134–147	142–161	5′ 1″	105–113	110–122	118–134
5′ 7″	132–141	138–152	147–166	5′ 2″	108–116	113–126	121–138
5′ 8″	136–145	142–156	151–170	5′ 3″	111–119	116–130	125–142
5′ 9″	140–150	146–160	155–174	5′ 4″	114–123	120–135	129–146
5′ 10″	144–154	150–165	159–179	5′ 5″	118–127	124–139	133–150
5′ 11″	148–158	154–170	164–184	5′ 6″	122–131	128–143	137–154
6′ 0″	152–162	158–175	168–189	5′ 7″	126–135	132–147	141–158
6′ 1″	156–167	162–180	173–194	5′ 8″	130–140	136–151	145–163
6′ 2″	160–171	167–185	178–199	5′ 9″	134–144	140–155	149–168
6′ 3″	164–175	172–190	182–204	5′ 10″	138–148	144–159	153–173

6. What is the title of the table on the left? _____

7. What is the title of the table on the right? _____

8. What are the four column headings used in both tables?

   _____   _____   _____   _____

9. What is the desirable weight range for a woman who is 5 feet 3 inches tall and has a medium frame? _____

10. What is the desirable weight range for a man who is 5 feet 11 inches tall and has a large frame? _____

11. What is the lowest desirable weight for a 5-foot, 8-inch man with a small frame? _____

12. What is the highest desirable weight for a 4-foot, 10-inch woman with a medium frame? _____

Check your answers on page 205.

Reading Circle Graphs

Circle graphs are named for their shape. They are also called pie charts. The circle represents the whole of something, that is, 100%. The parts of the circle represent the parts, or percentages, of the whole.

Scientists use circle graphs when they want to show what portion of a whole thing one part is. When reading a circle graph, you can easily make comparisons between the parts. There are three steps in reading a circle graph.

How to Read a Circle Graph

STEP 1: Read the title.
STEP 2: Read the labels on the parts of the circle graph.
STEP 3: Read the circle graph to find details.

The following example applies these three steps to this circle graph.

WHAT A TYPICAL CELL IN THE HUMAN BODY IS MADE OF

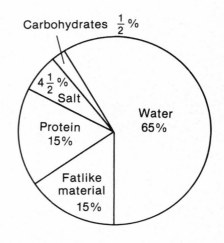

STEP 1: Read the title.

The title of a circle graph lets you know what the circle represents. The title is *What a Typical Cell in the Human Body Is Made Of.* This tells you that the circle represents a cell in the human body.

STEP 2: Read the labels on the parts of the circle graph.

The purpose of this step is to give you a quick overview of the circle graph. It is divided into five parts. The five parts represent the five substances that make up most cells in the human body. When you add the percentages of all five parts, they total 100%.

STEP 3: Read the circle graph to find details.

There are many details on the graph. For example, the largest part of the circle graph shows that water makes up most of a typical human cell—65%.

TRY THIS

Answer the following questions, which are based on the circle graph.

What percent of an average cell is protein? _____

What percent of an average cell is salt? _____

What two substances make up equal parts of a human cell?

_____ and _____

An average cell contains 15% protein and 4½% salt. Protein and fatlike material make up equal parts of a human cell: each makes up 15%.

Questions 1 to 6 are based on the following two circle graphs.

GASES THAT HUMANS INHALE

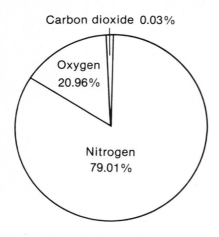

Carbon dioxide 0.03%

Oxygen 20.96%

Nitrogen 79.01%

GASES THAT HUMANS EXHALE

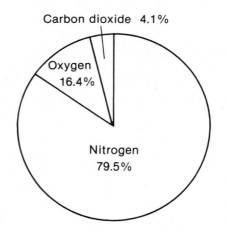

Carbon dioxide 4.1%

Oxygen 16.4%

Nitrogen 79.5%

1. What is the title of the circle graph on the left? _____

2. What is the title of the circle graph on the right? _____

3. Name the three gases that humans inhale and exhale.

_____ _____ _____

4. What percent of the gases that humans inhale is nitrogen?

_____

5. What percent of the gases that humans exhale is carbon dioxide?

_____

6. The gases that humans exhale contain
   (1) more oxygen than the gases they inhale
   (2) the same amount of oxygen as the gases they inhale
   (3) less oxygen than the gases they inhale

Check your answers on page 205.

Lesson 19

Reading Bar Graphs

Like circle graphs, bar graphs make it easy to compare things. However, unlike circle graphs, which compare the parts of one thing, bar graphs compare different things. Bar graphs are named for the bars that show the amounts being compared. There are three steps in reading a bar graph.

How to Read a Bar Graph

STEP 1: Read the title.
STEP 2: Read the labels on the horizontal and vertical axes.
STEP 3: Read the bar graph to find details.

The following example applies these three steps to this bar graph.

CALORIES BURNED WHILE EXERCISING

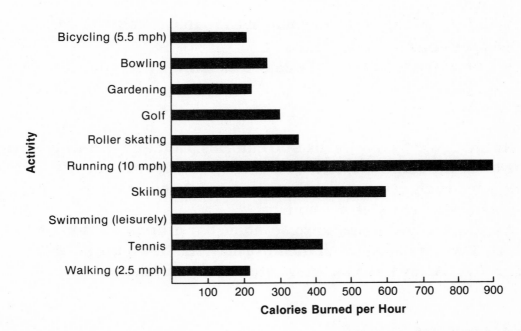

STEP 1: Read the title.

The title of the bar graph is *Calories Burned While Exercising*.

STEP 2: Read the labels on the vertical and horizontal axes.

Bar graphs have two **axes** that intersect, or meet. The line that

> *Axes* is the plural of *axis*.

runs from top to bottom along the left side of the graph is called the **vertical axis**. The line that runs from left to right along the bottom of the graph is called the **horizontal axis**.

The vertical axis of the bar graph in the example is labeled *Activity*. Along the axis is a list of ways to exercise. *Bicycling* is at the top, and *walking* is at the bottom. The horizontal axis of the graph is labeled *Calories Burned per Hour*. The numbers along the axis range from 100 to 900.

STEP 3: Read the bar graph to find details.

On this graph, the bars run parallel to the horizontal axis. They show how many calories are burned per hour when doing each kind of exercise. For instance, the bar for roller skating shows that a person burns 350 calories per hour doing this kind of exercise.

TRY THIS

Answer the following questions, which are based on the bar graph.

How many calories are burned while running for 1 hour?

_____

Which two activities shown burn the same number of calories per hour? _____ and _____

Which activity burns more calories, skiing or tennis?

_____

Running for 1 hour burns 900 calories. Golf and leisurely swimming burn the same amount of calories—300 per hour. Skiing burns more calories than tennis: skiing—nearly 600 calories per hour; tennis—about 420 calories per hour.

As you will see in the exercise, some bar graphs are double bar graphs. They are used when the information shown is divided into two groups. A key lets you know what each bar stands for.

Questions 1 to 10 are based on the following double bar graph. (Notice that the bars in this graph run parallel to the vertical axis.)

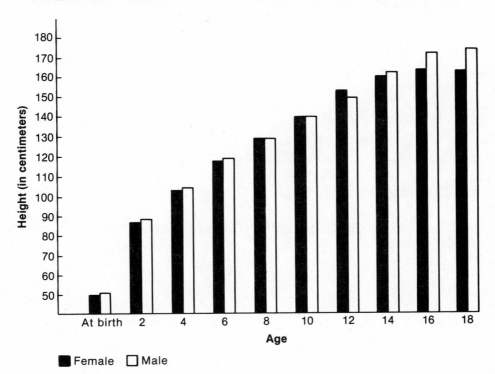

AVERAGE HEIGHTS OF CHILDREN AND ADOLESCENTS

■ Female □ Male

1. What is the title of the bar graph? _____
2. What does the horizontal axis show? _____
3. What does the vertical axis show? _____
4. What do the black bars on the graph stand for? _____
5. What do the white bars on the graph stand for? _____
6. What is the average height of 6-year-old girls?
    (1) 87 centimeters   (2) 117 centimeters   (3) 163 centimeters
7. What is the average height of 16-year-old boys?
    (1) 160 centimeters   (2) 163 centimeters   (3) 172 centimeters
8. At what two ages are the average heights of boys and girls the same? _____
9. At what age are girls taller than boys? _____
10. Between what ages is there no change in the average height of girls? _____

Check your answers on page 206.

Reading Line Graphs

Line graphs show change, often over a period of time. Like bar graphs, line graphs have horizontal and vertical axes. However, instead of bars, they use lines to show amounts. There are three steps in reading a line graph.

How to Read a Line Graph

STEP 1: Read the title.
STEP 2: Read the labels on the horizontal and vertical axes.
STEP 3: Read the line graph to find details.

The following example applies these three steps to this bar graph.

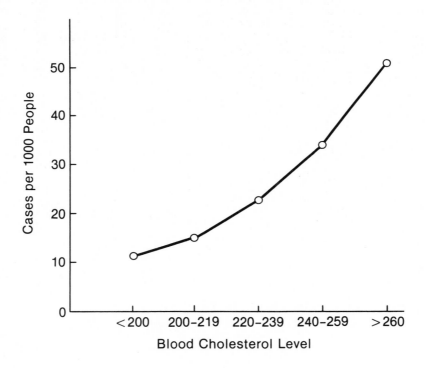

RISK OF DEVELOPING HEART DISEASE

STEP 1: Read the title.

The title of the line graph is *Risk of Developing Heart Disease.*

STEP 2: Read the labels on the vertical and horizontal axes.

The vertical axis of the bar graph is labeled *Cases per 1000 People.* The numbers along this axis range from 10 to 50. The horizontal axis is labeled *Blood Cholesterol Level.* The blood cholesterol levels shown range from less than 200 (<200) to more than 260 (>260).

STEP 3: Read the line graph to find details.

Dots above each label on the horizontal axis show how many people developed heart disease at each cholesterol level. The line of the graph connects the dots. For instance, one dot on the line graph is above *<200* on the horizontal axis and across from *10* on the vertical axis. This means that 10 out of 1000 people whose blood cholesterol level was below 200 developed heart disease.

Sometimes you have to estimate when you read a line graph. For example, there is a dot above *200–219* on the horizontal axis. You need to estimate how far up the vertical axis this dot is. It's about halfway between *10* and *20*, so it is at about 15.

The graph shows a **trend**, or pattern of change. As the level of blood cholesterol rises, the number of cases of heart disease increases. The main purpose of many line graphs is to show a trend, not to give exact figures.

EXERCISE 20

Questions 1 to 5 are based on the following line graph.

INFANT MORTALITY RATE

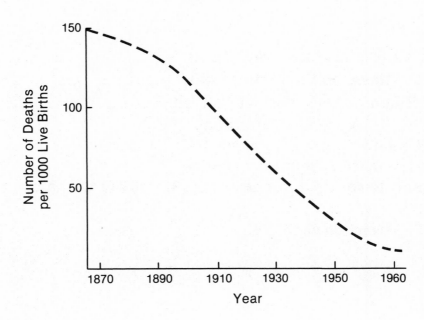

NOTE: The infant mortality rate is the number of deaths of children up to age one.

1. What is the title of the graph? _____

2. What is shown on the vertical axis? _____

3. What is shown on the horizontal axis? _____

4. In 1910, how many infants died per 1000 live births?
    (1) about 90   (2) about 125   (3) about 150

5. Since 1870 the infant mortality rate has
    (1) gone up   (2) gone down   (3) stayed the same

Questions 6 to 10 are based on the following line graph.

LIFE EXPECTANCY

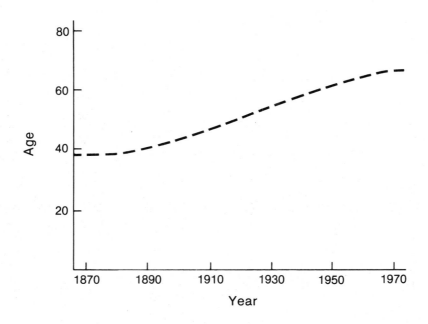

6. What is the title of the graph? _____

7. What is shown on the vertical axis? _____

8. What is shown on the horizontal axis? _____

9. In 1940 life expectancy was about
    (1) 50 years   (2) 60 years   (3) 70 years

10. Since 1870 life expectancy has
    (1) gone down   (2) gone up   (3) stayed the same

Check your answers on page 206.

SCIENCE READINGS 1

This section of the unit contains science readings. These readings can help you prepare for the science test of the GED in three ways. You can use them to

- review what you already know about science
- expand your general knowledge of science
- practice the reading skills covered in Unit 1

WHAT IS SCIENCE?

Science is the existing body of knowledge about the universe. As more facts are uncovered, this body of knowledge grows. Science is divided into four main branches: **biology**, **earth science**, **chemistry**, and **physics**.

Biology is the study of life. Biologists study the <u>structure</u> and <u>function</u> of living

> STRUCTURE: how something is put together
> FUNCTION: how something works

things. A biologist often specializes in one of the divisions of biology. **Anatomy** is the study of the <u>structure</u> of organisms. **Physiology** is the study of the <u>functions</u> of organisms. **Zoology** is the study of animals. **Botany** is the study of plants. Finally, **ecology** is the study of how life forms relate to each other and to their environment.

Earth science is the study of the earth. Like a living organism, the earth has been changing slowly since its birth about 4.5 billion years ago. Earth scientists try to figure out how the planet was formed and how it changes. Earth science is divided into four main branches. **Geology** is the study of the land. **Meteorology** is the study of the air surrounding the earth. **Oceanography** is the study of the oceans. **Astronomy** is the study of the universe beyond the earth.

Chemistry is the study of matter. Matter is everything that has size and weight. Chemistry deals with what matter is made of and how it changes. Scientists who study matter are called chemists.

Physics is the study of how matter and energy relate to each other. Physics includes the study of such subjects as light, sound, gravity, and the laws of motion. Scientists who study physics are called physicists.

1. What are the four branches of earth science?

   _____   _____

   _____   _____

2. Which sentence in the first paragraph states the main idea of the passage?

   _____

3. How are the details in the second paragraph organized?
   (1) by cause and effect
   (2) by comparison
   (3) by list structure
   (4) by time order

4. Match the word in Column A with its definition in Column B.

   Column A
   ___ A. science
   ___ B. meteorology
   ___ C. oceanography
   ___ D. physics
   ___ E. chemistry
   ___ F. anatomy

   Column B
   (1) deals with weather conditions
   (2) includes the study of light
   (3) studies how organisms are put together
   (4) focuses on the changes in matter
   (5) studies the sea
   (6) studies the whole universe

CLASSIFICATION OF LIVING THINGS

All scientists use the same system to classify, or group, living things. Each living thing is classified in seven groups and subgroups: a kingdom, a phylum, a class, an order, a family, a genus, and a species. A kingdom is the biggest group a living thing belongs to. A phylum is smaller than a kingdom, a class is smaller than a phylum, and so on. A species is the smallest group. It is made up of only one kind of living thing.

There are two **kingdoms**. All living things are members of either the **plant kingdom** or the **animal kingdom**. The following table shows the classification of three members of the animal kingdom. The names of each group are in Latin.

	Human	Chimpanzee	Lion
KINGDOM	Animalia	Animalia	Animalia
PHYLUM	Chordata	Chordata	Chordata
CLASS	Mammalia	Mammalia	Mammalia
ORDER	Primates	Primates	Carnivora
FAMILY	Hominidae	Pongidae	Felidae
GENUS	*Homo*	*Pan*	*Panthera*
SPECIES	*sapiens*	*troglodytes*	*leo*

The animal kingdom is divided into **phyla**. Humans, chimpanzees, and lions

> *Phyla* is the plural form of *phylum*.

all belong to the same phylum, Chordata, which includes all animals with backbones.

Phyla are divided into smaller groups called **classes**. All the animals listed in the table belong to the class Mammalia. Members of this class, mammals, feed their young with breast milk and have hair.

Classes are divided into **orders**. Humans and chimpanzees are members of a highly developed order of mammals called Primates. Primates have fingers and toes and walk on two legs. The lion is a member of the order Carnivora.

At this point, humans and chimpanzees go their separate ways. As the table shows, humans belong to a different **family**, **genus**, and **species** than chimpanzees.

5. Which of the following groups is the biggest?
   (1) kingdom
   (2) class
   (3) species

6. Which of the following is not a trait of mammals?
   (1) feed young with breast milk
   (2) have hair
   (3) walk on two legs

7. Which of the following are members of the phylum Chordata?
   (1) animals without backbones
   (2) animals with backbones
   (3) all animals

8. What is the family of the lion?
   (1) Carnivora
   (2) Felidae
   (3) Pongidae

HOW THE HUMAN BODY IS STRUCTURED

The human body is made up of cells, tissues, organs, and systems. **Cells** are the smallest units of life. **Tissues** are groups of cells. **Organs** are groups of tissues. **Systems** are groups of organs.

Cells. Humans have many different kinds of cells. Each kind does a special job. For instance, red blood cells carry oxygen to all parts of the body. Muscle cells enable the body to move, and nerve cells carry messages throughout the body.

Tissues. Cells that do the same job in the body are grouped together to form tissues. The body has four main kinds of tissues. **Epithelial tissue** lines and protects the body. The skin is made up of epithelial tissue. **Connective tissue** connects the parts of the body. Bones, tendons, ligaments, and blood are made of connective tissue. **Muscle tissue** allows the body to move. Finally, **nerve tissue** controls the organs and their functions.

Organs. Groups of different tissues that work together are called organs. Each organ has a certain job to do. The eyes, lungs, kidneys, brain, and heart are organs. Some organs, like the heart, are made up of all four kinds of tissue. Epithelial tissue protects the heart. Connective tissue holds the heart in place. Muscle tissue makes the heart pump. Finally, nerve tissue connects the heart to the brain.

Systems. Groups of organs that work together to perform certain functions are called systems. The human body has 11 systems. Each system does a job that keeps the body alive.

9. **Which of the following sentences from the passage states the main idea?**
   (1) The human body is made up of cells, tissues, organs, and systems.
   (2) Some organs, like the heart, are made up of all four kinds of tissue.
   (3) Groups of organs that work together to perform certain functions are called systems.

10. **Which cells bring oxygen to all parts of the body?**
   (1) red blood cells
   (2) muscle cells
   (3) nerve cells

11. **A group of organs that work together is called a**
   (1) cell
   (2) tissue
   (3) system

12. **Which kind of tissue covers the body?**
   (1) connective
   (2) epithelial
   (3) muscle
   (4) nerve

13. **Which kind of tissue connects the heart to the brain?**
   (1) connective
   (2) epithelial
   (3) muscle
   (4) nerve

THE ELEVEN SYSTEMS IN THE HUMAN BODY

The following table shows the 11 systems in the human body, their jobs, and their parts. Some systems have many jobs and parts. In such cases, only some of their jobs and parts are listed.

System	Job	Parts
Respiratory	Supplies the body with oxygen; removes carbon dioxide from the body	Nasal passages, trachea, lungs
Digestive	Takes nutrients from food so that the body can use them	Mouth, esophagus, stomach, liver, pancreas, intestines
Circulatory	Carries nutrients, water, and oxygen to cells; removes waste from cells	Heart, veins, arteries, capillaries
Nervous	Controls all activities of the body	Brain, spinal cord, nerves
Skeletal	Gives the body shape and support; protects organs	Bones, cartilage, joints, ligaments
Muscular	Controls movement	Muscles
Integumentary	Protects the body	Skin
Endocrine	Secretes hormones that help regulate certain body activities	Glands
Immune	Finds and destroys organisms that are not part of the body	Thymus gland, white blood cells, spleen
Excretory	Removes various wastes produced by the body	Kidneys, bladder
Reproductive	Produces children	Ovaries, testes

14. **Which of the following systems protects the organs?**
   (1) skeletal
   (2) reproductive
   (3) nervous

15. **What do the glands in the endocrine system do?**
   (1) control body movements
   (2) find and destroy foreign organisms
   (3) secrete hormones

16. **Which of the following organs is part of the excretory system?**
   (1) brain
   (2) kidneys
   (3) lungs

17. **Which of the following systems controls all activities of the body?**
   (1) nervous system
   (2) immune system
   (3) muscular system

18. **Which of the following organs is part of the respiratory system?**
   (1) lungs
   (2) ovaries
   (3) skin

THE DIGESTIVE SYSTEM

The human body needs food to grow and to stay healthy. However, most foods cannot be used directly by the body. During digestion, the **digestive system** breaks food down into nutrients that the body can use. Each organ in the digestive system performs part of the process.

Digestion begins in the **mouth** where food is chewed and made smaller. The enzymes in saliva change some of the nutrients in food into simpler substances.

Food that has been chewed passes through the **esophagus** to the stomach. The **stomach** is a large sac that can store food for as long as six hours. In the stomach, food is churned into smaller pieces.

From the stomach, food moves into the **small intestine**, a narrow tube about 25 feet long. Most digestion takes place there. **Bile**, which is secreted by the **liver**, separates fats into tiny balls. Digestive juices from the **pancreas** break down starches and proteins. Finally, digestive juices made by the small intestine break down all other nutrients.

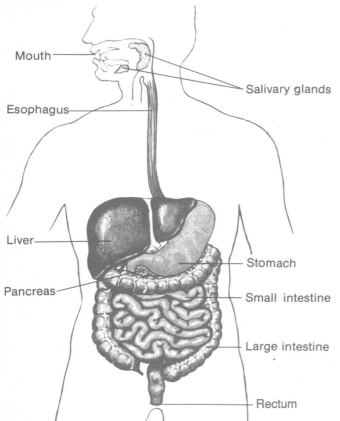

Mouth
Salivary glands
Esophagus
Liver
Stomach
Pancreas
Small intestine
Large intestine
Rectum

Digested food leaves the small intestine and enters the body's bloodstream. Blood carries digested food to the rest of the body. Undigested food passes from the small intestine into the **large intestine**, a wide, coiled tube. The body absorbs the water from the remains of the food while it is in the large intestine. Then, the unused solid waste leaves the body through the **rectum**.

19. What is the topic of the passage?

_____

20. Where does digestion start?

_____

21. About how long is the small intestine?

_____

22. What breaks down fat? _____

23. Which organ makes digestive juices that break down starches and proteins?
    (1) the liver
    (2) the pancreas
    (3) the small intestine

24. How are the details in the passage organized?
    (1) by cause and effect
    (2) by comparison
    (3) by list structure
    (4) by time order

25. Which of the following sentences from the passage is the main idea?
    (1) The stomach is a large sac that can store food for as long as six hours.
    (2) Digested food leaves the small intestine and enters the body's bloodstream.
    (3) During digestion, the digestive system breaks food down into nutrients that the body can use.

THE ATMOSPHERE

The earth is covered by a "blanket" of air called the **atmosphere**. The atmosphere is held close to the earth by gravity. Without the atmosphere, the earth would be a dry and barren place.

The atmosphere is a mixture of invisible gases. These gases are necessary for the survival of all living things. Nitrogen makes up 78% of the atmosphere. Plants use compounds containing nitrogen to make protein. Oxygen makes up 21% of the atmosphere. It is needed for respiration in plants and animals. The air also includes small amounts of other gases such as carbon dioxide and argon.

The atmosphere, which is about 350 miles thick, has four layers. The layer closest to the earth is the **troposphere**. It is 5 miles thick at the poles of the earth and 11 miles thick at the equator.

The next layer is the **stratosphere**. The stratosphere extends about 30 miles out from the earth. It is a zone of cloudless air with temperatures much like those near the earth's surface. It contains a layer of ozone, a form of oxygen gas that shields the earth from the sun's ultraviolet rays.

Beyond the stratosphere is the **mesosphere**. It extends another 50 miles from the earth. The mesosphere is the coldest layer of the atmosphere.

The outside layer of the atmosphere is the **thermosphere**. Its name means "heat sphere." It is the hottest layer of the atmosphere, with temperatures reaching 3600°F.

26. What is the topic of the passage?

_____

27. Which three of the following gases make up the atmosphere?
    ____ (a) carbon dioxide
    ____ (b) carbon monoxide
    ____ (c) hydrogen
    ____ (d) oxygen
    ____ (e) nitrogen

28. How many miles thick is the troposphere at the equator? _____

_____

29. In which part of the atmosphere is the ozone layer? _____

30. Which is the outside layer of the atmosphere? _____

31. What does *therm* mean? _____

The **universe** is the name for everything that exists. Most of the universe is empty **space**. In this empty space, there is nothing—not even air. The rest of the universe is made up of matter and energy.

Everything that has weight and takes up space is **matter**. All matter—every solid, liquid, and gas in the universe—is made up of **atoms**. We are made up of atoms. So are the food we eat, the air we breathe, and the sun that gives us warmth and light. We cannot see the atoms that make up everything around us. Atoms are very tiny. There are billions and billions of atoms in a drop of water—more than there are people in the world.

Atoms have three parts: **protons**, **neutrons**, and **electrons**. Protons and neutrons are contained in the center of the atom, called the **nucleus**. Electrons move in orbits around the nucleus.

OXYGEN ATOM

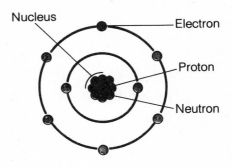

32. What is in empty space? _____

33. What is matter? _____

34. What is all matter made of? _____

35. Which of the following sentences from the second paragraph is the main idea?
    (1) Everything that has weight and takes up space is matter.
    (2) All matter—every solid, liquid, and gas in the universe—is made up of atoms.
    (3) Atoms are very tiny.

In the universe, besides space and matter, there is also energy. **Energy** is the ability to do work—that is, the ability to cause something to move.

There are two forms of energy: kinetic and potential. **Kinetic energy** is energy of motion. A person skiing down a mountain has kinetic energy. On the other hand, **potential energy**, or stored energy, is energy of position. For example, a person standing on the top of a mountain ready to ski down has potential energy. When the person is not skiing, the energy to do work, or ski down the mountain, is stored energy. When the person waiting to ski begins skiing, the potential energy becomes kinetic energy. It moves the person to the bottom of the mountain. Kinetic and potential energy are constantly changing forms.

36. What is the topic of the passage?

_____

37. What is energy? _____

38. Which of the following sentences from the second paragraph is the main idea?
    (1) There are two forms of energy: kinetic and potential.
    (2) Kinetic energy is energy of motion.
    (3) On the other hand, potential energy, or stored energy, is energy of position.

39. How are the details in the second paragraph organized?
    (1) by cause and effect
    (2) by comparison
    (3) by list structure
    (4) by time order

Check your answers on page 206.

SCIENCE READINGS 1 SKILLS CHART

To review the reading skills covered by the questions in Science Readings 1, study the following parts of Unit 1.

Unit 1		*Question Number*
Chapter 1	Prereading Strategies	19, 26, 36
Chapter 2	Word Parts	31
Chapter 3	Details in Passages	1, 4, 5, 6, 7, 10, 11, 12, 13, 20, 21, 22, 23, 27, 28, 29, 30, 32, 33, 34, 37
Chapter 4	The Stated Main Idea	2, 9, 25, 35, 38
Chapter 5	Patterns of Organization	3, 24, 39
Chapter 6	Tables and Graphs	8, 14, 15, 16, 17, 18

GED PRACTICE 1

This section will give you practice in answering questions like those on the GED. The Science Test of the GED has 66 multiple-choice questions. Each question has 5 choices. The 10 questions in this Practice are all multiple-choice, like the ones on the GED.

As you do this Practice, use the reading skills you've studied in this unit:

- Before you read a paragraph or table, preview it.
- Preview the questions, too. This way you will read for the details you need to answer the questions.
- As you read a passage, note its organization. This will help you to find main ideas and understand details.

Directions: Choose the one best answer to each item.

Items 1 and 2 are based on the following information.

An immunity to a disease is a resistance to it. People have two types of immunity: natural and acquired. Natural immunity is present at birth. It protects people from diseases that can infect other living things. For example, people cannot get tobacco mosaic disease, a plant disease. Acquired immunity, however, develops during a person's lifetime. Once a person has had a disease such as chicken pox, for example, he or she will probably not get it again.

1. Which of the following statements from the passage states the main idea?

   (1) People have two types of immunity: natural and acquired.
   (2) Natural immunity is present at birth.
   (3) For example, people cannot get tobacco mosaic disease, a plant disease.
   (4) Acquired immunity, however, develops during a person's lifetime.
   (5) Once a person has had a disease such as chicken pox, for example, he or she will probably not get it again.

2. The passage explains the difference between

   (1) plant diseases and animal diseases
   (2) chicken pox and tobacco mosaic disease
   (3) natural immunity and acquired immunity
   (4) disease and resistance
   (5) immunity in humans and immunity in plants

Item 3 is based on the following information.

An allergy is a disorder of the immune system. Allergic reactions occur when the immune system responds to a false alarm. That is, the immune system attacks a harmless substance as if it were a threat to the body. The immune system of an allergy sufferer attacks a harmless substance such as pollen, cat hair, or dust. The allergic reaction often causes symptoms like those of a cold or the flu—sore throat, runny nose, itchy eyes. The most common types of allergies are hay fever, asthma, and hives.

3. An allergic reaction takes place when

   (1) a hairy animal is in the area
   (2) the immune system reacts against something that is harmless
   (3) cat hair or house dust threatens to harm the body
   (4) a person is ill with a cold or the flu
   (5) the immune system is attacked by a virus

Items 4 to 6 are based on the following information.

Angioplasty is a medical procedure that can widen clogged heart arteries. It doesn't involve surgery. First, a doctor inserts a thin plastic tube, called a catheter, into an artery

GED Practice 1   85

in an arm or leg. The tube is guided through the artery until it reaches the clogged heart artery. Then, a smaller catheter with a balloon tip is passed through the first tube. Next, the balloon is inflated at the point of the blockage. This enlarges the blood vessel so blood can flow more easily to the heart. Finally, the balloon is deflated, and the catheters are withdrawn.

4. What is a catheter?

   (1) a thin plastic tube
   (2) a small balloon
   (3) an enlarged blood vessel
   (4) a clogged artery
   (5) a heart specialist

5. After the second catheter is passed through the first one, what is the next step in the procedure?

   (1) A tube is guided to the clogged heart artery.
   (2) A catheter is inserted into an artery in an arm or leg.
   (3) The catheters are removed.
   (4) A balloon is inflated.
   (5) A balloon is deflated.

6. Which of the following statements from the passage states the main idea?

   (1) Angioplasty is a medical procedure that can widen clogged heart arteries.
   (2) It doesn't involve surgery.
   (3) First, a doctor inserts a thin plastic tube, called a catheter, into an artery in an arm or leg.
   (4) The tube is guided through the artery until it reaches the clogged heart artery.
   (5) Finally, the balloon is deflated and the catheters are withdrawn.

Items 7 to 10 are based on the following information.

A blood pressure reading is reported as two numbers, as in 120/80. The first number is the systolic pressure. This is the amount of pressure the blood puts on the walls of the arteries when the heart contracts, or beats. The second number is the diastolic pressure. This is the amount of pressure the blood puts on the artery walls when the heart is relaxed between contractions. The higher the numbers, the harder it is for blood to flow through the arteries.

BLOOD PRESSURE CLASSIFICATIONS
(for persons 18 and older)

Systolic Pressure (first number)

Reading	Category
Lower than 140	Normal
140–159	Borderline isolated systolic hypertension
160 or higher	Isolated systolic hypertension

Diastolic Pressure (second number)

Reading	Category
Lower than 85	Normal
85–89	High normal
90–104	Mild hypertension
105–114	Moderate hypertension
115 or higher	Severe hypertension

7. The diastolic pressure is the pressure recorded when the

   (1) blood flows
   (2) heart beats
   (3) heart rests
   (4) arteries contract
   (5) arteries harden

8. A blood pressure reading tells about the pressure the

   (1) heart puts on the artery walls
   (2) arteries put on the heart
   (3) blood puts on the heart
   (4) blood puts on the artery walls
   (5) arteries put on the blood

9. Which of the following systolic blood pressure readings is normal?

   (1) 170
   (2) 160
   (3) 150
   (4) 140
   (5) 130

10. A diastolic blood pressure reading of 110 would place a person in which of the following categories?

   (1) normal blood pressure
   (2) high normal blood pressure
   (3) mild hypertension
   (4) moderate hypertension
   (5) severe hypertension

Check your answers on page 207.

GED PRACTICE 1 SKILLS CHART

To review the reading skills covered by the items in GED Practice 1, study the following parts of Unit 1.

Unit 1		*Item Number*
Chapter 3	Details in Passages	3, 4, 7, 8
Chapter 4	The Stated Main Idea	1, 6
Chapter 5	Patterns of Organization	2, 5
Chapter 6	Tables and Graphs	9, 10

UNIT 2

Inferring as You Read

Making inferences is something you do all the time. For example, when you smell smoke, you probably infer that something is burning, even though you do not see the fire. You also make inferences when you read. The skill of inferring as you read is the ability to understand the meaning that is not directly stated.

To diminish risks to water supplies, the Environmental Protection Agency has developed new protective standards for landfills.

Unit 2 Overview

Chapter 1   Inferences
Chapter 2   The Implied Main Idea

Science Readings 2
GED Practice 2

INFERENCES

In the lessons in this chapter, you will practice making inferences. First, you will use context clues to help you figure out the meanings of new words. Then, you will determine whether an answer to a question is directly stated or implied in something you have read. Finally, you will use details as clues to help answer inference questions.

Lesson 21

Inferring Word Meaning

A word in a sentence is surrounded by other words. These other words are its **context**. Sometimes you may not know the meaning of a word. Often the word's context can help you figure out its meaning.

TRY THIS

Use the underlined context clues to help you figure out the meaning of the word in dark type.

Marty is **ambidextrous**. He uses his right hand when he eats, and his left hand when he writes. He is a left-handed golfer, but a right-handed pitcher. Marty's son, Mort, is not **ambidextrous**. He uses his right hand to do everything.

An ambidextrous person
(1) is right-handed
(2) is left-handed
(3) can use both hands with ease

An ambidextrous person can use both hands with ease (3). The word's context gives examples of what a person who is ambidextrous can do: Marty does things with both hands. The paragraph contrasts Marty's ability with his son's. Mort, who is not ambidextrous, uses only his right hand to do things.

Many kinds of context clues can help you figure out the meanings of words. As in the above paragraph, the context may give you examples of the new word. In other cases, the context may define the new word or another word that has the same meaning as the new word. The context may also define a word that has a meaning opposite that of the new word.

The ability to use context clues is a valuable skill. It can help you better understand something you are reading. It can also help you increase your vocabulary. It is especially helpful when no dictionary is available.

EXERCISE 21

Use context clues to help you figure out the meanings of the words in dark type. Answer the question that follows each passage.

Question 1 is based on the following paragraph, in which context clues are underlined.

Natural resources are materials people need or use that are supplied by nature. All natural resources are either renewable or **nonrenewable**. Water and soil are renewable resources. They are always being replaced by natural processes, so they can't be used up. Minerals and coal are **nonrenewable** resources.

1. Nonrenewable resources are resources that
   (1) are not supplied by nature
   (2) are quickly replaced by nature
   (3) can be used up

Question 2 is based on the following passage.

A mineral is a solid substance that occurs naturally in the earth. There are over 2000 different minerals. The rocks that make up the earth's crust are made of minerals.

Some minerals, such as gold, are made of a single element.

> ELEMENTS: the chemical substances out of which everything in the universe is made

Others are **compounds**. The mineral halite is a **compound**. It is made up of two elements, sodium and chlorine. Some **compounds** are made up of more than two elements.

2. Compounds are made up of
   (1) only one element
   (2) two or more elements
   (3) sodium and chlorine

Question 3 is based on the following passage.

Metals are elements that have certain properties. Metals are shiny. They also **conduct** heat and electricity. In addition, metals are malleable. This means that they can be hammered or pressed into different shapes without breaking. Metals are also ductile. That is, they can be drawn or stretched thin without breaking. Iron, aluminum, and copper are elements that are metals.

Nonmetal elements have the opposite properties. They are not shiny. Nonmetals cannot carry heat or electricity. Furthermore, they are not malleable or ductile. In fact, they break apart very easily. Carbon, sulfur, and phosphorus are elements that are nonmetals.

3. *Conduct* means
   (1) carry
   (2) break apart very easily
   (3) stretch

Question 4 is based on the following paragraph.

A few metals, such as gold and silver, are found in their pure state. However, most metals are combined with other elements in ores. After ores are taken from the earth, metals can be

ORES: minerals that contain useful metals and nonmetals

extracted from them. For example, during a process called smelting, ore is heated in such a way that metal can be separated from it.

4. *Extracted* means
   (1) blended
   (2) removed
   (3) heated

Question 5 is based on the following paragraph.

Both aluminum and gold are metals. Because aluminum is the most **abundant** metal on earth, it is not expensive. Gold, because it is a very rare metal, is quite expensive.

5. *Abundant* means
   (1) plentiful
   (2) scarce
   (3) expensive

Question 6 is based on the following paragraph.

Conservationists are people who protect the earth's natural resources. They want natural resources to be used in a way that causes the least amount of harm to the environment. They try to make sure that people do not **exhaust** the earth's supply of non-renewable resources. They also try to protect the earth from <u>pollution</u>.

> POLLUTION: harmful or unwanted substances added to the environment

6. *Exhaust* means
   (1) protect
   (2) replace
   (3) use up

Questions 7 to 9 are based on the following passage.

Air pollution occurs when harmful substances are added to the air. Pollutants such as ash, soot, and gas are **emitted** when coal and oil are burned for fuel.

Air pollution speeds up the <u>weathering</u> process. It also kills

> WEATHERING: the slow process by which all substances exposed to the air are worn down

plants that people depend on for food. However, the most **detrimental** effect of air pollution is the health problems it

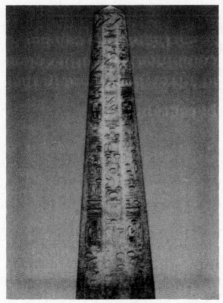

Cleopatra's Needle, a stone structure, stood in an Egyptian desert for 3500 years with little damage (*left*). A few years after it was moved to Central Park in New York City, it showed signs of weathering by air pollution and moisture (*right*).

causes in humans. Regular exposure to air pollution can cause respiratory problems or **aggravate** those that already exist.

7. *Emitted* means
   (1) destroyed
   (2) released
   (3) used

8. *Detrimental* means
   (1) useful
   (2) harmless
   (3) harmful

9. *Aggravate* means
   (1) make worse
   (2) improve
   (3) cure

Questions 10 to 12 are based on the following passage.

The presence of harmful substances in bodies of water is called water pollution. The processes used to make many different products—tires, paper, paint, etc.—create chemical wastes. These chemicals, many of which are **toxic,** are often dumped into rivers and other bodies of water.

Pesticides also **contaminate** water. Pesticides are **toxic** chemicals used to kill insects and other pests that damage crops. When pesticides are used, a certain amount may run off the land into streams and rivers. Pesticides can also leak down into ground water.

> GROUND WATER: water beneath the earth's surface

Even the oceans are showing signs of abuse. In the summer of 1988, many beaches were closed because of other kinds of pollution. Raw sewage and medical waste began to wash up on the

> RAW SEWAGE: untreated waste from sinks, bathtubs, and toilets

shore. The **refuse** from hospitals included hypodermic needles, bags filled with blood, and dead laboratory rats.

The effects of water pollution are quite serious. When pollutants **contaminate** water, it cannot be used for drinking, bathing, or recreation. Fish and other organisms that live in the water become diseased or die.

10. *Toxic* means
    (1) poisonous
    (2) helpful
    (3) liquid

11. *Contaminate* means
    (1) to make pure
    (2) to make impure
    (3) to make safe

12. *Refuse* means
    (1) waste
    (2) equipment
    (3) lost supplies

Questions 13 to 15 are based on the following passage.

When you throw away a bag of garbage, do you think about where it will go? Years ago, most people did not think about what would happen to the milk cartons and cereal boxes they **discarded.** Today, awareness of the solid waste crisis is growing.

Many more people are now aware that things thrown away today will have to be put somewhere tomorrow.

For each person in America, about 3.6 pounds of garbage are thrown away per day. This adds up to about 160 million tons of trash per year. The problem is that we are running out of places to put garbage. Most communities are running out of landfill

LANDFILL: a place where garbage is buried

space. Some already ship their garbage to **disposal sites** in other states.

Solid waste is either buried or burned. Both disposal methods cause pollution. Burying garbage contaminates ground water. Burning garbage pollutes the air and creates toxic ash. However,

ASH: the powder that remains after something has been burned

these disposal methods are being improved.

The EPA has developed new protective standards for land-

EPA: Environmental Protection Agency, the government agency responsible for protecting the nation's land, air, and water

fills. Liners, covers, and collection systems that keep poisons from draining into the ground can greatly **diminish** risks to water supplies. Incinerators are now designed and run so that

INCINERATOR: a furnace for burning waste

they do not pose a public health threat. Also, the ash that remains is treated and disposed of in lined landfills.

Many communities use incinerators that turn the heat energy from burning garbage into electrical energy. These waste-to-energy plants put trash to use and reduce the volume of solid waste by 90%. The process works best when certain items are removed before the garbage is burned. These include items that do not burn well, items that create harmful emissions, and items that can be recycled.

Researchers are now working on ways to recycle nontoxic ash. By making things from ash instead of burying the ash in landfills, the end products in the waste cycle can be sold. Some products now made from ash are cement, concrete, cinder blocks, and fiberglass.

13. *Discarded* means
    (1) opened
    (2) used
    (3) threw away

14. *Disposal sites* are places where a community's garbage is
    (1) made
    (2) picked up
    (3) dumped
15. *Diminish* means
    (1) increase
    (2) reduce
    (3) improve

Check your answers on page 208.

Lesson 22

Identifying Stated and Implied Answers

When you understand something that is stated in a passage, your understanding comes from **reading the lines** that are written. In most passages, there is also a meaning **"between the lines"**—that is, in what is not written. When you read between the lines, you use details that are stated to help you grasp ideas that are not directly stated. It is similar to what you do when you use context clues to figure out the meaning of a new word.

Much of the meaning we get when we read comes from reading between the lines, or **making inferences**. When you have to answer a question about information in a passage, the question may be about stated information or about **implied** information, the information between the lines.

Here is a two-step strategy for finding out whether you need to read the lines or to read between the lines to answer a particular question about information in a passage.

How to Find Out If an Answer Is Stated or Implied

STEP 1: Scan the passage to see if the answer is stated directly. If not, go to Step 2.

STEP 2: Scan the passage to find the clues that lead to the answer.

The following example shows how to apply these two steps to questions about the following paragraph.

Water exists in three states: liquid, solid, and gas. At temperatures of 32°F and below, water freezes and is solid. At 212°F, the point of boiling, water becomes a gas.

Question A: At what temperature does water boil and become a gas?
   Answer: At 212°F.
Question B: Between what temperatures is water a liquid?
   Answer: Between 32°F and 212°F.

STEP 1: Scan the passage to see if the answer is stated directly. If not, go to Step 2.

The answer to Question A is **stated** in the third sentence of the paragraph. Therefore, you can find the answer by **reading the lines**.

The answer to Question B is **not directly stated** in the passage, so you need to go to Step 2.

STEP 2: Scan the passage to find the clues that lead to the answer.

The following clues lead to the answer to Question B: If water is solid at 32°F and below and becomes a gas at 212°F, it must be a liquid at temperatures between 32°F and 212°F. Therefore, you can find the answer by **reading between the lines**.

EXERCISE 22

The following passages and graph are each followed by questions and their answers. Use the two-step strategy to decide how the answers were found.

> **How to Find Out If an Answer Is Stated or Implied**
>
> Step 1: Scan the passage or graph to see if the answer is stated directly. If not, go to Step 2.
> Step 2: Scan the passage or graph to find the clues that lead to the answer.

Questions 1 and 2 are based on the following paragraph and on Questions A and B and their answers.

The **atmosphere** is a mixture of gases that surrounds the

> ATMOSPHERE: the air that we breathe

earth. It is made up mostly of nitrogen and oxygen. Living things need the atmosphere to survive. They need nitrogen to make protein, and they need oxygen for respiration.

Question A: What are nitrogen and oxygen?
Answer: Nitrogen and oxygen are gases.
Question B: Why do living things need nitrogen?
Answer: Living things need nitrogen to make protein.

1. How was Question A answered?
   (1) by reading the lines
   (2) by reading between the lines

2. How was Question B answered?
   (1) by reading the lines
   (2) by reading between the lines

Questions 3 and 4 are based on the following graph and on Questions C and D and their answers.

Question C: How much of the air is made up of nitrogen?
Answer: Seventy-eight % of the air is made up of nitrogen.
Question D: How much of the air is made up of carbon dioxide?
Answer: Less than 1% of the air is made up of carbon dioxide.

GASES IN THE ATMOSPHERE

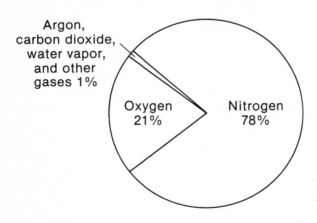

Argon, carbon dioxide, water vapor, and other gases 1%

Oxygen 21%

Nitrogen 78%

3. How was Question C answered?
   (1) by reading the lines
   (2) by reading between the lines

4. How was Question D answered?
   (1) by reading the lines
   (2) by reading between the lines

Questions 5 and 6 are based on the following paragraph and on Questions E and F and their answers.

Air changes at different **altitudes**. For example, the higher up

> ALTITUDE: the distance above sea level

you go, the colder the air gets. Also, as the altitude increases, the amount of oxygen in the air decreases. People who are not used to high altitudes can find it hard to breathe.

Question E: Why is it harder for people to breathe as the altitude increases?

Answer: There is less oxygen in the air.

Question F: How does the air temperature change as the altitude increases?

Answer: The higher up you go, the colder it gets.

5. How was Question E answered?
   (1) by reading the lines
   (2) by reading between the lines

6. How was Question F answered?
   (1) by reading the lines
   (2) by reading between the lines

Questions 7 and 8 are based on the following paragraph and on Questions G and H and their answers.

Air, like other kinds of matter, is affected by the force of

A gas fills its container. Therefore, without gravity, the gases that make up the atmosphere would try to fill *their* container—all of space.

gravity. Because of this, air has weight. The weight of air causes

GRAVITY: the force of attraction between objects.

air pressure. The upper layers of air push down on the lower layers. The more air there is above a place, the greater the air pressure is.

The change in air pressure is what causes your ears to pop when you reach a certain altitude.

Question G: What causes air pressure?

Answer: The weight of air causes air pressure.

Question H: What happens to the amount of air pressure as the altitude increases?

Answer: The amount of air pressure decreases as the altitude increases.

7. How was Question G answered?
   (1) by reading the lines
   (2) by reading between the lines

8. How was Question H answered?
   (1) by reading the lines
   (2) by reading between the lines

Check your answers on page 209.

Making Inferences

In the last lesson, you used a two-step strategy to decide whether a question was answered by reading the lines of a passage (finding details) or by reading between the lines (making inferences). In this lesson, you will use a similar strategy to find the answers to the same kinds of questions.

How to Answer Questions About Stated and Implied Details

STEP 1: Scan the passage to see if the answer is stated directly. If not, go to Step 2.

STEP 2: Scan the passage to find the clues that lead to the answer. Use these clues to figure out the answer to the question.

TRY THIS

Read the following paragraph and use the two-step strategy to answer the questions.

Oceans cover about 71% of the earth's surface. The Atlantic Ocean, the Pacific Ocean, and the Indian Ocean are the three major oceans. The Pacific Ocean is the largest and deepest. The Atlantic Ocean is the second largest.

About how much of the earth's surface is covered by oceans?

_____

Which of the three major oceans is the smallest? _____

Oceans cover about 71% of the earth's surface. This answer is directly stated in the first sentence of the paragraph. The Indian Ocean is the smallest of the three major oceans. The passage states that there are three oceans. It says that the Pacific Ocean is the largest and that the Atlantic Ocean is the second largest. Therefore, you can infer that the Indian Ocean is the smallest.

The following passages and graph are each followed by questions about stated and implied details. Use the two-step strategy to answer the questions.

> **How to Answer Questions About Stated and Implied Details**
>
> STEP 1: Scan the passage or graph to see if the answer is stated directly. If not, go to Step 2.
>
> STEP 2: Scan the passage or graph to find the clues that lead to the answer. Use these clues to figure out the answer to the question.

Questions 1 to 3 are based on the following graph.

TEMPERATURES OF THE OCEAN ZONES

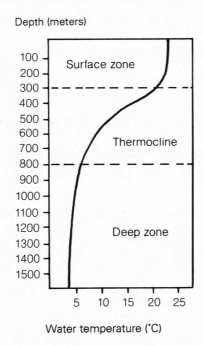

1. In which zone is the ocean's temperature warmest?

   _____

2. What is the temperature range in the thermocline zone?

   _____

3. Information on the graph suggests that oceans are warmed by heat from
   (1) the center of the earth
   (2) the sun
   (3) marine life

Questions 4 to 6 are based on the following paragraph.

Water covers nearly three-quarters of the earth, but 97% of this water is salt water in the oceans. This salt water cannot be used by the living things on land, which need fresh water to survive. Of the small amount of fresh water available, almost 85% cannot be used because it is trapped in polar ice caps and glaciers. The rest is found in rivers, streams, springs, ponds, lakes, swampy wetlands, and in the ground.

4. About how much of the earth is covered by water? _____

5. Where is most of the water on the earth found? _____

6. About what percent of the earth's fresh water can be used by

   living things on land? _____

Questions 7 to 9 are based on the following passage.

Tides are the rise and fall of the oceans. When the ocean rises, it is high tide. When it falls, it is low tide. The tide changes every 6 hours.

The pull of the moon's gravity causes tides. As the moon's

The earth's gravity keeps our feet on the ground!

gravity pulls on the earth, it causes the oceans to bulge in two

BULGE: to swell

places. They bulge on the side of the earth facing the moon and on the opposite side. Both bulges make high tides. At the same time, low tides occur between the two bulges.

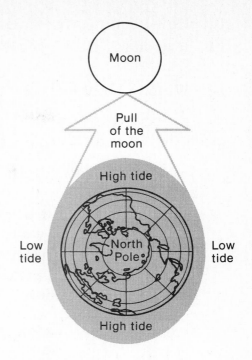

7. How often does the tide change?

_____

8. What causes tides?

_____

9. How many times a day is it high tide in the same place?

_____

Questions 10 to 12 are based on the following passage and illustration.

Earth and the other eight planets revolve around the sun. The time it takes a planet to make one revolution around the sun is a year on that planet. Mercury takes 88 earth-days to make one revolution. Therefore, a year on Mercury is 88 earth-days long. Venus makes a revolution in 225 earth-days. The planet farthest from the sun is Pluto. It takes Pluto 247.7 earth-years to revolve once around the sun.

Planets revolving around the sun.

10. How long in earth time is a year on Pluto? _____

11. How many days does it take the earth to revolve around the sun?
    _____

12. Which planet is closer to the sun, Mercury or Venus?
    _____

Question 13 and 14 are based on the following passage.

The tilt of the earth's axis causes the change in seasons. The axis always tilts in the same direction. As the earth revolves around the sun, the Northern Hemisphere leans away from the sun for part of the year, and toward the sun for the other part. When the Northern Hemisphere leans toward the sun, it is summer in that hemisphere. At the same time, it is winter in the Southern Hemisphere.

> The Northern Hemisphere extends from the equator—an imaginary line around the earth—to the North Pole. The Southern Hemisphere extends from the equator to the South Pole.

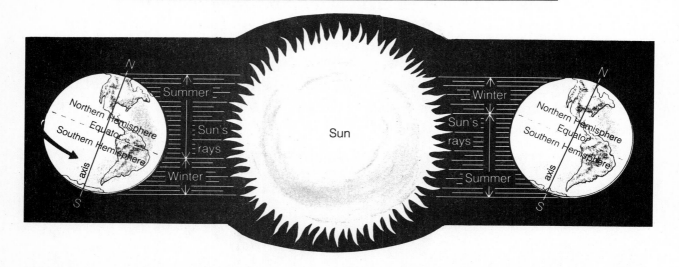

13. Does the Southern Hemisphere lean toward or away from the sun when it is summer there? _____

14. When it is autumn in the Southern Hemisphere, what season is it in the Northern Hemisphere? _____

Questions 15 to 17 are based on the following passage.

Each planet rotates on its axis. The time it takes a planet to make one rotation is called a day on that planet. Saturn takes about 10.5 hours to rotate on its axis. Therefore, a day on Saturn is 10.5 hours long. Mars makes one rotation in 24.5 hours. Mercury takes about 59 earth-days to rotate on its axis.

15. How long does it take Earth to rotate on its axis? _____

16. How long is a day on Mercury? _____

17. Which of the following planets has the shortest day?
    (1) Earth
    (2) Mars
    (3) Mercury
    (4) Saturn

Check your answers on page 209.

Chapter

2 THE IMPLIED MAIN IDEA

Suppose you want to let someone know that you are angry. You can make a direct statement by saying "I am angry." Or, you can **imply** your point by slamming doors and refusing to speak. Likewise, writers often imply their main ideas rather than state them directly.

In Lessons 10 and 11, you found directly stated main ideas. In this chapter, you will practice **inferring main ideas** when they are **implied**.

Lesson 24

Inferring the Heading for a Word List

Inferring the main idea of a paragraph, which you will do in the next lesson, is similar to inferring a heading for a word list.

In Lesson 9, you found the headings for word lists when they were listed among the other words on the lists. When the heading is not part of a list, you can infer what it should be by figuring out what the items on the list have in common.

TRY THIS

Infer the heading for this list.

_____

Earth
Mars
Mercury
Neptune
Venus

Because all the words on the list are names of planets, the word *Planets* should be the heading for the list.

Infer the heading for each list.

1. _____
   blue
   green
   orange
   red
   yellow

2. _____
   lakes
   oceans
   ponds
   rivers
   streams

3. _____
   carbon dioxide
   helium
   hydrogen
   nitrogen
   oxygen

4. _____
   astronomy
   biology
   ecology
   meteorology
   oceanography

5. _____
   Africa
   Antarctica
   Asia
   Australia
   Europe
   North America
   South America

Check your answers on page 210.

Lesson 25

Inferring the Main Idea of a Paragraph

In Lesson 24, you inferred the headings for word lists. In this lesson, you will put the information in a paragraph together to infer its main idea. Three steps can help you infer the main idea of a paragraph.

> **How to Infer the Main Idea of a Paragraph**
>
> STEP 1: Find the topic of the paragraph.
> STEP 2: Put the information in the sentences together and decide what important and general idea they imply about the topic.
> STEP 3: Test the proposed main idea to make sure that most of the sentences support it.

To see how these three steps can help you infer the main idea of a paragraph, do the following example.

TRY THIS

Use the three-step strategy to infer the main idea of the following paragraph. Answer the questions.

The land, or the solid body of the earth, is called the lithosphere. The earth's waters are called the hydrosphere. Finally, the earth's air is called the atmosphere.

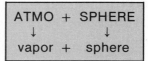

LITH(O) + SPHERE	HYDR(O) + SPHERE	ATMO + SPHERE
↓ ↓	↓ ↓	↓ ↓
stone + sphere	water + sphere	vapor + sphere

What is the topic of the paragraph? _____
The main idea of the paragraph is that
   (1) water covers most of the earth
   (2) the earth has three spheres
   (3) the planets have three spheres

The topic of the paragraph is the earth. Each sentence in the paragraph is about the earth. Choice (2) is the main idea of the paragraph. Each sentence supports the main idea by defining one of the three spheres of the earth.

Choice (1) cannot be the main idea because all the sentences in the paragraph are not about the water that covers most of the earth. Choice (3) cannot be the main idea because the paragraph is about the spheres of the earth, not the spheres of other planets.

The following table shows how the topic, the main idea, and the supporting sentences are related to each other.

The **topic** is a word or phrase.	**the earth**
The **main idea** is a statement **about** the topic.	**The earth** has three spheres.
The **supporting ideas** relate to the main idea.	The land, or the solid body of **the earth**, is called the **lithosphere**. **The earth's** waters are called the **hydrosphere**. Finally, **the earth's** air is called the **atmosphere**.

Use the three-step strategy to infer the main idea of each paragraph. Answer the questions.

How to Infer the Main Idea of a Paragraph

STEP 1: Find the topic of the paragraph.

STEP 2: Put the information in the sentences together and decide what important and general idea they imply about the topic.

STEP 3: Test the proposed main idea to make sure that most of the sentences support it.

Questions 1 and 2 are based on the following paragraph.

In forests, there is usually very little <u>erosion</u> of fertile soil.

EROSION: the process by which rock and soil particles are moved from one place to another by wind or water

The roots of trees hold the soil in place and absorb some of the water. The trees are so close together that they catch and hold a large portion of even the heaviest rainfall. Most of the rain that does reach the soil is easily absorbed. In contrast, when a forest is cut down, much of the topsoil is eventually washed or blown away.

1. What is the topic of the paragraph? _____

2. Which of the following is the main idea of the paragraph?
   (1) Trees prevent soil erosion.
   (2) Heavy rainfall can destroy forests.
   (3) Cutting down forests endangers wildlife.

Questions 3 and 4 are based on the following paragraph.

Running water is the major cause of erosion. Rivers, streams, and <u>runoff</u> flow over the earth's surface and change it.

RUNOFF: water that flows over the earth's surface after it rains or snows

The powerful waves of the oceans constantly erode and shape the shoreline. The wind is the most active cause of erosion in deserts, plowed fields, and beaches. In all of these areas, the wind picks up and carries loose sand and soil. Finally, glaciers are a powerful cause of erosion. As a glacier moves through a valley, rocks, gravel, and silt are carried along with it and pushed along in front of it.

3. What is the topic of the paragraph? _____
4. The main idea of the paragraph is that
   (1) erosion causes beaches to get smaller
   (2) water erosion changes the land
   (3) erosion is caused by running water, waves, wind, and glaciers

Questions 5 and 6 are based on the following paragraph.

Igneous rocks are formed when <u>magma</u> from beneath the

MAGMA: hot liquid rock

earth's crust cools and hardens. Granite is one of the most common igneous rocks. **Sedimentary rocks** are formed when <u>sediments</u> are pressed together. Sandstone and shale are exam-

SEDIMENTS: remains of plants and animals or pieces of rocks or shells that have been carried to and deposited in new places by wind, water, or ice

ples of sedimentary rocks. **Metamorphic rocks** are formed when igneous or sedimentary rocks are changed by heat or pressure. Heat and pressure change limestone into marble, for example.

5. What is the topic of the paragraph? _____
6. What is the main idea of the paragraph?

_____

Questions 7 and 8 are based on the following paragraph.

Some humans have lived as long as 117 years. The maximum life span recorded for another mammal, the blue whale, is 100 years. However, a dog cannot be expected to live for more than 20 years. The adult mayfly, an insect, lives no longer than 1 day. The marigold, a common plant, has a maximum life span of 8 months. In contrast, another plant, the bristlecone pine, has been known to live for 5500 years.

7. What is the topic of the paragraph? _____
8. What is the main idea of the paragraph?

_____

Questions 9 and 10 are based on the following paragraph.

Mercury, the planet closest to the sun, is much smaller than Earth. Unlike Earth, it has no hydrosphere or atmosphere. Mercury has only one-third the amount of gravity that Earth has. In addition, it takes Mercury much longer to rotate on its axis than it takes Earth, so its days are longer than Earth's days.

9. What is the topic of the paragraph? _____

10. What is the main idea of the paragraph?

_____

Check your answers on page 210.

Inferring the Main Idea of a Passage

Like the main idea of a paragraph, the main idea of a passage is often unstated. There is a four-step process you can use to infer the main idea of a passage. It is similar to the three-step process for inferring the main idea of a paragraph.

> **How to Infer the Main Idea of a Passage**
>
> STEP 1: Find the topic of the passage.
> STEP 2: Find the main idea of each paragraph.
> STEP 3: Put the main ideas together and decide what important and general idea they imply about the topic.
> STEP 4: Test the proposed main idea by making sure the main ideas of most of the paragraphs support it.

To see how these four steps can help you infer the main idea of a passage, do the following example.

TRY THIS

Use the four-step strategy to infer the main idea of the following passage. Answer the questions.

Water is a renewable resource. It evaporates from the surfaces of ponds, lakes, and oceans. The water vapor rises into the air. As the water vapor cools, it changes back into liquid water. It then returns to the earth in the form of rain, snow, sleet, or hail. Then, it evaporates again. This reuse of water, which continues endlessly, is called the water cycle.

Three important gases in the air—carbon dioxide, oxygen, and nitrogen—are also renewable resources. They are renewed through processes that involve living things. Animals take in oxygen and give off carbon dioxide when they breathe. Green plants take in carbon dioxide and release oxygen when they make food. Plants use nitrogen from the air to make proteins. These

> PROTEIN: a substance used to build and repair cells

proteins enter the bodies of animals when the animals eat plants. When plants and animals die and decay, the nitrogen they carry in proteins returns to the soil, and from there to the air.

Soil is another renewable resource. It provides plants with the minerals they need to grow. When soil is rich in such minerals, it is said to be fertile. As plants grow, they remove minerals from the soil. Then, when plants die and decay, the minerals are returned to the soil. In this way, soil remains fertile.

What is the topic of the passage? _____
Which sentence in each paragraph states the main idea?
Paragraph 1: _____
Paragraph 2: _____
Paragraph 3: _____
Infer the main idea of the passage.

_____

The topic of this passage is renewable resources because each paragraph discusses a different renewable resource. The main ideas of the paragraphs are their first sentences: *Water is a renewable resource* (Paragraph 1). *Three important gases in the air—carbon dioxide, oxygen, and nitrogen—are also renewable resources* (Paragraph 2). *Soil is another renewable resource* (Paragraph 3). The common bond that exists among the paragraphs is that they all tell about renewable resources. Therefore, you can infer the following main idea for the passage: Water, air, and soil are renewable resources.

To test the proposed main idea, see if the main ideas of the paragraphs in the passage support it. In this case the main ideas of the paragraphs do support the proposed main idea because each talks about one of the three renewable resources mentioned in the main idea.

The following table shows how a passage's topic and main idea are related and how the main idea is related to the other paragraphs' main ideas.

The **topic** is a word or phrase.	**renewable resources**
The **main idea of a passage** is the most important and /or most general point the passage makes about the topic.	Water, air, and soil are **renewable resources**.
The main ideas of the paragraphs **support** the main idea of the passage.	Water is a **renewable resource.** Three important gases in the air—carbon dioxide, oxygen, and nitrogen—are also **renewable resources.** Soil is another **renewable resource.**

EXERCISE 26

Use the four-step strategy to infer the main ideas of the following passages. Answer the questions.

> **How to Infer the Main Idea of a Passage**
> STEP 1: Find the topic of the passage.
> STEP 2: Find the main idea of each paragraph.
> STEP 3: Put the main ideas together and decide what important and general idea they imply about the topic.
> STEP 4: Test the proposed main idea by making sure the main ideas of most of the paragraphs support it.

Questions 1 to 3 are based on the following passage.

In the first step of the water cycle, called **evaporation,** water on the earth's surface changes to a **vapor,** or gas. The sun's heat causes large amounts of water to evaporate from the oceans and fresh-water sources. Water also evaporates from the soil, from plants, and from animals. Winds carry the water vapor up into the air.

> The water cycle illustrates that water exists in three states.

During the second step of the water cycle, called **condensation,** vapor changes back into a liquid. Condensation occurs when warm air containing water vapor rises and cools. When warm air cools, it can no longer hold as much water vapor. Most of the water vapor condenses into droplets of water that form clouds.

The third step of the water cycle, called **precipitation,** occurs when water returns to the earth as rain, snow, sleet, or hail. This happens when the water droplets that form clouds become too numerous and heavy to remain floating in the air. The water that falls to the earth is fresh water.

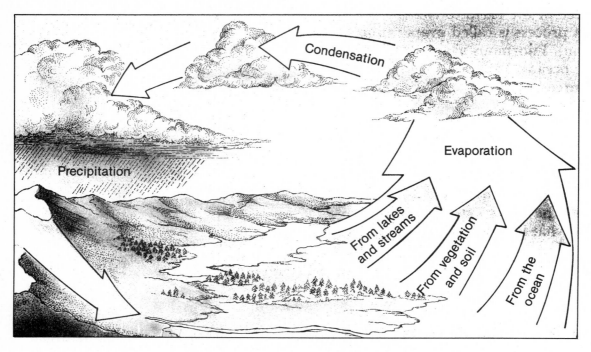

1. What is the topic of the passage? _____

2. Which sentence in each paragraph states the main idea?

   Paragraph 1: _____

   Paragraph 2: _____

   Paragraph 3: _____

3. Infer the main idea of the passage.

   _____

Questions 4 to 6 are based on the following passage.

An endangered species is one that will probably disappear unless it is given special protection. Animals such as the dodo and the passenger pigeon are already extinct. Fortunately, many species have been saved from extinction by laws such as the Endangered Species Act. Today many species of animals are

> ENDANGERED SPECIES ACT: a U.S. law enacted in 1973 to protect plants and animals in danger of becoming extinct

endangered. Among them are the Florida panther and the California condor.

Many species of animals are endangered because their habitats are being destroyed. As the human population increases, more and more forests are cleared to grow crops and build towns. When a forest is destroyed, forest dwellers lose their homes. Many species are threatened by deforestation in tropical rain for-

> DEFORESTATION: the clearing of forests

ests. Fifty to eighty percent of all the species on earth live in these forests. However, each year thousands of acres of rain forests are cut down and burned, leaving many species homeless.

In the past 10 years, poachers have killed a half million Afri-

> POACHERS: people who hunt illegally

can elephants for their ivory tusks. Poachers have also slaughtered large numbers of black rhinoceroses for their horns, which are ground into a powder and sold as medicine in Asia. The blue whale is also endangered. It has been hunted and killed in great numbers for products such as oil, food, and fertilizer. Unfortunately, many animals are endangered by hunting.

Chemical pollution also endangers many animals. Toxic chemicals from agriculture and industry wash into streams, rivers, and oceans. When these chemicals are eaten by animals or absorbed by plants, they enter the food chain. When an animal

> FOOD CHAIN: the transfer of energy in the form of food from one living thing

eats a plant or another animal that has been poisoned, it ingests the poison, too. This process continues as each animal is eaten by a larger animal. Eventually, the largest animals in the food chain take in the most poison.

4. What is the topic of the passage? _____
5. Which sentence in each paragraph states the main idea?
   Paragraph 1: _____
   Paragraph 2: _____
   Paragraph 3: _____
   Paragraph 4: _____
6. Infer the main idea of the passage.

   _____

Check your answers on page 210.

This section of the unit contains science readings. These readings can help you prepare for the GED in three ways. You can use them to
- review what you already know about science
- expand your general knowledge of science
- practice the reading skills covered in Units 1 and 2

ATOMS

All matter is made up of **atoms**. Atoms have three parts: **protons**, **neutrons**, and **electrons**. Protons and neutrons are contained in an atom's nucleus, while electrons whirl around the nucleus.

The **atomic number** of an atom shows how many protons are in its nucleus. The atomic number of carbon is 6. This means that a carbon atom has 6 protons in its nucleus. No other atom has 6 protons in its nucleus. The atomic number of sodium is 11; the atomic number of chlorine is 17.

Substances made up of only one kind of atom are called elements. For example, oxygen, gold, and silver are **elements**. There are 109 known elements.

Substances made up of two or more different kinds of atoms are called **compounds**. Water is a compound. It is made up of one hydrogen atom and two oxygen atoms. The smallest particle of a compound is called a **molecule**.

1. What are the three parts of an atom?
   —————— , —————— , and ——————
2. What is a compound made of?
   _____
3. What is the smallest part of a compound called? _____
4. Which of the sentences in the third paragraph states the main idea?
   _____
5. How many protons are there in the nucleus of a sodium atom? _____

GALAXIES

The big-bang <u>theory</u> may explain how

> THEORY: a possible explanation for something that happens in nature

the <u>universe</u> was formed. According to

> UNIVERSE: everything that exists

this theory, at one time all the matter and energy that make up the universe were packed together in an extremely small, hot space. Then, about 15 billion years ago, a great explosion—the big bang—shot this matter and energy out in all directions. The big bang caused the universe to expand. It has been expanding ever since.

SODIUM ATOM

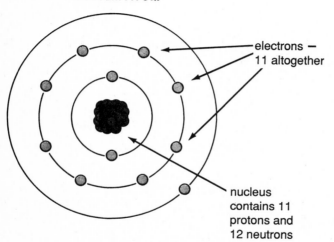

electrons — 11 altogether

nucleus contains 11 protons and 12 neutrons

After the big bang, the force of gravity began to affect all the matter racing out-

> Gravity causes larger objects to pull smaller objects toward themselves.

ward in every direction. Gravity began to pull the matter into clumps. These clumps became galaxies.

A galaxy is a huge group of stars. Astronomers believe that there are about 100 billion major galaxies in the universe. A typical galaxy contains about 100 billion stars. This means that there are more stars in space than there are grains of sand on all the beaches in the world!

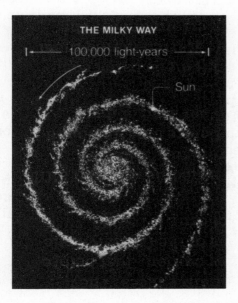

THE MILKY WAY

|←——— 100,000 light-years ———→|

Sun

Our sun and the other stars we can see are part of the Milky Way galaxy. Scientists estimate that our galaxy is about 100,000 light-years in diameter. There-

> LIGHT-YEAR: the distance that light travels in 1 year—about 6 trillion miles. Distances in space are measured in light-years.

fore, it would take light about 100,000 years to travel across the Milky Way. The sun is located 30,000 light-years from the center of the galaxy.

6. *Expand*, as it is used in the first paragraph, means
   (1) explode
   (2) get smaller
   (3) spread out

7. What may the big-bang theory explain? _____

8. What is a galaxy? _____

9. At the speed of light, how many years would it take to travel from the sun to the center of the Milky Way? _____

THE SOLAR SYSTEM

If an object smaller than a star gets close enough to that star, it gets caught in the star's field of gravity. When this happens, a <u>solar</u> system is formed. The

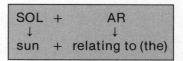

SOL	+	AR
↓		↓
sun	+	relating to (the)

star at the center of a solar system is its sun.

Our solar system includes the sun, Earth and the eight other planets that revolve around the sun, and other small bodies. The planets travel in paths, or orbits, around the sun. They take different lengths of time to complete their orbits, and they orbit at different distances from the sun. Closest to the sun, the inner planets—Mercury, Venus, Earth, and Mars—are solid. They have metal cores and rocky mantles. The outer planets—Jupiter, Saturn, Uranus, Neptune, and Pluto—are made up mostly of gases.

The solar system also includes thousands of smaller bodies: moons, asteroids, meteoroids, and comets. Moons are satellites that revolve around planets. Asteroids and meteoroids are small chunks of rock that orbit the sun. Asteroids move around the sun between Mars and Jupiter. Meteoroids can leave their orbits and fall to the earth. Comets are chunks of ice, dust, and gas. They also orbit the sun.

10. How many planets are there in our solar system? _____

11. Which of the following sentences states the main idea of the third paragraph?
    (1) The solar system also includes thousands of smaller bodies: moons, meteoroids, asteroids, and comets.
    (2) Moons are satellites that revolve around planets.
    (3) Asteroids and meteoroids are small chunks of rock that orbit the sun.

12. Which of the following sentences from the passage states the main idea of the passage?
    (1) If an object smaller than a star gets close enough to that star, it gets caught in the star's field of gravity.
    (2) The star at the center of a solar system is its sun.
    (3) Our solar system includes the sun, Earth and the eight other planets that revolve around the sun, and other small bodies.

13. Which of these planets is farthest from the sun?
    (1) Venus
    (2) Mercury
    (3) Uranus

14. Which of these bodies is the largest in our solar system?
    (1) the sun
    (2) Jupiter
    (3) Earth
    (4) Earth's moon

THE LAYERS OF THE EARTH

The earth's outer layer of rock is called its **crust.** This layer is covered by soil, water, and rocks. The crust is thinner in some places than in others. Its thickness ranges from 8 to 32 kilometers. Compared to the size of the earth, the crust is very thin. It is like the skin of an apple compared to the whole fruit.

The layer under the earth's crust is called the **mantle.** The mantle is about 2900 kilometers thick. It makes up 80% of the volume of the earth. Scientists have taken rock samples from the upper part of the mantle by drilling through the earth's crust under the ocean. The samples show that the mantle is made up of much the same material as the crust. The material of the mantle, however, is very hot. Its temperature ranges from 870°C in the upper mantle to 2200°C in the lower part. The material in the lower mantle is under great pressure. Scientists believe that in the mantle, solid rock flows, or changes shape.

The earth's center, or **core,** has two separate layers. Both layers are made up of iron and nickel. The **outer core** extends about 2250 kilometers under the mantle.

The temperature of the outer core may be as high as 5000°C. Scientists believe that the outer core is at least partly liquid. The **inner core** is about 2600 kilometers across. It is probably solid. Some scientists believe that the solid iron and nickel in the inner core create a magnetic field around the earth.

15. Infer the main idea of the passage.

   _____

16. Where is the earth's crust most likely the thinnest?

   _____

17. Which layer of the earth is the thickest? _____

18. What is the temperature range in the mantle? _____

ECOSYSTEMS

An **ecosystem** is an area in which organisms interact with each other and the nonliving things that surround them. An ecosystem can be small, like a fish tank, or large, like a forest.

The living members of an ecosystem form a **community.** The community is named for the ecosystem in which the organisms live. A pond community, for example, includes the fish, frogs, insects, plants, and all the other living things—small and large—in and near a pond.

Every type of organism in a community has its own **habitat,** or living area. A living thing's habitat provides it with food and shelter. An earthworm's habitat is deep in the soil, for example, where it finds small organisms to eat. A bird's habitat may be the high branches of a tree.

Each organism in a community has a **niche,** or a special role to play. For example, an earthworm's niche includes eating small organisms so that it can grow and become food for a bird. Part of a beaver's niche is to build a dam.

An organism's niche can affect the lives of other organisms. For example, when a beaver builds a dam across a

stream, part of a stream ecosystem becomes a pond ecosystem. Because the stream no longer rushes along, its banks stop eroding. Plants begin to grow on what are now the pond's banks. Songbirds begin to nest along the quiet banks. Fish, such as trout, make their homes in the pond. A whole new pond community develops.

19. Match the word in Column A with its definition in Column B.

   Column A
   ___ A. ecosystem
   ___ B. community
   ___ C. habitat
   ___ D. niche
   ___ E. organism

   Column B
   (1) an organism's living area
   (2) an area in which many different organisms interact with each other and their environment
   (3) a living thing
   (4) a group made up of all the living things in an area
   (5) the role an organism plays in a community

20. Which of the following sentences from the third paragraph states the main idea?
   (1) Every type of organism in a community has its own habitat, or living area.
   (2) A living thing's habitat provides it with food and shelter.
   (3) An earthworm's habitat is deep in the soil, for example, where it finds small organisms to eat.

21. According to the passage, part of a beaver's niche is to
   (1) live high in the branches of a tree
   (2) build dams
   (3) eat earthworms

THE RESPIRATORY SYSTEM

Every cell in the human body needs a steady supply of energy to stay alive. This energy comes from combining food with oxygen. The respiratory system takes in oxygen from the air and gets rids of the waste gas, carbon dioxide.

Breathing is a mechanical process that takes place about 14 times per minute. Air moves into and out of the lungs when people breathe. The air that people take in, or inhale, contains oxygen. The air that people breathe out, or exhale, contains waste—carbon dioxide and water.

When the **diaphragm**, a muscle, contracts, air is pulled into the respiratory system—usually through the **nostrils**. Nose hairs trap dust particles and bacteria to prevent them from going any farther into the respiratory system. If these particles irritate the nose, a sneeze forces them out. Because the nose filters the air, it is healthier to breathe air through the nose than through the mouth. But when the nose is blocked, such as when a person has a cold, the mouth acts as a backup organ so that breathing can continue.

Air passes from the nose into the **throat**. It moves past the voicebox, or **larynx**, and into the windpipe, or **trachea**. Air is allowed into the trachea by the **epiglottis**, a lid that opens the trachea for air during breathing but closes it against food during swallowing.

The trachea is a single breathing tube. As air moves through it, tiny hairs lining the trachea trap dirt particles and bacteria that have managed to get through the nose. The trachea reacts to irritations by producing a cough.

The trachea branches into two tubes. These **bronchial tubes** carry air to the **lungs,** the main organs of the respiratory system. Inside the lungs, the bronchial tubes divide into smaller and smaller tubes, much as a tree limb divides into branches. At the ends of the thinnest branches are tiny **air sacs**. The walls of each air sac are lined with thin, moist pouches that look like bunches of tiny grapes. These are the **alveoli.** The alveoli are surrounded by capillaries. It is here that the blood picks up oxygen and releases carbon dioxide.

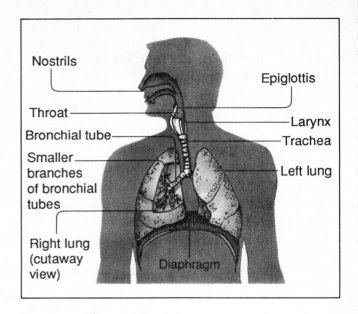

22. What is the name of the process by which air moves in and out of the lungs? _____

23. What is combined with oxygen to give the body energy? _____

24. In which part of the respiratory system are carbon dioxide and oxygen exchanged? _____

25. In which two parts of the respiratory system are dust and bacteria trapped? _____

26. Which of the following sentences from the passage states the main idea of the passage?
    (1) Every cell in the human body needs a steady supply of energy to stay alive.
    (2) The respiratory system takes in oxygen from the air and gets rids of the waste gas, carbon dioxide.
    (3) Breathing is a mechanical process that takes place about 14 times per minute.

Check your answers on page 210.

SCIENCE READINGS 2 SKILLS CHART

To review the reading skills covered by the questions in Science Readings 2, study the following parts of Units 1 and 2.

Unit 1		*Question Number*
Chapter 3	Details in Passages	1, 2, 3, 7, 8, 10, 17, 18, 19, 21, 22, 23, 24, 25
Chapter 4	The Stated Main Idea	4, 11, 12, 20, 26

Unit 2		
Chapter 1	Inferences	5, 6, 9, 13, 14, 16
Chapter 2	The Implied Main Idea	15

This section will give you practice answering questions like those on the GED. The Science Test of the GED has 66 multiple-choice questions. Each question has 5 choices. The 10 questions in this Practice are all multiple-choice, like the ones on the GED

As you do this Practice, use the reading skills you've studied so far in this book.

Directions: Choose the <u>one best answer</u> to each item.

<u>Items 1 and 2</u> are based on the following graph.

ELEMENTS IN THE EARTH'S CRUST

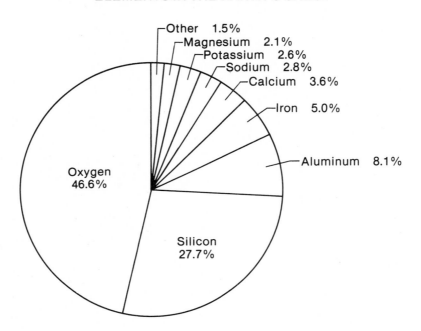

1. Which of the following elements accounts for 8.1% of the earth's crust?

   (1) potassium
   (2) sodium
   (3) calcium
   (4) iron
   (5) aluminum

2. The element that makes up nearly half of the earth's crust is a

   (1) metal
   (2) solid
   (3) gas
   (4) liquid
   (5) mineral

Items 3 and 4 are based on the following passage.

Americans produce about 400,000 tons of solid waste a day. Much of it is made of plastic. Unfortunately, a lot of that plastic waste ends up in the ocean. Because it does not dissolve in water, plastic can remain in the ocean and threaten animal life for years, even decades.

Each year, about 2 million seabirds and 100,000 marine mammals, including whales, die because of plastic pollution. Some marine animals get trapped and tangled in plastic trash. Sea turtles choke on plastic bags. Young seals and sea lions get six-pack rings caught around their necks and slowly suffocate. When six-pack rings get stuck around their bills, pelicans eventually die.

3. The main idea of the passage is that
   (1) Americans throw too much plastic away
   (2) most solid waste is plastic
   (3) plastic doesn't dissolve in the ocean
   (4) plastic waste kills marine animals
   (5) plastic should be recycled

4. How does some plastic waste kill pelicans?
   (1) It chokes them.
   (2) It poisons them.
   (3) It keeps them from eating.
   (4) It keeps them from swimming.
   (5) It drowns them.

Items 5 to 7 are based on the following passage.

Bald eagles almost became extinct in the 1950s and the 1960s because of the widespread use of DDT, a pesticide. DDT makes the shells of eagles' eggs so fragile that the eggs break before they are ready to hatch. The banning of DDT in the early 1970s helped to save the eagle and other birds.

The American alligator was hunted for its meat and leather. As a result, the animal almost disappeared from the waters of the southeastern part of the United States. In 1967, the alligator was declared an endangered species, so it could no longer be hunted. The alligator has since made a strong comeback. Most experts agree that the alligator is now alive and well. In fact, these aquatic reptiles have become a serious problem in some areas. They attack children and pets and invade swimming pools.

5. The main idea implied by the passage is that
   (1) the bald eagle and the American alligator will never again become endangered species
   (2) both the bald eagle and the American alligator were saved from extinction
   (3) the American alligator can be dangerous
   (4) many birds have been harmed by DDT
   (5) the bald eagle and the American alligator were hunted for sport

6. The American alligator was saved from extinction because
   (1) people stopped killing it
   (2) DDT was banned
   (3) manufacturers stopped using alligator leather
   (4) experts decided it was alive and well
   (5) it began to make its home in swimming pools

7. In the United States, a species that is declared endangered
   (1) is extinct
   (2) cannot be hunted
   (3) will not become extinct
   (4) attacks children and pets
   (5) has disappeared from the Southeast

Items 8 to 10 are based on the following passage.

On July 20, 1976, seven years after man first landed on the moon, NASA's unmanned spacecraft, Viking 1, touched down on Mars. Biologists back on Earth were eager to find out if there was life on Mars or not. They waited as Viking's mechanical arm scooped up some red soil and put it in a tiny lab. At first, there seemed to be signs of life. However, after a series of tests, the Martian soil proved to be sterile.

Mars, the fourth planet from the sun, is a cold desert. It is colored red by rust, or iron oxide. Its atmosphere is made up mainly of carbon dioxide. It has white caps at its poles made mostly of frozen carbon dioxide, or dry ice, instead of snow. Except for a small amount of water vapor in the air, what water there is on Mars is frozen deep beneath the planet's surface.

Although the "red planet" appears to be dead now, it may not always have been. New evidence suggests that around the same time life appeared on Earth—some four billion years ago—Mars may have been alive. If it was ever alive, it had to be warm and wet. Many scientists believe that Mars once had great rivers of water. Photographs of the planet's surface show small valleys that look like riverbeds on Earth.

8. The word <u>sterile</u> at the end of the first paragraph means

   (1) full of life
   (2) without living organisms
   (3) very clean
   (4) iron oxide
   (5) warm and wet

9. Which of the following statements is NOT true?

   (1) Mars is colored by rust.
   (2) Mars' atmosphere is mostly carbon dioxide.
   (3) Mars is the fourth planet from the sun.
   (4) Mars was explored by astronauts.
   (5) There may have been life on Mars at one time.

10. According to the passage, <u>Viking 1</u> collected evidence about life on Mars by

   (1) making soil tests
   (2) taking temperature readings
   (3) measuring the carbon dioxide in the atmosphere
   (4) measuring the water vapor in the air
   (5) taking photographs

Check your answers on page 212.

GED PRACTICE 2 SKILLS CHART

To review the reading skills covered by the items in GED Practice 2, study the following parts of Units 1 and 2.

Unit 1		Item Number
Chapter 3	Details in Passages	1, 7, 9, 10

Unit 2		
Chapter 1	Inferences	2, 4, 6, 8
Chapter 2	The Implied Main Idea	3, 5

UNIT 3

Applying Information You Read

When you use your knowledge in a new situation, you apply it. You apply your knowledge many times each day. For instance, you apply math skills to do a variety of things, such as balance your checkbook. The basic science principles covered in this book have countless practical applications.

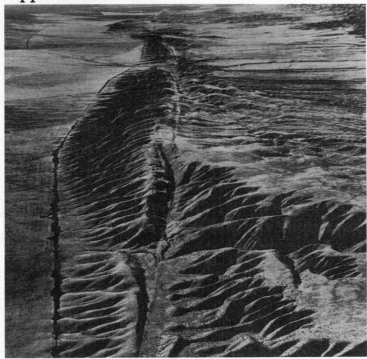

Earthquakes are common along the San Andreas fault in California.

Unit 3 Overview

Lesson 27   Applying Information About Categories
Lesson 28   Applying Information from Passages
Lesson 29   Applying Information from Passages and Graphics
_____

Science Readings 3
GED Practice 3

Applying Information About Categories

In this lesson, you will apply information about categories to specific situations. The information about a category describes one kind of person, place, or thing. To apply this information, you need to connect it to a specific situation.

TRY THIS

Read the following definition and answer the question that follows it.

HERBIVORES: animals that eat only plants

Which two of the following animals are herbivores?

_____ Gorillas are vegetarians.

_____ Vultures eat dead animals.

_____ Most caterpillars eat only leaves.

_____ Sea otters eat crabs and shellfish.

Gorillas and most caterpillars are herbivores. Gorillas are vegetarians, which means that they eat only plants. Most caterpillars eat only the leaves of plants. Both vultures and sea otters eat meat.

To answer this question, you applied information about herbivores to examples of specific animals. You used your knowledge about herbivores to figure out which animals are herbivores.

NOW TRY THIS

Read the following definitions and answer the questions that follow.

CARNIVORES: Animals that eat only other animals
HERBIVORES: Animals that eat only plants
OMNIVORES: Animals that eat both plants and animals

The tyrannosaur had a heavy neck, powerful jaws, and teeth 6 inches long. It ate only other dinosaurs. What kind of animal was the tyrannosaur? _____

The Kodiak bear, a type of brown bear, eats salmon, fruit, and grass. What kind of animal is the Kodiak bear?

_____

The koala bear of Australia feeds only on the leaves and young bark of eucalyptus trees. What kind of animal is the koala bear?_____

The tyrannosaur was a carnivore because it ate only the flesh of other dinosaurs. The Kodiak bear is an omnivore because it eats both plants and animals. The koala bear is an herbivore because it eats only plants.

To answer these questions, you used your knowledge about three types of animals to figure out what category each of three specific animals belongs to.

EXERCISE 27

Read the following lists of descriptions and answer the questions that follow each list.

Questions 1 to 5 are based on the following information.

Descriptions of four kinds of drugs that are commonly abused are listed below.

DEPRESSANTS slow down, or depress, the <u>nervous system</u>. This

> NERVOUS SYSTEM: the system that controls all the functions of the body

causes all bodily functions to slow down. Depressants relieve anxiety and bring on sleep. People who have taken high doses slur their words, stagger, and lose muscle coordination. They also lose control of their emotions and lack sound judgment. People quickly build up a tolerance to these depressants and find themselves taking more and more to get the same effect. This can lead to taking an overdose.

HALLUCINOGENS cause people to hallucinate. This means that they see and hear things that exist only in their minds. When taking these drugs, people have a distorted sense of reality. They may become very fearful, or they may think that nothing will harm them. They may not be able to tell the difference between themselves and their surroundings.

OPIATES are also called narcotics. They are powerful painkillers. They also create euphoria—a state of dreamlike happiness. Opiates reduce depression and anxiety. They are highly addictive.

STIMULANTS increase, or stimulate, the activity of the nervous system. This causes all bodily functions to speed up. Stimulants reduce fatigue and depression and suppress the appetite. People under the influence of stimulants become very confident and talk a lot. The drug creates a feeling of well-being—until it wears off. When users "come down," or "crash," they often become sad and depressed.

1. A couple of hours after taking LSD, Sandy walked into traffic. All the cars looked like rubber cars with smiling faces. They looked as though they were moving in slow motion. Just before she was knocked down, Sandy thought one of the friendly little cars was coming to greet her. What kind of drug is LSD?

   _____

2. Richard is a busy dentist. His demanding schedule makes it difficult for him to relax when he gets home from the office. He wrote himself a prescription for Seconal. Before long, he found that he needed the drug just to function. What kind of drug is Seconal? _____

3. Suzanne is a principal dancer with a world-famous ballet company. She is hooked on amphetamines. She started taking them to boost her energy before rehearsals and performances. The pills also helped her stay thin. Now she needs them to get her going as soon as she wakes up. What kind of drug are amphetamines? _____

4. Charlie pulled the muscles in his lower back while lifting weights. He asked his doctor for a drug that would relieve his backache. The doctor prescribed Percodan. The drug not only made Charlie's back feel better, but it also lifted his spirits. When his back was completely healed, Charlie could not stop taking the drug. Now, unless he uses the drug, he begins to feel very sick from withdrawal symptoms. What kind of drug is Percodan? _____

5. Carrie is an alcoholic. She started drinking because alcohol helped her feel more at ease in social situations. After a few drinks, she would lose her inhibitions and become the life of the party. At the end of the evening, however, Carrie could not speak clearly or walk without stumbling. She would often pass out in her car. What kind of drug is alcohol? _____

Questions 6 to 10 are based on the following information.

A machine is any object that helps people do work. Simple machines do work with one movement. The six simple machines are described below.

A **LEVER** is a bar that moves on a fixed point. Levers are used to lift heavy loads and to pry things apart.

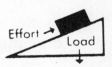

An **INCLINED PLANE** is a flat, slanted surface. Inclined planes are used to raise heavy loads.

A **WEDGE** is a small inclined plane that is movable. It has one thick end and one thin, sharp end. Wedges are used to split things in two.

A **SCREW** is a small inclined plane wrapped around a cylinder to form a spiral. A screw can pull things together or push them apart.

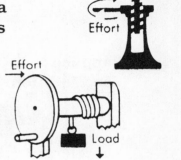

A **WHEEL AND AXLE** is a cylinder, or axle, and a larger wheel. The larger wheel turns around the axle. A wheel and axle is used to move loads.

A **PULLEY** is a wheel with a grooved rim over which a rope, chain, or belt is passed. Pulleys are used to make lifting or pulling easier.*

6. Kathy and Alan are playing on a seesaw. What kind of simple machine are they using? _____

7. Brian used an ax to chop down a dead tree for firewood. What kind of simple machine did he use? _____

8. Jeremy pulled his brothers home from the baseball field in his wagon. What kind of simple machine did he use? _____

9. Dominick's motorcycle broke down on a country road. When his friend arrived with his pickup, they used two boards to make a ramp and wheeled the motorcycle into the truck. What kind of simple machine did they use? _____

*Illustrations from *The World Book Encyclopedia.* (c) 1991 World Book, Inc. By permission of the publisher.

10. Aunt Nellie was bringing the wash in through her second-story window. Her clothesline was attached to a big oak tree at the end of the yard. Because she was able to move the line toward her and away from her, she could hang her clothes outside to dry without leaving the house. What kind of simple machine was she using? _____

Questions 11 to 15 are based on the following information.

Newton's three laws of motion describe what happens when a force moves an object from one place to another.

NEWTON'S FIRST LAW OF MOTION. An object at rest will stay at rest unless an outside force moves it. Likewise, an object in motion will stay in motion unless an outside force stops it.

NEWTON'S SECOND LAW OF MOTION. Two things affect an object's change in motion: (1) its <u>mass</u> and (2) the size of the outside force

MASS: the amount of matter in an object

applied to it. The greater the mass of the object, the smaller the <u>acceleration</u>. The greater the force, the greater the

ACCELERATION: the rate of change in speed and/or direction

acceleration. The change in motion takes place in the direction in which the force acts. In other words, if an object is pushed to the right, it will move to the right.

NEWTON'S THIRD LAW OF MOTION. For every action, there is an equal and opposite reaction. That is, when one object exerts a force on a second object, the second object exerts an equal and opposite force on the first object.

11. Earth and the other eight planets revolve around the sun. Which of Newton's laws of motion does this illustrate? _____

12. Rudy Falco went bowling. He tried an 8-pound ball and a 16-pound ball. Rudy decided to use the 8-pound ball because, given his strength, the 8-pound ball rolled down the alley faster than the 16-pound ball. Which of Newton's laws of motion does this illustrate? _____

13. Tom is practicing target shooting with his rifle. As the bullet

moves forward, the rifle recoils, or kicks backward against his
shoulder. Which of Newton's laws of motion does this illustrate?
_____

14. When a rocket is launched into space, the burning gases shoot
downward from the bottom of the rocket. The rocket moves upward. Which of Newton's laws of motion does this illustrate?

_____

15. A car suddenly stopped when it was cut off by a truck. Of course,
all the passengers continued to move forward. Luckily, everyone
was wearing a safety belt, so no one was injured. Which of
Newton's laws of motion does this illustrate? _____

Check your answers on page 212.

Lesson 28

Applying Information from Passages

In this lesson, you will apply information to new contexts as you did
in the last lesson. However, the information you will apply is embed-
ded in passages. Therefore, before you can answer a question, you
will need to find the information in the passage that relates to it.

TRY THIS

Read this passage and answer the questions that follow it.

Celsius and Kelvin
thermometers measure
temperature. The Celsius scale is
part of the metric system. People in
most major countries use the
Celsius scale for everyday
temperature measurement. On the
Celsius scale, 0° is the freezing
point of water and 100° is the
boiling point of water.

The Kelvin scale is the
international standard for scientific
measurement. On a Kelvin
thermometer, the freezing point of
water is 273 kelvins, and its boiling
point is 373 kelvins.

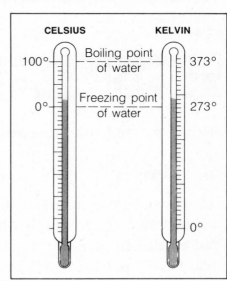

You can convert a Celsius temperature to a Kelvin temperature by using this formula:

Celsius temperature + 273 = Kelvin temperature.

Likewise, you can convert a Kelvin temperature to a Celsius temperature by using this formula:

Kelvin temperature − 273 = Celsius temperature.

On a Celsius thermometer, normal human body temperature is 37°. What is it on the Kelvin scale? _____
Mercury freezes at 233 kelvins. At what temperature does it freeze on the Celsius scale? _____

Normal human body temperature is 310 kelvins. Mercury freezes at −40° Celsius. The formulas you need to answer the questions are in the third paragraph. By applying the second formula, you can figure out normal human body temperature on the Kelvin scale:

Celsius temperature + 273 = Kelvin temperature
37° + 273 = 310 kelvins

By applying the first formula, you can figure out the temperature at which mercury freezes on the Celsius scale.

Kelvin temperature − 273 = Celsius temperature
233 kelvins − 273 = −40°

In the following exercise, you will apply scientific principles to new contexts.

EXERCISE 28

Read each passage and answer the questions.

Question 1 is based on the following paragraph.

Most substances—solids, liquids, and gases—take up more space when their temperature increases. This occurs because the molecules that make up these substances move farther apart when they are heated. This is called **thermal expansion**.

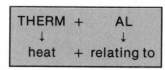

THERM + AL
↓ ↓
heat + relating to

Solids expand when heated, so expansion links are part of bridge surfaces.

1. Which three of the following events can be explained by the principle of thermal expansion?

____ (a) Jeffrey felt feverish and took his temperature. The mercury in the thermometer rose to 100.6°F, two degrees above normal.

____ (b) During the summer, the door to Joe's closet is hard to close. In winter, it closes easily.

____ (c) After Christmas, Patty could not fit all her new sweaters into her dresser drawers.

____ (d) The phone rang while Lorraine was running the water for a bath. By the time she returned to shut it off, the tub was filled to the top. When she got in, some water overflowed.

____ (e) Red checked the pressure in his car tires on a hot summer day. It was higher than when he filled the tires on a cool day in the spring.

Question 2 is based on the following paragraph.

Most kinds of matter expand when heated and contract when cooled. One exception is water, which expands when it is frozen. Therefore, when water is frozen, its <u>volume</u> increases. One cubic

> VOLUME: the amount of space an object takes up

meter of water becomes 1.08 cubic meters of ice. However, as the volume increases, the <u>density</u> decreases because the same num-

> DENSITY: the amount of mass in a given volume of a substance

ber of molecules fill more space. Thus, ice floats on liquid water.

2. Which four of the following choices illustrate the above principles about water?

_____ (a) On a hot summer day, Bette filled a glass with ice. An hour later, the glass was half full of water.

_____ (b) During a severe cold spell, the water pipe leading to Bill's house cracked.

_____ (c) Liz finds that her plants need more water in the summer than they do in the winter.

_____ (d) Lucille told her son not to go ice skating because the pond was not safe. She explained that under the thin sheet of ice on the pond's surface there was about 4 feet of water that had not yet frozen.

_____ (e) Vinnie forgot to put antifreeze in his car, and the water in the radiator froze. The radiator cracked.

Questions 3 and 4 are based on the following passage.

Matter on the earth exists in three states: **solid**, **liquid**, and

> MATTER: anything that has weight and takes up space

gas. The particles of matter are the closest together in solids. This closeness, or tight structure, gives a definite shape and volume to a solid. A glass and an apple are examples of solids.

The particles of matter in liquids are not as close together as those in solids. They are close enough to give a liquid a definite volume but not a definite shape. For example, a cup of milk takes up a certain amount of space, but it has no definite shape. It will take the shape of whatever container it is poured into.

The particles of matter in a gas are the farthest apart. That is why a gas has neither a definite shape nor a definite volume. A gas completely fills its container regardless of its size or shape. For example, when an apple pie is baking, gases from the pie spread out and fill the kitchen, which is their container. That's what makes the pleasant aroma in the air.

3. In the following illustration, the circles represent particles of matter. Which picture represents the solid? the liquid? the gas?

O O	OOOOOOOOO	O O O
	OOOOOOOOO	O O
O	OOOOOOOOO	O O O
O	OOOOOOOOO	O O

(a) _____   (b) _____   (c) _____

4. A jar holds 2 quarts. Which of the following will completely fill the jar?
   (1) 2 cups of beans
   (2) 1 quart of water
   (3) 1 ounce of oxygen

Question 5 is based on the following passage.

The **boiling point** is the temperature at which a liquid becomes a gas. At the boiling point, the molecules of a liquid absorb

| MOLECULE: a combination of atoms; the smallest particle of a compound |

so much heat that they move faster and farther apart. They fill whatever space they are in.

Air pressure changes the boiling point of a liquid. At altitudes above sea level, air pressure is lower than it is at sea level.

| SEA LEVEL: the altitude at the ocean's surface |

The lower the air pressure, the lower the boiling point will be. The lower the boiling point, the less time it takes a substance to boil.

5. Water boils at 100°C at sea level. Ethyl alcohol boils at 79°C. When salt is added to a liquid, it raises its boiling point. Which of these liquids would take the longest to boil?
   (1) ethyl alcohol heated in the mountains
   (2) water heated above sea level
   (3) salt water heated at sea level

| ETHYL ALCOHOL: the alcohol in alcoholic drinks |

Question 6 is based on the following passage.

The **melting point** is the temperature at which a solid changes to a liquid. At the melting point, the molecules of a solid absorb so much heat energy that they move faster and farther apart. The tight structure of the solid breaks down, and the matter begins to melt, or become a liquid.

Matter holds together because molecules are attracted to each other. The stronger the force of attraction between the molecules of a solid, the higher the solid's melting point. The molecular bonds between hydrogen molecules are very weak, so it has a low melting point: −260°C. On the other hand, the bonds between platinum molecules are very strong. Therefore, it has a high melting point: 1770°C. Tungsten has the highest melting point of all metals: 3410°C. It is used to make filaments, the tiny wires that glow inside electric light bulbs.

6. Which of the following metals has the strongest molecular bonds?
    (1) gold (melting point: 1063°C)
    (2) silver (melting point: 961°C)
    (3) lead (melting point: 328°C)

Question 7 is based on the following passage.

A **mixture** is a combination of two or more substances. The substances are not chemically combined; they are simply mixed together. Each substance in a mixture keeps its identity. For example, soil is a mixture. It is a combination of sand, rock, and clay. In a handful of soil, each of the substances in soil can be seen.

A **solution** is a kind of mixture that is formed when one substance dissolves in another. All solutions have two important properties. One is that the particles that have dissolved are too small to see. Another is that the dissolved particles are evenly spread out. Therefore, unlike in a mixture, in a solution all parts of it look the same. For example, ocean water is a solution of various salts in water. The salt particles are evenly spread out and too small to see, so all parts of a jar of salt water look the same.

Not all solutions are liquids. Solids and gases can also be solutions. For example, metal solutions, called **alloys**, are solids dissolved in solids. Gold jewelry is made of a solid solution of gold and copper. Air is a gas solution made of oxygen and other gases dissolved in nitrogen.

7. Various mixtures and solutions are listed below. Which of the following are mixtures and which are solutions?
    (a) tossed salad _____
    (b) a cup of coffee _____
    (c) a dish of pudding _____
    (d) garlic salt _____
    (e) sterling silver _____

Check your answers on page 213.

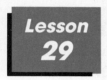

Lesson 29

Applying Information from Passages and Graphics

As you know, when you apply information, you use it in a new way. So far in this unit, you have applied information about categories to specific situations. You have also applied the information in passages in new contexts. In this lesson, you will apply information from both passages and graphics in new contexts.

TRY THIS

Read the following passage and table. Then answer the questions.

All <u>atoms</u> have an atomic number and a mass number. The

> ATOM: the smallest particle of an element having the properties of that element

atomic number is the number of protons in an atom's nucleus. The atoms of each element have a different number of protons. For example, oxygen has 8, and gold has 79. The **mass number** of an atom is the sum of the number of protons and the number of neutrons in its nucleus. Helium's mass number is 4 because it has 2 protons and 2 neutrons in its nucleus.

ATOMIC AND MASS NUMBERS OF SOME COMMON ELEMENTS

Name	Atomic Number	Mass Number
Aluminum	13	27
Carbon	6	12
Fluorine	9	19
Helium	2	4
Hydrogen	1	1
Nitrogen	7	14
Oxygen	8	16
Sodium	11	23

How many protons are there in a nitrogen atom? _____

How many neutrons are there in a fluorine atom? _____

To answer these questions, you need to apply information from both the passage and the table. The passage tells what *atomic number* and *mass number* mean, and the table gives examples.

There are 7 protons in the nucleus of a nitrogen atom. You can infer this because nitrogen's atomic number is 7. There are 10 neutrons in a fluorine atom. You can infer that there are 9 protons in the nucleus of an atom of fluorine because its atomic number is 9. If you subtract 9 from 19, fluorine's mass number, the result will be 10, which is the number of neutrons in the nucleus.

As in the above examples, as you do the following exercise, you will need to consider each passage and the related table or graph as a whole. Both the passage and the graphic will provide information you need to answer the questions.

EXERCISE 29

Read each of the following passages together with the related table or graph. Answer the questions.

Questions 1 to 3 are based on the following information.

Minerals can be identified by **hardness**. Hardness is the ability of a mineral to resist being scratched. The hardness of a mineral can be tested by scratching it with other minerals. Only a harder mineral can scratch a softer one.

Frederich Mohs worked out a hardness scale for minerals. It lists 10 minerals from the softest to the hardest. The softest mineral, talc, is given the number 1. The hardest mineral, diamond, is given the number 10.

Mineralogists who use the Mohs scale keep a set of these 10 minerals. To find the hardness of an unfamiliar mineral, they scratch it with the minerals listed on the scale until they determine its hardness. A mineral will scratch only another mineral that has a lower number. A mineral will be scratched only by another mineral that has a higher number. Minerals that are equally hard have the same number.

MOHS HARDNESS SCALE

Mineral	Hardness	Mineral	Hardness
Talc	1	Feldspar	6
Gypsum	2	Quartz	7
Calcite	3	Topaz	8
Fluorite	4	Corundum	9
Apatite	5	Diamond	10

Diamond is the hardest mineral, so it ranks 10 on the Mohs Hardness Scale.

1. Stibnite is a gray and black mineral. It scratches talc and is scratched by calcite. According to the Mohs scale, what is the hardness of stibnite?

    (1) 1
    (2) 2
    (3) 3

2. Orthoclase is a white or pale pink mineral. It scratches apatite and is scratched by quartz. According to the Mohs scale, what is the hardness of orthoclase?

    (1) 4
    (2) 5
    (3) 6

3. Galena is a metallic gray mineral. It scratches gypsum and is scratched by calcite. According to the Mohs scale, what is the hardness of galena?

    (1) 2½
    (2) 3
    (3) 3½

Questions 4 to 7 are based on the following information.

Density is the amount of mass in a given volume of a substance. A piece of lead has more mass than a piece of aluminum of the same size. Therefore, lead has a higher density than aluminum.

Density, mass, and volume are three physical properties of matter.

The density of a substance determines its ability to float on a fluid. For example, substances that are less dense than water

FLUID: any substance, liquid or gas, that can flow or change shape

will float on water. However, substances with a greater density than that of water will sink.

An object's mass is usually expressed in **grams.** An object's volume is often expressed in **cubic centimeters.** Therefore, density is often expressed in **grams per cubic centimeter,** or g/cm^3.

DENSITY OF SOME COMMON SUBSTANCES

Substance	Density (g/cm^3)	Substance	Density (g/cm^3)
Helium	0.0002	Seawater	1.025
Air	0.0013	Aluminum	2.7
Cork	0.24	Steel	7.8
Gasoline	0.7	Copper	8.9
Wood (oak)	0.85	Silver	10.5
Oil	0.90	Lead	11.3
Water (solid)	0.92	Mercury	13.6
Water (liquid)	1.0	Gold	19.3

4. If a cork falls into a glass of water, will it sink or float? _____

5. Mercury is a metal that is a liquid at room temperature. Which two of the following will float in mercury?

_____ (a) a gold wedding band

_____ (b) a copper penny

_____ (c) an aluminum can

6. Why do balloons filled with helium rise? _____

7. Which two of the following will float on liquid water?

_____ (a) oil

_____ (b) ice cubes

_____ (c) liquid mercury

Questions 8 to 12 are based on the following information.

Acids and bases are chemical compounds that have opposite properties. **Acids** taste sour. They also give off hydrogen ions.

> IONS: atoms that carry an electrical charge

Bases, also called **alkalis**, taste bitter and feel slippery. Instead of giving off hydrogen ions, they combine with hydrogen ions.

Strong acids and strong bases are both highly corrosive. This means that they corrode, or wear away, other substances. They can burn through many layers of material and cause serious damage to the skin, for example.

Strong acids and bases are also poisonous. Therefore, it is never a good idea to taste chemicals to identify them. One way to find out if a solution contains an acid or a base is to use <u>litmus</u>

> LITMUS: a dye made from plants called lichens

paper, a special kind of paper used by chemists. Blue litmus paper turns red when dipped in an acid. Red litmus paper turns blue when dipped in a base.

Many foods contain acids. Citrus fruits, such as oranges, lemons, and grapefruits, contain citric acid. Vinegar contains acetic acid. Yogurt and tea also contain acid. Ascorbic acid is the chemical name for vitamin C.

Many household products contain bases. Deodorants, soap, ammonia, and lye are bases. Ammonia is used as a household cleaner because it cuts grease. Lye is used to unclog drains.

When an acid and a base are combined, a chemical change takes place. The properties of the acid and the base change and they produce water and a salt. This process is called **neutralization**.

The **pH scale** is a series of numbers from 0 to 14. This scale

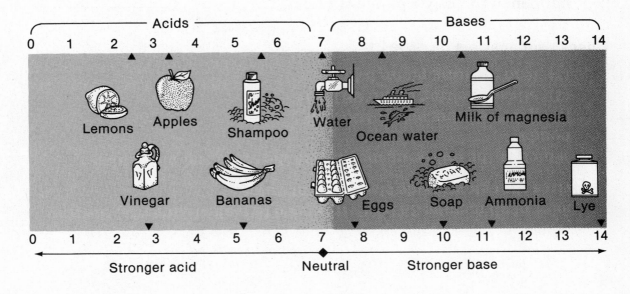

is used to rate the strength of an acid or a base. Neutral substances, like pure water, have a pH value of 7. A substance with a pH lower than 7 is an acid. A substance with a pH higher that 7 is a base.

8. Which of the following is a base?
   (1) an egg
   (2) a banana
   (3) vinegar

9. Which of the following is the most acidic?
   (1) an apple
   (2) a lemon
   (3) lye

10. Hydrochloric acid in the stomach helps us digest many kinds of food. However, too much hydrochloric acid causes acid indigestion. Milk of magnesia is used as an antacid. It neutralizes acid in the stomach. Is milk of magnesia an acid or a base? _____

11. Some gases released by burning fossil fuels combine with water vapor in the air to form weak acids. These acids fall to the earth's surface with rain or snow. This is called **acid rain**. Among the many problems it causes, acid rain pollutes bodies of water. Fish and other forms of life die when the acid content of the water is too high. Limestone is added to some lakes to neutralize the harmful effects of acid rain. Is limestone an acid, a base, or a salt? _____

12. Tony, a 2-year-old, wanted to clean up the grape juice he had spilled on the floor. He poured drain cleaner on the stain. He knelt down to clean up the purple stain. When he stood up, there were holes in the knees of his pajamas. What had most likely happened to Tony's pajamas? _____

Check your answers on page 214.

This section of the unit contains science readings. These readings can help you prepare for the GED in three ways. You can use them to
- review what you already know about science
- expand your general knowledge of science
- practice the reading skills that you learned in Units 1 to 3

MATTER AND ENERGY

Everything in the universe is either matter or energy. **Matter** is anything that occupies space and has mass. People, flowers, and cars are examples of matter. **Energy** is the ability to do work. Energy has many forms, such as heat energy, light energy, and electrical energy. Physics is the study of the relationship between matter and energy.

Matter and energy can be neither created nor destroyed. However, matter can be converted to energy, and energy can be converted to matter. Matter is changed into energy when an atom is split into smaller atoms. This is called atomic fission. When this happens, the total amount of matter and energy remains the same.

In 1905, Albert Einstein discovered a way to figure out how much energy appears when a given amount of matter disappears. He expressed his discovery in a formula. The formula is part of his famous **theory of relativity**.

Einstein's formula is $E = mc^2$. E stands for energy; m stands for mass; c stands for the speed of light. The formula means that the energy of matter equals the product of its mass and the square of the speed of light. With this formula, Einstein was saying that matter is energy in another form, or that matter and energy are two forms of the same thing and can be converted into each other.

SQUARE OF THE SPEED OF LIGHT: the speed of light multiplied by itself. Light travels 186,000 miles per second, so the square of the speed of light is 186,000 X 186,000, or 34,596,000,000.

1. What is the meaning of *converted* as it is used in the second paragraph?

   _____

2. Matter is another form of
   (1) the speed of light
   (2) Einstein's theory of relativity
   (3) energy

3. Which of the following statements is true, according to the information in the passage?
   (1) When a candle burns, matter (the wax and wick) becomes energy (heat and light).
   (2) The universe is constantly expanding. Therefore, each year the amount of energy and matter in the universe increases.
   (3) Each time a living thing dies, there is less matter and energy on the earth.

PHYSICAL AND CHEMICAL PROPERTIES OF MATTER

All matter has two kinds of properties, or characteristics—**physical properties** and **chemical properties**. The combination of properties a certain substance has makes it different from all other substances, or kinds of matter.

All substances have the physical properties of mass, weight, volume, and density. Some substances also have other physical properties: color, odor, shape, and hardness. The physical properties of matter are those that you can observe through your senses of sight, smell, taste, and touch.

It is possible to distinguish among many different substances just by observing physical properties. For example, you can tell the difference between a moth ball and a cotton ball by observing their physical properties. Many elements can be identified just by their physical properties. Iron, for example, is a hard, whitish metal that is more strongly attracted to a magnet than any other metal; neon is a gas that glows orange-red when electricity passes through it.

Some elements have many of the same physical properties. For example, hydrogen and oxygen are both colorless, odorless, tasteless gases. Their chemical properties distinguish them from one another, however.

Chemical properties determine how a substance reacts with other substances. For example, the ability to burn is a chemical property. The ability to support burning is another chemical property. Hydrogen has the ability to burn. Oxygen does not, but it supports burning. Therefore, hydrogen and oxygen can be distinguished from each other by their chemical properties.

4. Which of the following sentences from the passage states the main idea of the passage?
   (1) Chemical properties determine how a substance reacts with other substances.
   (2) All matter has two kinds of properties, or characteristics—physical properties and chemical properties.
   (3) All substances have the physical properties of mass, weight, volume, and density.

5. What is neon?
   (1) a hard, whitish metal
   (2) a gas that glows orange-red
   (3) a gas that burns easily

6. Which one of the following describes a chemical property of an element?
   (1) Copper is a red metal that conducts heat and electricity.
   (2) Boron is hard and brittle.
   (3) Helium freezes at $-272°C$.
   (4) Like water, the metal bismuth expands when it is frozen.
   (5) Phosphorus is used to make matches because it combines quickly with oxygen and burns.

PHYSICAL AND CHEMICAL CHANGES

The basic particle of matter is the atom, but few substances exist as single atoms. Most matter consists of two or more atoms united to form a single molecule.

> MOLECULE: the smallest particle of a compound

Matter is always changing. Matter changes in two ways—through physical change and chemical change. After a physical change, both the physical and chemical properties of a substance are still the same. In contrast, after a chemical change, both the physical and chemical properties of a substance are different.

During a physical change, matter changes its shape, size, or state. However, the matter is still made of the same molecules. Therefore, its physical and chemical properties remain the same. For example, when water freezes, it is still water. Only the state of the water changes—from liquid to solid.

In a chemical change, the molecules in a substance change. Atoms in the molecules of the substance break away from their "partner atoms" and combine with different atoms to form new molecules. When molecules change, a new substance is made. For example, when sodium, a soft, silver metal, and chlorine, a poisonous, green gas, combine chemically, they make a completely different substance: table salt. Thus, both the physical and chemical properties of sodium and chlorine change.

7. Which one of the following processes is an example of a physical change?
   (1) evaporation: a liquid changes to a gas
   (2) photosynthesis: plants use the sun's energy, carbon dioxide, and water to make their own food
   (3) respiration: food combines with oxygen to produce energy

8. Which one of the following causes a chemical change?
   (1) burning wood
   (2) chopping wood
   (3) painting wood

9. What is table salt made of? _____

FOOD CHAINS

All living things need energy to carry on their life processes. The sun is the main source of energy for all living things. Energy passes from one organism to another when one of them eats the other. This transfer of energy is known as the **food chain**.

Because green plants use the sun's energy to make their own food, they are called **producers**. They produce food for themselves and become food for the animals that eat them. The energy from plants passes along a food chain as each animal eats another.

Animals are called consumers because they eat plants or other animals. A **primary consumer** eats plants. It is the first consumer to get the energy stored in a plant F—energy that came from the sun. The animal that eats a primary consumer is a **secondary consumer**—the second animal to get the energy. The next animal in the chain is called a **tertiary consumer**. The last animal in a food chain is the one that is not eaten by another animal.

The last animal becomes food for **decomposers,** bacteria and fungi. These organisms decompose, or break down,

wastes and remains of dead animals into materials that go into the soil. From the soil, these materials begin to be recycled when plants use them for nourishment.

Each link in the food chain is a **feeding level**. The amount of energy in the chain decreases as it passes from one level to the next. This happens because at each level animals use some of the energy to carry out their life activities.

The loss of energy as it moves through a food chain can be pictured as an energy pyramid. An energy pyramid shows the decreasing amount of energy available at each feeding level. There are fewer and fewer animals at each new feeding level because there is less energy—and food—available. An area that has thousands of crickets as primary consumers, for example, may have only a few hawks at the top feeding level in the food chain.

An energy pyramid is pictured below.

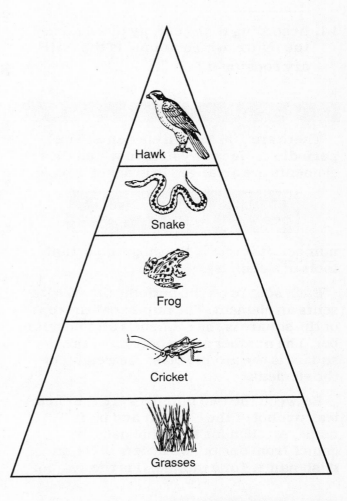

Hawk

Snake

Frog

Cricket

Grasses

10. What is the primary source of energy for all organisms on the earth?

_____

11. What is the role of the human in this food chain?

GRASS → COW → HUMAN

(1) producer
(2) primary consumer
(3) secondary consumer
(4) tertiary consumer
(5) decomposer

12. The Kim family sat down to a dinner of brown rice and stir-fried vegetables. What is the role of the Kim family in this food chain?

(1) producer
(2) primary consumer
(3) secondary consumer
(4) tertiary consumer
(5) decomposer

13. According to the energy pyramid in the figure, what does the frog eat?

_____

14. According to the energy pyramid in the figure, which animal is the tertiary consumer? _____

THE PERIODIC TABLE

There are 109 known elements. The **periodic table** is a system in which these elements are arranged in order of atomic

ATOMIC NUMBER: the number of protons in the nucleus of an atom

number. It is one of the most important tools of a chemist.

Each square on the periodic table represents an element. The number at the top of the square is the element's atomic number. The number at the bottom of the square is the atomic mass, or weight, of the element.

Between the two numbers are the chemical symbol of the element and its full name. An element's symbol usually comes from one or two letters of its English name. For example, **O** is the symbol for oxygen. **Ar** is the symbol for argon; **Cl** is the symbol for chlorine. Some symbols come from the Latin names for the elements. The symbol for iron is **Fe**, from the Latin word *ferrum.*

Columns of elements in the periodic table are called **groups,** or **families.** Elements in the same family have similar properties. For example, the elements in Column 1 of the table are all soft, silver-white, shiny metals. They are also highly reactive chemicals. This means that they easily combine with other elements. In contrast, all the elements in Column 18 are called noble, or inert, gases. These gases rarely take part in chemical reactions.

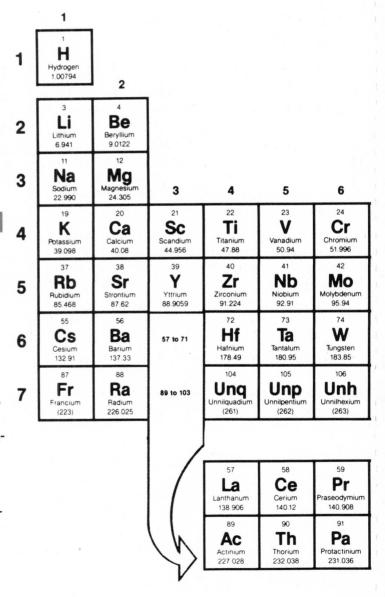

Each horizontal row of elements in the periodic table is called a **period**. The elements in a period do not have similar properties, but there is a pattern. The first element is a very active solid, and the last element is an inactive gas.

15. The symbol for tin is **Sn**. What is the atomic number of tin? _____

16. The symbol for Barium is **Ba**. What is the atomic mass of barium? _____

17. Which of the following symbols comes from the element's English name?
    (1) **Al**
    (2) **Pb**
    (3) **Cu**

18. Where does the chemical symbol for potassium most likely come from, its English name or its Latin name? _____

19. Which of the following elements is a highly reactive metal?
    (1) lithium
    (2) krypton
    (3) neon

20. Does radon react easily with other chemicals or not? _____

Key

6	Atomic number
C	Element's symbol
Carbon	Element's name
12.011	Atomic mass

18
2
He
Helium
4.003

13	14	15	16	17	
5	6	7	8	9	10
B	**C**	**N**	**O**	**F**	**Ne**
Boron	Carbon	Nitrogen	Oxygen	Fluorine	Neon
10.81	12.011	14.007	15.999	18.998	20.179
13	14	15	16	17	18
Al	**Si**	**P**	**S**	**Cl**	**Ar**
Aluminum	Silicon	Phosphorus	Sulfur	Chlorine	Argon
26.98	28.086	30.974	32.06	35.453	39.948

7	8	9	10	11	12						
25	26	27	28	29	30	31	32	33	34	35	36
Mn	**Fe**	**Co**	**Ni**	**Cu**	**Zn**	**Ga**	**Ge**	**As**	**Se**	**Br**	**Kr**
Manganese	Iron	Cobalt	Nickel	Copper	Zinc	Gallium	Germanium	Arsenic	Selenium	Bromine	Krypton
54.938	55.847	58.9332	58.69	63.546	65.39	69.72	72.59	74.922	78.96	79.904	83.80
43	44	45	46	47	48	49	50	51	52	53	54
Tc	**Ru**	**Rh**	**Pd**	**Ag**	**Cd**	**In**	**Sn**	**Sb**	**Te**	**I**	**Xe**
Technetium	Ruthenium	Rhodium	Palladium	Silver	Cadmium	Indium	Tin	Antimony	Tellurium	Iodine	Xenon
(98)	101.07	102.906	106.42	107.868	112.41	114.82	118.71	121.75	127.60	126.905	131.29
75	76	77	78	79	80	81	82	83	84	85	86
Re	**Os**	**Ir**	**Pt**	**Au**	**Hg**	**Tl**	**Pb**	**Bi**	**Po**	**At**	**Rn**
Rhenium	Osmium	Iridium	Platinum	Gold	Mercury	Thallium	Lead	Bismuth	Polonium	Astatine	Radon
186.207	190.2	192.22	195.08	196.967	200.59	204.383	207.2	208.98	(209)	(210)	(222)
107	108	109									
Uns	**Uno**	**Une**									
Unnilseptium	Unniloctium	Unnilennium									
(262)	(265)	(266)									

60	61	62	63	64	65	66	67	68	69	70	71
Nd	**Pm**	**Sm**	**Eu**	**Gd**	**Tb**	**Dy**	**Ho**	**Er**	**Tm**	**Yb**	**Lu**
Neodymium	Promethium	Samarium	Europium	Gadolinium	Terbium	Dysprosium	Holmium	Erbium	Thulium	Ytterbium	Lutetium
144.24	(145)	150.36	151.96	157.25	158.925	162.50	164.93	167.26	168.934	173.04	174.967
92	93	94	95	96	97	98	99	100	101	102	103
U	**Np**	**Pu**	**Am**	**Cm**	**Bk**	**Cf**	**Es**	**Fm**	**Md**	**No**	**Lr**
Uranium	Neptunium	Plutonium	Americium	Curium	Berkelium	Californium	Einsteinium	Fermium	Mendelevium	Nobelium	Lawrencium
238.029	237.048	(244)	(243)	(247)	(247)	(251)	(252)	(257)	(258)	(259)	(260)

PLATE TECTONICS AND EARTHQUAKES

The earth's crust is not solid. It is made up of several blocks of rock, called **plates**. These plates are like the pieces of a jigsaw puzzle. They float on top of the hot liquid <u>mantle</u>.

> MANTLE: the layer of the earth below the crust

Material from the earth's mantle slowly oozes up to the earth's crust. The constant creation of a new crust causes the plates to move around. Plates are either forced together, are pulled apart, or scrape past each other. This system of plates and their movements is called **plate tectonics**.

Plate tectonics explains how surface features of the land are formed. For example, when two plates move together, one slides under the other and a mountain is formed. When two plates slide past each other, a <u>fault</u> is created. Plates move very

> FAULT: a crack in the earth's crust

slowly. Mountains, faults, and other structures are created over very long periods of time.

The theory of plate tectonics also explains earthquakes. An earthquake is any trembling or shaking of the earth's crust. As plates move, they create pressure on the rocks along their edges. The rocks can take being squeezed together or pulled apart for just so long. Finally, they reach their "breaking point." When rocks beneath the earth's surface break or move, the land shakes.

Almost 95% of all earthquakes occur at the edges of plates. Most earthquakes seem to be caused by sudden movements along faults, which are cracks in the earth's crust. Most faults are under the earth's surface. However, some faults are visible. Parts of the San Andreas Fault, a 600-mile fault that extends through California, can be seen. The San Andreas Fault is one of the most active sources of earthquakes in the world.

An earthquake always begins someplace below the earth's surface along a fault. The point at which the earthquake begins is called the **focus**. The point on the earth's surface immediately above the focus is called the **epicenter**. The most violent shaking occurs at the epicenter.

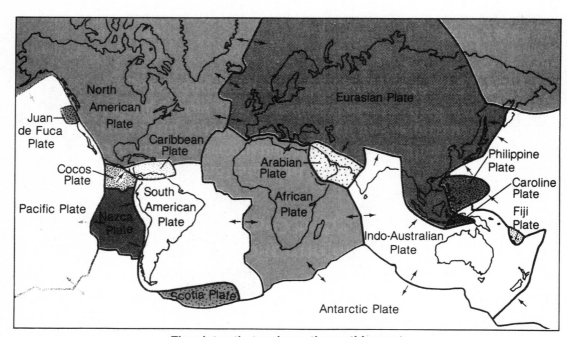

The plates that make up the earth's crust.

Although as many as a million earthquakes may occur in a single year, most of them occur beneath the sea. Others shake the ground so slightly that they pass unnoticed. However, at least one severe earthquake occurs each year.

21. According to the information in the passage, which two of the following statements are true?
    ____ (a) The earth's crust is solid.
    ____ (b) The earth's crust is made up of pieces of rock.
    ____ (c) The earth's crust is always changing.

22. Which two of the following are explained by the theory of plate tectonics?

____ (a) how mountains are formed
____ (b) exactly when an earthquake will occur
____ (c) where an earthquake is likely to occur

23. What is an earthquake? _____

24. What causes earthquakes? _____

25. Where does the most violent shaking of an earthquake occur? _____

26. Where is the earth's crust the most stable?
    (1) above the edge of plates
    (2) above the middle of plates
    (3) along faults

Check your answers on page 214.

SCIENCE READINGS 3 SKILLS CHART

To review the reading skills covered by the questions in Science Readings 3, study the following parts of Units 1 to 3.

Unit 1		*Question Number*
Chapter 3	Details in Passages	2, 5, 9, 10, 21, 22, 23, 24, 25
Chapter 4	The Stated Main Idea	4
Chapter 6	Tables and Graphs	13
Unit 2		
Chapter 1	Inferences	1, 26
Unit 3	Applying Information You Read	3, 6, 7, 8, 11, 12, 14, 15, 16, 17, 18, 19, 20

This section will give you practice in answering questions like those on the GED. The Science Test of the GED has 66 multiple-choice questions. Each question has 5 choices. The 10 questions in this section are all multiple-choice, like the ones on the GED.

As you do this Practice, use the reading skills you've studied so far in this book.

Directions: Choose the one best answer to each item.

Item 1 is based on the following passage.

Friction is the force that works against the motion of an object. When a moving object is in contact with another object, friction acts in the direction opposite that of the motion of the moving object. The moving object slows down and finally stops. Without friction, you could not walk. The friction between the soles of your shoes and the ground keeps you from slipping and sliding.

1. Each of the following describes a way to increase or decrease friction. Which one would cause friction to decrease?
   (1) changing from regular tires to snow tires
   (2) changing from loafers to sneakers to play basketball on a wooden floor
   (3) waxing a wooden floor
   (4) spreading sand on a snow-covered road
   (5) putting a rubber mat on a shower floor

Item 2 is based on the following passage.

The meaning of work in physics is different from its common meaning. According to scientists, work is performed when a force moves an object. The object must move in the same direction as the force. For an object to move, a force greater than the resisting force of the object must be applied to it. If you push against a brick building with all your strength, you will not be able to move it. This is because the force you apply to the wall is not greater than the resisting force of the wall. Therefore, you will not be doing work.

2. Which of the following is not an example of work as scientists define it?
   (1) A body builder lifts a barbell over his head.
   (2) A woman carries a box of books downstairs to her basement.
   (3) A man vacuums his living room.
   (4) A mason pushes a wheelbarrow full of bricks.
   (5) A child pulls a wagon up a hill.

Items 3 and 4 are based on the following passage and table.

A chemical formula shows which elements make up a compound. For instance, the formula for the compound water is H_2O. A molecule of water is made up of two atoms of hydrogen (H_2) and one atom of oxygen (O).

COMMON ELEMENTS

Element	Symbol	Element	Symbol
Calcium	Ca	Hydrogen	H
Carbon	C	Nitrogen	N
Chlorine	Cl	Oxygen	O
Fluorine	F	Sodium	Na
Helium	He		

3. The formula for the poisonous gas methane is CH. What two elements make up methane?
   (1) calcium and hydrogen
   (2) carbon and helium
   (3) carbon and hydrogen
   (4) chlorine and hydrogen
   (5) chlorine and nitrogen

4. Freon is a coolant used in refrigerators and air conditioners. Its formula is CCl_2F_2. How many atoms of chlorine are there in one molecule of Freon?

 (1) one
 (2) two
 (3) three
 (4) four
 (5) five

Items 5 to 7 are based on the following passage and graph.

Ozone is a compound made of three atoms of oxygen. Ozone is both a blessing and a curse in the environment. In the upper atmosphere, ozone shields the earth from harmful radiation given off by the sun. At ground level, however, high levels of ozone are a major health concern.

Ozone is the main gas in smog. Ozone is made when sunlight reacts with certain chemicals in car exhaust, paint fumes, and emissions from factories and power plants. The hotter the weather, the higher the ozone level.

Ozone causes health problems because it tends to break down cells and tissues. The EPA says the ozone level is dangerous when it is higher than 120 parts per billion—that is, when there are over 120 ozone molecules for every billion molecules of air. Recent studies show that high levels of ozone affect not only people with impaired respiratory systems, but also healthy adults and children. Even at low levels, exposure to ozone for only a few hours has been found to reduce lung function in healthy people during periods of exercise. This decrease in lung function usually causes chest pain, coughing, wheezing, and congestion. When there is too much ozone in the air, it's wise to limit the time you spend outdoors.

5. Which of the following sentences from the passage states the main idea of the passage?

 (1) In the upper atmosphere, ozone shields the earth from harmful radiation given off by the sun.
 (2) At ground level, however, high levels of ozone are a major health concern.
 (3) Ozone is the main gas in smog.
 (4) This decrease in lung function usually causes chest pain, coughing, wheezing, and congestion.
 (5) Ozone is a compound made of three atoms of oxygen.

6. The graph shows how much ground-level ozone there is in the air in Anaheim, California, during a typical day. According to the graph, the worst time of the day to exercise outdoors in Anaheim is

 (1) before sunrise
 (2) before 11:00 A.M.
 (3) between 11:00 A.M. and 4:00 P.M.
 (4) after 4:00 P.M.
 (5) after sunset

7. On a hot day in a city with a lot of air pollution, the least healthy way to exercise is probably to

 (1) jog in a park
 (2) ride a stationary bike at home
 (3) lift weights in a gym
 (4) swim in an indoor pool
 (5) bowl at a bowling alley

Items 8 to 10 are based on the following passage.

The ozone layer in the upper atmosphere is 30 miles above the earth's surface. It shields the earth from the sun's ultraviolet

OZONE LEVELS IN A DAY

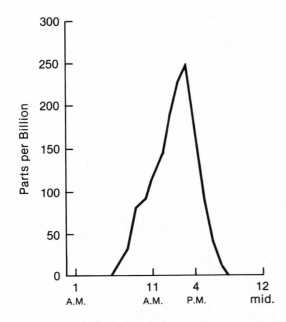

(UV) rays. However, there is a "hole" in this paper-thin shield above the continent of Antarctica. This hole is caused by chemicals called CFCs (chlorofluorocarbons). These CFCs are made up of chlorine, fluorine, and carbon atoms.

CFCs are present in the cooling fluids in refrigerators and air conditioners. They are used to make packaging and insulating foams, like styrofoam. They are also used as propellants in aerosol spray cans.

After CFCs are used, they slowly float up to the ozone layer above the earth and destroy it. This journey takes a CFC molecule about 7 to 10 years. The sun's UV rays break the bonds of the CFC molecule after it reaches its destination, and chlorine atoms are released. A free chlorine atom pulls one atom of oxygen away from the three atoms that form a molecule of ozone. What's left is the kind of oxygen that we breathe. Each chlorine atom can destroy between 10,000 and 100,000 molecules of ozone during the 75 to 130 years before it becomes inactive.

UV rays harm humans and other living things. UV rays cause skin cancer and eye cataracts in humans. They also break down the human immune system. UV light damages crops. It also slows down the growth of single-celled plants called phytoplankton, which are the first link in the ocean's food chain.

The damaging effects of CFCs far outweigh their benefits. The United States and other countries plan to produce 50% fewer CFCs in the next 10 years. However, many scientists believe that a complete ban on CFCs is necessary.

8. If the ozone in the upper atmosphere is not protected, UV rays from the sun will probably
   (1) burn a hole in the atmosphere
   (2) destroy the CFCs we need for refrigeration
   (3) destroy the oxygen we need to breathe
   (4) cause increasing harm to many living things
   (5) melt the ice that covers Antarctica

9. How many atoms of oxygen make up each molecule of the oxygen that we breathe?
   (1) one
   (2) two
   (3) three
   (4) ten
   (5) thirty

10. If we stopped using CFCs today, how long would it take before they stopped destroying the ozone layer?
   (1) 7 to 10 years
   (2) 75 to 130 years
   (3) about 140 years
   (4) about 10,000 years
   (5) about 100,000 years

Check your answers on page 216.

GED PRACTICE 3 SKILLS CHART

To review the reading skills covered by the items in GED Practice 3, study the following parts of Units 1 to 3.

Unit 1		*Item Number*
Chapter 3	Details in Passages	8
Chapter 4	The Stated Main Idea	5
Unit 2		
Chapter 1	Inferences	9, 10
Unit 3	Applying Information You Read	1, 2, 3, 4, 6, 7

UNIT 4
Analyzing and Evaluating What You Read

When you analyze and evaluate what you are reading, you are reading critically. When you **analyze** what you are reading, you closely examine its parts. When you **evaluate** what you are reading, you make a judgment about it. Before you can evaluate something, you need to analyze it.

Chapter 1 of this unit will give you basic practice in analyzing and evaluating. In Chapters 2 and 3 you will do some of the kinds of analysis and evaluation that are required on the GED.

Lightning discharges electricity from thunderstorm clouds to the ground or to other clouds.

Unit 4 Overview

RELEVANT AND IRRELEVANT INFORMATION

In Units 1 and 2, you found the main ideas of single paragraphs and longer passages. As you know, the main idea is the most important and general statement made about the topic. Any information that supports or relates to a main idea is **relevant** to it. In contrast, any information that does not support or relate to a main idea is **irrelevant** to it. Throughout this chapter, you will practice distinguishing between relevant and irrelevant information.

Lesson 30

Analyzing Word Lists

The heading is the controlling idea of a word list. The items in the list are details related to the heading. In Lessons 9 and 24 you found the headings of word lists. In this lesson, you will decide whether each word on a list is relevant to its heading or not. A word that is relevant is related to the heading of the list. A word that is irrelevant is not related to the heading and doesn't belong on the list.

TRY THIS

Read the following word list and answer the question that follows it.

Fuels
coal
gasoline
oil
bricks
kerosene
wood

The heading of the list is *Fuels*. Which word in the list names something that is not a fuel? _____

A fuel is any material that is burned for energy. Because bricks do not burn, they cannot be used as a fuel. Therefore, the word *bricks* is irrelevant to the list's heading. All the other items are relevant to the heading because they are burned for energy.

EXERCISE 30

Part A. Find the one irrelevant item in each of the following lists.

1. **Colors**

____ red
____ yellow
____ green
____ orange
____ apple
____ blue

2. **Things That Run on Electricity**

____ toaster
____ sink
____ refrigerator
____ hair dryer
____ light bulb
____ vacuum cleaner

3. **Gases**

____ nitrogen
____ helium
____ aluminum
____ hydrogen
____ oxygen
____ radon

Part B. In each list, take out the irrelevant word and replace it with a word that is relevant to the heading.

1. **Parts of the Circulatory System**

____ arteries
____ capillaries
____ heart
____ lungs

_____
(replacement word)

2. **Bodies in the Solar System**

____ asteroids
____ galaxies
____ meteoroids
____ moons
____ sun

_____
(replacement word)

3. **Metals**

____ copper
____ gold
____ iron
____ ozone
____ silver
____ tin

_____
(replacement word)

Check your answers on page 217.

Evaluating Sentences in Paragraphs

In the last lesson, you saw that all the words in a list should be relevant to the heading of the list. The same thing applies to the sentences in a paragraph. They should all be relevant to the main idea.

TRY THIS

Read the following paragraph. In it the sentences are numbered and the main idea is underlined. Answer the question that follows the paragraph.

(1) <u>There are many forms of energy</u>. (2) The energy that comes from the sun is radiant energy. (3) Mechanical energy is the energy of motion. (4) Electrical energy is produced when atoms gain or lose electrons. (5) After a series of experiments, Ben Franklin proved that lightning is a form of electricity. (6) The motion of the particles in matter is heat energy.

Which sentence is irrelevant to the main idea? _____

Sentence 5 is irrelevant to the main idea of the paragraph. Sentence 1 states the main idea—that there are many forms of energy. Sentences 2, 3, 4, and 6 tell what some forms of energy are. Sentence 5, however, does not tell about a form of energy. It tells about Franklin and his experiments with lightning. This sentence does not belong in the paragraph because the paragraph is about forms of energy—not Franklin, experiments, lightning, or electricity.

In order to find out if there is an irrelevant sentence in a paragraph, you need to read the whole paragraph. You should look for a sentence that does not belong in the paragraph because it does not support the main idea. An irrelevant sentence introduces a new idea that is not relevant to the paragraph.

EXERCISE 31

Part A. Read each paragraph and answer the question that follows it. In each paragraph, the sentences are numbered and the main idea is underlined.

Question 1 is based on the following paragraph.

(1) Chemical energy turns into heat energy when gasoline burns in the engine of a car. (2) The heat energy then changes into mechanical energy that moves the car. (3) Compact cars burn less gas for energy than larger luxury models do. (4) Electrical energy changes into heat energy in a hair dryer. (5) In a lamp, electrical energy changes into both light and heat energy. (6) Thus, energy changes forms.

1. Which sentence is irrelevant to the main idea of the paragraph?

_____

Question 2 is based on the following paragraph.

(1) Electricity is produced by electric generators. (2) Moving

GENERATOR: a machine that changes mechanical
energy into electrical energy

water or steam turns large wheels called turbines. (3) As a turbine rotates, it moves large coils of wires through a magnetic

MAGNETIC FIELD: an area where a magnetic force exists
(A magnetic force pulls two things—such as an iron
magnet and pins—together or apart.)

field, and electricity is produced. (4) Cars have generators.

2. Which sentence is irrelevant to the main idea of the paragraph?

_____

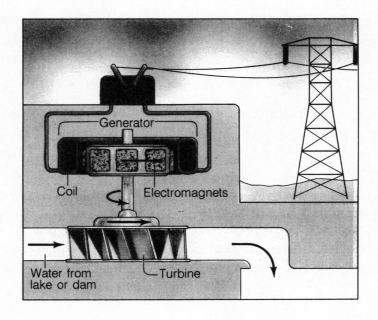

Question 3 is based on the following paragraph.

(1) All power plants that make electricity need some form of energy to spin the turbines. (2) In a hydroelectric power plant, the force of falling water spins the turbines. (3) In a thermal power plant, the power of steam spins the turbines. (4) In most thermal power plants, the heat that turns water into steam comes from burning coal. (5) The process of burning coal releases by-products that pollute the air. (6) In other thermal power plants, the heat needed to make steam comes from splitting atoms.

THERM
↓
heat

3. Which sentence is irrelevant to the main idea of the paragraph?

_____

Question 4 is based on the following paragraph.

(1) Nuclear energy is used to generate electricity in nuclear power plants. (2) Nuclear energy is the energy stored in the nucleus of an atom. (3) During nuclear fission, heat is released.

NUCLEAR FISSION: the process by which energy is released when the nucleus of an atom is split

(4) The heat turns water into steam, the steam spins turbines, and electricity is produced. (5) The Nuclear Regulatory Commission makes sure that nuclear power plants operate safely.

4. Which sentence is irrelevant to the main idea of the paragraph?

_____

Part B. Read each paragraph and answer the questions that follow it. The sentences in each paragraph are numbered.

Questions 1 and 2 are based on the following paragraph.

(1) Coal, oil, and natural gas are fossil fuels. (2) Coal, the most abundant fossil fuel in the United States, is a solid. (3) Oil, the most widely used energy resource in the United States, is a liquid. (4) Natural gas, which is found with oil, is made up mostly of methane gas. (5) Carbon monoxide, a deadly gas, is created when fossil fuels are burned in a fire that does not get enough oxygen.

1. Which sentence states the main idea of the paragraph? _____
2. Which sentence is irrelevant to the main idea of the paragraph?

_____

Questions 3 and 4 are based on the following paragraph.

(1) Fossil fuels are formed from the remains of dead plants and animals that were preserved long ago in the earth's crust. (2) These dead organisms were buried under sediments such as mud, sand, and clay. (3) Some sediments contain bones that have helped scientists figure out how dinosaurs probably looked. (4) Over hundreds of millions of years, heat has changed the sediments into rock and the dead matter into fossil fuels.

3. Which sentence states the main idea of the paragraph? _____

4. Which sentence is irrelevant to the main idea of the paragraph?

_____

Questions 5 and 6 are based on the following paragraph.

(1) Fossil fuels are hydrocarbons, which contain the elements hydrogen and carbon. (2) Carbon is part of more than 2 million compounds. (3) When hydrocarbons are combined with oxygen at high temperatures, they burn. (4) This process, called combustion, releases heat and light energy. (5) Therefore, their chemical composition makes fossil fuels useful energy sources.

5. Which sentence states the main idea of the paragraph? _____

6. Which sentence is irrelevant to the main idea of the paragraph?

_____

Questions 7 and 8 are based on the following paragraph.

(1) Coal is a solid fossil fuel. (2) There are four kinds of coal: peat, lignite, bituminous coal, and anthracite. (3) **Peat** is a soft

Counterclockwise from top left, the four types of coal: peat, lignite, bituminous coal, and anthracite.

substance made of decayed plant fibers. (4) When rocks above it put pressure on peat, it changes into **lignite,** a soft coal with a woody texture. (5) With more pressure, lignite turns into **bituminous coal,** which is often called soft coal. (6) It takes tremendous pressure to change bituminous coal into **anthracite,** a very hard and brittle coal.

7. Which sentence states the main idea of the paragraph? _____
8. Which sentence is irrelevant to the main idea of the paragraph?

_____

Check your answers on page 217.

Chapter

2 FACTS AND OPINIONS

A **fact** is something that is known with certainty. It can be proved. An **opinion** is a statement that is based on a person's beliefs or values. Unlike a fact, an opinion cannot be checked and proved true. In this chapter, you will learn to distinguish between facts and opinions in sentences and passages you read.

Lesson 32

Analyzing Lists of Sentences

It is a <u>fact</u> that Marie and Pierre Curie discovered the element radium. It can be checked in an encyclopedia or another reliable source and proved true.

However, to say that Marie Curie was a better scientist than her husband, Pierre, is an <u>opinion</u>. Two people can argue endlessly about which scientist was better. Both may back up their opinions with very sound reasons, but neither of them will be able to prove that his or her beliefs are true.

Although many people may share an opinion, it is not a fact unless it can be proved true. You may agree with someone else's opinion, but that doesn't make it a fact.

> FACT: a statement that can be tested or checked and proved true
> OPINION: a statement, based on a person's beliefs or values, that cannot be proved true

Ask yourself these questions to decide whether a statement is a fact or an opinion:

Can you prove it?
     If you can prove it, it's a **fact**.
Can you agree or disagree with it but not prove it?
     If you can agree or disagree with it but cannot prove it, it's an **opinion**.

The first sentence is a fact. You can prove that it is true by checking in a science book or an encyclopedia. The second sentence states an opinion. Some people may think that another planet is the most beautiful. You cannot prove that the earth is the most beautiful, but you can agree or disagree with the idea.

Opinions are subjective. That is, they vary from person to person. Beauty, for example, is in the eye of the beholder. What is beautiful to one person may not be beautiful to someone else. Facts, on the other hand, are objective. Their truth is not affected by how a person feels about them.

Unlike facts, opinions often contain "judgment words" that express a feeling about someone or something. Examples of judgment words are _beautiful, ugly, best, worst, good,_ and _bad._

EXERCISE 32

Tell which of the sentences in each list state facts and which express opinions.

List 1

_____ 1. The sun heats and lights the earth.
_____ 2. Without the sun, living things could not exist on the earth.
_____ 3. More people should use solar energy to heat their homes.
_____ 4. Too much exposure to the sun can cause skin cancer.
_____ 5. People who lie in the sun to get a tan are foolish.

List 2

_____ 6. Bituminous coal is the most plentiful type of coal on the earth.

_____ 7. Coal near the surface of the ground is obtained by a process called strip mining.

_____ 8. Strip mining causes land pollution.

_____ 9. Many coal miners get lung disease.

_____10. Coal mining is a dangerous job.

List 3

_____11. People in the oil business do not care about the environment.

_____12. Most oil is contained in the pores of underground rocks.

_____13. Oil is obtained by drilling.

_____14. Oil from wells is processed in refineries.

_____15. Oil that spills out of tankers harms the environment.

List 4

_____16. Nuclear energy is the energy contained in the nucleus, or center, of an atom.

_____17. Nuclear weapons will prevent a third world war.

_____18. People who build nuclear power plants place the desire for profits far above their concern for public safety.

_____19. All nuclear power plants should be closed down.

_____20. On March 18, 1979, an accident occurred at the Three Mile Island nuclear power plant in Middletown, Pennsylvania.

At Three Mile Island, radiation escaped into the atmosphere when the nuclear core overheated because of a cooling system failure in the reactor.

Check your answers on page 218.

Analyzing Facts and Opinions in Passages

The word *science* comes from the Latin word *scire*, which means "to know." Scientists seek answers to questions about the world around them. They uncover basic truths, or facts, about the universe. Therefore, the purpose of most science writing is to explain scientific knowledge. When you read about science, you usually read facts.

The following passage, for example, states facts about nuclear waste:

> Nuclear power plants in the United States produce nearly 2000 tons of waste each year. This waste is radioactive. Unless it is disposed of safely, it is a hazard to all living things.

The first sentence in the paragraph can be proved a fact by examining nuclear power plant waste disposal records. The second and third sentences can be proved factual by referring to scientific studies on nuclear wastes and the effects they have on living things.

People form opinions based on scientific facts. In the following paragraph, each sentence states an opinion about nuclear energy. The opinions are based on these three facts, even though the facts aren't stated in the paragraph: (1) Nuclear waste is hazardous to life; (2) air pollution caused by burning fossil fuels and by oil spills is a hazard to life; and (3) there have been accidents at nuclear power plants.

> The U.S. government should close all nuclear power plants because the hazards are far too great to make them worthwhile. Radioactive waste threatens life on Earth more than oil spills or air pollution. In addition, it is certain that there will be another major accident in the near future unless nuclear plants are closed.

The first sentence is an opinion based on the writer's values. The writer thinks that the hazards of nuclear power are *too* great, so plants should be closed. The opinion in the second sentence is that nuclear power is more dangerous than pollution from fossil fuels. Other people have the opposite opinion. Neither opinion is a fact. The last sentence makes a prediction. A prediction is clearly an opinion, because it is a statement about something that hasn't happened yet.

Since most opinions are based on facts, it is common to read passages in which both facts and opinions are stated. For this reason, it is important to recognize the difference between them. You don't want to mistake someone else's opinion for a fact, but you need to get the facts in order to form an opinion of your own. In addition, questions on the GED may ask you to decide if a statement is a fact or an opinion.

Low-level radioactive waste being buried at a dump site.

EXERCISE 33

Read the following passages and answer the questions.

Questions 1 and 2 are based on the following paragraph in which the sentences are numbered.

(1) The problem with nuclear power is that we don't know enough about how to use it safely or wisely. (2) At one time, people in great numbers protested the passing of airplanes overhead. (3) Nuclear power is at about that stage right now. (4) We fear it and damn it because we are not yet fully its masters, as we now consider ourselves to be masters of the airplane. (5) Trying to ban the airplane did not work. (6) Banning nuclear energy is not the answer. (7) Not far down the road, our supply of fossil fuels will, indeed, be gone. (8) The sun and the wind are not the answer. (9) Nuclear power can be. (10) But we must first become its masters.

1. Which sentences in the paragraph state facts? _____
2. Which sentences in the paragraph express opinions? _____

Question 3 is based on the following passage in which the sentences are numbered.

(1) On April 26, 1986, an accident occurred at the Chernobyl nuclear power plant near Kiev in the Soviet Union. (2) An explo-

sion in the nuclear reactor, which caused its roof to blow off, started a fire that burned for days. (3) A cloud of radioactive particles rose into the air and was carried by winds throughout Europe.

(4) Several people were killed instantly by the explosion at the Chernobyl plant. (5) Others died soon after from burns or radiation poisoning. (6) Everyone affected by the accident at Chernobyl has suffered greatly. (7) How many more people will die in future years as a result of radiation remains unknown.

3. All the sentences in the passage state facts except one. Which one expresses an opinion? ____

Question 4 is based on the following passage.

THE NATION CRIES OVER SPILLED OIL

On March 24, 1989, the largest oil spill in U.S. history occurred. An oil tanker owned by the Exxon Corporation, the *Exxon Valdez*, crashed into Bligh Reef in Prince William Sound, Alaska. The rocky reef ruptured eight of the eleven oil tanks aboard the ship, and 11 million gallons of oil spilled out into the sea.

Twelve hours passed before efforts were made to contain the oil. As a result, only about 13% of the oil was recovered. The crude oil blackened 1100 miles of the once pristine Alaskan coastline.

The oil spill proved to be fatal for many animals who lived in the sound. The corpses of about 1000 sea otters, 148 eagles, and 34,000 other birds were found. Some were poisoned by the toxic chemicals in the oil. Others died of <u>hypothermia</u> because either their fur or feathers stuck together and could not protect them from the cold water. Many birds drowned because an oil coating made it hard for them to float.

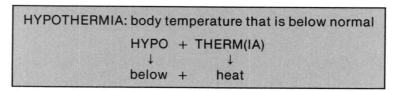

HYPOTHERMIA: body temperature that is below normal

HYPO + THERM(IA)
↓   ↓
below   +   heat

Scientists believe that the dead animals may represent only 10% to 30% of the total number of animals harmed by the spill. As many as half of the estimated 5000 eagles who make their home in the sound may have been poisoned by the oil. In addition, the salmon and herring that live in the icy waters may have been tainted. Only time will tell how many animals will be damaged as the poisonous chemicals make their way up the food chain.

Some of the survivors of the spill may be permanently handicapped. Some eagles were blinded by oil poisoning. Other eagles who were affected crashed and broke their wings while flying. Some had to have their wings amputated.

Exxon spent about 5½ months and $1 billion trying to clean up the oil. Despite its efforts, extensive damage was done to the ecosystem. The accident harmed more animals than any other oil spill. In addition, many experts believe that the sound will be forever tainted by what has been called America's worst industrial accident.

4. Is the passage made up mainly of facts or of opinions?_____

Questions 5 and 6 are based on the following passage in which the sentences are numbered.

(1) Oil spills are killing our wildlife, destroying our beaches, and upsetting the whole ecosystem of our oceans. (2) We must put a stop to this before our environment is further destroyed.

(3) We feel one way to solve this problem is to get more responsible workers to control the transportation of oil. (4) At times they are just inattentive or careless. (5) We cannot have this any longer.

(6) Not only do the oil spills affect our environment, but they affect the health and safety of people. (7) Pollution like this gets into the water we drink. (8) We are destroying ourselves and future generations by not putting a stop to this now. (9) Even though it gets expensive to prevent these oil spills and to clean them up, we should not let money stop us.

5. Which sentences in the passage state facts? _____
6. Which sentences in the passage express opinions? _____

Check your answers on page 218.

3 CONCLUSIONS AND SUPPORTING INFORMATION

In this chapter, you will evaluate conclusions and supporting information. You will determine which conclusions can be drawn from the given information. You will also identify the information that leads to a given conclusion.

Lesson 34

Evaluating Conclusions

Writers often present a lot of information and then draw a conclusion from that information. There are different kinds of conclusions. Based on the information presented, a conclusion may (1) provide a kind of summary, (2) draw an inference, or (3) state an opinion. No matter what kind of conclusion a writer draws, it is a valid conclusion only if it is based on the information that has been presented.

TRY THIS

Read the paragraph and answer the question that follows it.

Burning fossil fuels and splitting atoms to produce energy harms human health. Air pollution caused by the burning of fossil fuels can damage the lungs and respiratory tract. When combined with other air pollutants, fossil fuel pollutants contribute to many other human ailments. Nuclear fission produces radioactive waste, which is also harmful to humans. An accident at a nuclear power plant can release radiation into the air. Radiation sickness can kill people or make them very sick.

Which of the following conclusions is supported by the information in the paragraph?
(1) Fossil fuels and nuclear fission are safe sources of energy.
(2) Fossil fuels will always be used as a source of energy.
(3) The world needs to use safer sources of energy.

Conclusion (3) is the only one that is supported by all the information in the paragraph. It states an opinion. The paragraph tells how dangerous burning fossil fuels and splitting atoms are. It is reasonable to conclude that the world should use safer sources of energy.

Conclusion (1) seems to be a summary of the paragraph, but it is an inaccurate one. Because the paragraph is about the dangers of burning fossil fuels and splitting atoms, it is not logical to conclude that they are safe sources of energy.

Conclusion (2) seems to be an inference, but the paragraph does not present enough information to support the inference. It is true that fossil fuels are used for energy now, but that does not mean that they will be used for energy in the future.

When you evaluate a conclusion, you decide whether it is supported by all the information that is given. You must consider every piece of information. If even one small detail does not support it, the conclusion is not valid.

EXERCISE 34

Read each paragraph and answer the question that follows it.

Question 1 is based on the following passage.

> Water is a powerful source of energy. It is a clean energy source that does not pollute the environment. It is also renewable, which means it cannot be used up.
>
> Hydroelectric power plants use falling or flowing water to make electricity. The rush of water, which is controlled by dams, spins the blades of the turbines in an electric generator.
>
> Unfortunately, there are not many areas in the world where dams can be built.

1. Which one of the following conclusions is supported by the information in the passage?
   (1) Hydroelectric power plants are more expensive to build than other kinds of power plants.
   (2) Water power will probably never meet a large portion of the world's energy needs.
   (3) Water power will probably become a major source of energy.

Question 2 is based on the following graph.

SOURCES OF ENERGY USED IN THE UNITED STATES

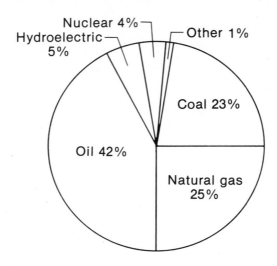

Nuclear 4%
Hydroelectric 5%
Other 1%
Coal 23%
Oil 42%
Natural gas 25%

2. The data in the circle graph show that most of the energy used in the United States comes from
   (1) coal
   (2) atoms
   (3) fossil fuels

Question 3 is based on the following paragraph.

Direct solar energy is taken straight from the sun. There are two types of direct solar energy: passive and active. When windows in a house let a lot of sunlight in, that house is warmed by passive solar energy. Active solar energy involves gathering the sun's energy into solar collectors. A solar collector is usually a panel of aluminum, copper, or steel that is painted black and covered with plastic or glass. Water is pumped into the collector where it is heated by the sun's rays. It is then pumped into tanks until it is needed to provide heat and hot water.

3. Which of the following conclusions is supported by the information in the passage?
   (1) Both passive and active solar energy can be used to warm a house at night.
   (2) Equipment that provides passive solar energy is more expensive than equipment that provides active solar energy.
   (3) The black paint on solar collectors helps them absorb energy.

Question 4 is based on the following table.

PRODUCTS PRODUCED FROM A BARREL OF CRUDE OIL

4. Which of the following conclusions is supported by the data in the table?
    (1) More than half of all oil is used for transportation.
    (2) Most oil is used to heat homes.
    (3) Oil is not a very useful product.

	% Yield
Gasolines	46.7
Fuel oil	28.6
Jet fuel	9.1
Petrochemicals and Miscellaneous products	3.8
Coke	3.5
Asphalt and road oil	3.1
Liquified gases	2.9
Lubricants	1.3
Kerosene	0.9
Waxes	0.1

Question 5 is based on the following passage.

During nuclear fission the nucleus of an atom is split apart. In a process called **fusion**, the nuclei of two atoms can be fused together.

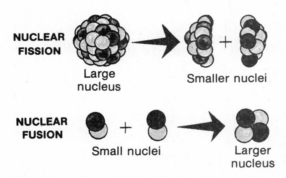

NUCLEAR FISSION   Large nucleus   Smaller nuclei

NUCLEAR FUSION   Small nuclei   Larger nucleus

Fusion reactions can take place only at very high temperatures—at least 100,000,000°C. At such high temperatures, matter does not exist as a solid, a liquid, or a gas. It exists in a fourth state, called **plasma**. Fusion reactions give the sun and other stars the tremendous energy they emit as heat and light.

5. Which of the following conclusions is supported by the information in the passage?
    (1) The matter that makes up stars exists in a liquid state.
    (2) The temperature of the sun must be at least 100,000,000°C.
    (3) Nuclear fission produces more energy than nuclear fusion.

Check your answers on page 218.

Evaluating Supporting Statements

In Lesson 34, you identified conclusions that were supported by the information in passages and graphics. In this lesson, you will do the opposite. You will read several details about a topic and decide which of them support a given conclusion.

In a group of sentences, each statement may be a fact. However, a given conclusion may be based on only a few of the sentences. To find out which sentences support a certain conclusion, you need to evaluate each sentence.

TRY THIS

Read the following conclusion and answer the question about it.

Unless people conserve energy and develop new sources of energy, there could be an energy shortage.

Which two of the following statements support this conclusion?

_____ (a) Fossil fuels are being used up.

_____ (b) The world population doubles every 33 years.

_____ (c) Companies make large profits selling fossil fuels.

Only Choices (a) and (b) support the conclusion. According to Choice (a), fossil fuels are being used up. If we don't conserve these energy sources, one day there won't be any left. This will cause an energy shortage unless new energy sources are developed. Choice (b) says that the world population is growing. It stands to reason that a growing population will use more and more energy. With more people and with no new sources of energy, a shortage could develop. Companies do make money selling fossil fuels, as Choice (c) says. However, even if companies did not make profits, we would still need to conserve energy and develop new resources to avoid an energy shortage. So, Choice (c) does not support the conclusion.

Read each conclusion and answer the question about it.

Question 1 is based on the following conclusion.

Wind power comes indirectly from the sun's energy.

1. Which one or more of the following statements support the above conclusion?

_____ (a) Wind is caused by uneven heating of the earth.

_____ (b) Windmills have been used for hundreds of years to grind grain and pump water.

_____ (c) The movement of wind causes a windmill to spin.

Wind is a source of energy. In this California "windmill farm," several thousand windmills drive turbines, which give generators the power to create an electric current.

Question 2 is based on the following conclusion.

There are many benefits of solar heating.

2. Which one or more of the following statements support the above conclusion?

_____ (a) The sun's rays are free.

_____ (b) The energy that reaches the earth from the sun is 500,000 times the amount of energy generated by all the power plants in the United States.

_____ (c) When it is cloudy, the water in solar collectors does not get hot.

Question 3 is based on the following conclusion.

Nuclear fusion is a safer form of energy than nuclear fission.

3. Which one or more of the following statements support the above conclusion?

____ (a) Unlike fission reactions, fusion reactions must take place at very high temperatures.

____ (b) Fusion reactions cannot cause explosions the way fission reactions can if they go out of control.

____ (c) Unlike fission reactions, fusion reactions do not produce dangerous radioactive wastes.

Question 4 is based on the following conclusion.

At this time, geothermal energy is not a major source of energy.*

4. Which one or more of the following statements support the above conclusion?

____ (a) The supply of geothermal energy is limitless.

____ (b) Geothermal energy is now used in several countries.

____ (c) In most areas of the world, geothermal heat is too deep to be reached by existing equipment.

Question 5 is based on the following conclusion.

As people's lives become more comfortable, the demand for energy increases.

5. Which one or more of the following statements support the above conclusion?

____ (a) People have begun to recycle newspapers, aluminum cans, bottles, and other garbage.

____ (b) People are using more electrical appliances such as air conditioners and dishwashers.

____ (c) Many families have two or more cars.

Check your answers on page 218.

*Geothermal energy comes from heat deep inside the earth. In geothermal power plants, this natural heat is used to spin the turbines that drive electric generators.

SCIENCE READINGS 4

This section of the unit contains science readings. These readings can help you prepare for the GED in three ways. You can use them to

- review what you already know about science
- expand your general knowledge of science
- practice the reading skills that you have learned in this book

THE SCIENTIFIC METHOD

To find answers to questions, scientists use a step-by-step approach called the **scientific method.** They use common sense to draw conclusions based on information they gather through research and experimentation.

Here are the basic steps of the scientific method:

1. State the problem.
2. Gather information.
3. Form a hypothesis.
4. Perform experiments to test the hypothesis.
5. Record data.
6. Analyze the data and draw a conclusion.

The following example shows how the scientific method is used to answer a question about antifreeze.

1. **State the problem.** Clearly stating the problem lets the scientist know how to proceed. The problem can take the form of a question.

   Example: How does antifreeze prevent water in a car's engine from freezing?

2. **Gather information.** The scientist brings together all the available information related to the problem.

   Example:
   a. Antifreeze is needed only where air temperatures go below the freezing point of water.
   b. Water becomes ice at its freezing point.
   c. The colder the temperature is, the more antifreeze is needed to keep the water in a car's engine from freezing.

3. **Form a hypothesis.** A hypothesis is an educated guess. After considering all the available information, the scientist proposes a hypothesis, or possible solution to the problem.

   Example: Antifreeze lowers the freezing point of water.

4. **Perform experiments to test the hypothesis.** The scientist performs an experiment to test the hypothesis.

   Example:
   Fill one jar with water.
   Fill another jar with water and antifreeze.
   Put a thermometer in each jar.
   Begin lowering the temperature of the liquids in both jars.

5. **Record data.** Data are records of measurements and observations. The scientist writes down all the important data collected during the experiment.

   Example: Record the temperatures at which the liquids in the jars freeze.

6. **Analyze the data and draw a conclusion.** The scientist examines the data carefully and draws a conclusion.

   Example: Antifreeze lowers the freezing point of water.

The conclusion in the sixth step is the same as the hypothesis in the third step because the experiments showed that the hypothesis is correct.

1. Match the step of the scientific method listed in Group A with its example in Group B.

   Group A
   ____ A. State the problem.
   ____ B. Form a hypothesis.
   ____ C. Perform experiments to test the hypothesis.
   ____ D. Record data.

   Group B
   (1) The more sunlight string bean plants get, the more they will grow.
   (2) Keep a height chart for each string bean plant. Record each plant's height every week.
   (3) How does sunlight affect the growth of string bean plants?
   (4) Give two groups of string bean plants different amounts of sunlight each day from May 15 to September 15. Give one group 2 hours of sunlight. Give the other group 5 hours of sunlight.

MUSCLES

When you are awake, you use your muscles in a variety of ways: walking, working, and exercising. Even when you are asleep, many of your muscles are still working to keep you alive. The muscles of your heart contract to pump blood. Your chest muscles help to move air in and out of your lungs. The muscles of your digestive tract move food through your body.

Muscles are made of long, thin fibers. They run beside one another and are held together in bundles by connective tissue. Muscle tissue has the special ability to shorten, or contract. As muscle tissue shortens, it causes movement in the body.

In order to contract, muscles need the energy that comes from food and oxygen. When a muscle contracts, the chemical energy in food is changed into mechanical energy, or the energy of movement.

There are three types of muscle tissue: **smooth** muscle, **cardiac** muscle, and **skeletal** muscle. Smooth muscles work all the time without any effort on your part. For this reason, they are called **involuntary** muscles. The muscles used in breathing and digestion are smooth muscles.

Cardiac muscle tissue is found only in the heart. Like smooth muscles, cardiac muscles are involuntary. Their contractions make the heart beat.

Unlike smooth muscles and cardiac muscles, skeletal muscles are **voluntary** muscles. They move only when you want them to. There are over 600 skeletal muscles in the body. Their function is to move all the parts of the body. When they contract, they move your arms, legs, head, and other body parts. Skeletal muscles are attached to bones by tendons.

SKELETAL MUSCLES

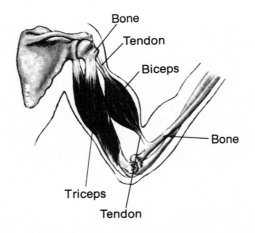

Bone
Tendon
Biceps
Bone
Triceps
Tendon

Skeletal muscles always work in pairs. For instance, the biceps and triceps in your upper arm form a pair. When you "make a muscle," or bend your arm upward, the biceps in the front of your arm contracts. At the same time, the triceps in the back of your arm relaxes.

Muscles perform better when they are used frequently. Regular exercise increases muscle size and strength, but when muscles are not used, they shrink.

2. What are the three kinds of muscle tissue?

_____ _____ _____

3. What is the function of skeletal muscles? _____

4. What is the difference between voluntary and involuntary muscles?

_____

5. What happens to your biceps when you contract your triceps? _____

6. Sara broke her right leg. A doctor set her broken bone and put her leg in a cast for 6 weeks. She used crutches to walk so that she would not put any weight on her broken leg. What probably happened to the muscles in Sara's right leg while she was wearing the cast?
   (1) They grew stronger.
   (2) They shrank.
   (3) They became involuntary.

THE GREENHOUSE EFFECT

The earth's temperature is slowly increasing. If this warming continues at the current rate, the average temperature will be 3° to 10° higher by the middle of the 21st century. This may not seem like much, but the average <u>global</u> tempera-

> GLOBAL: worldwide

ture has not varied by more than 4° in the last 15,000 years.

This slow rise in the earth's temperature is caused by the **greenhouse effect.**

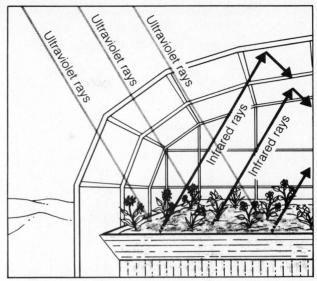

CO_2 and other gases in the atmosphere act like the glass windows in a greenhouse: they prevent heat from escaping.

Gases that accumulate in the atmosphere cover the earth like a glass building, or greenhouse. These gases let sunlight in but trap heat close to the earth's surface.

If this global warming trend continues, life on earth may change. Summers may be longer and hotter. The heat could melt the polar ice caps, which would cause the oceans to rise. In the United States, rainfall might decrease by as much as 40%. The United States alone generates 21% of the gases causing the greenhouse effect.

To slow down this increase in temperature, it is necessary to reduce the amount of carbon dioxide (CO_2) in the air. Although CO_2 is a natural part of the air, too much of it now surrounds the planet. CO_2 is the major cause of the greenhouse effect.

Most of the extra CO_2 comes from burning fossil fuels. If we stopped burning these fuels, we could cut the problem in half. But nothing is simple about the greenhouse effect.

Fossil fuels provide about 90% of the energy in the United States. These fuels give us heat and electricity. They help make our clothes and food. They also give our cars the power to run. Hence, the fuels that help to make us comfortable are slowly heating up the earth.

CARBON DIOXIDE PRODUCED BY BURNING FUELS

(in pounds per 1,000,000 Btu's* of heat)

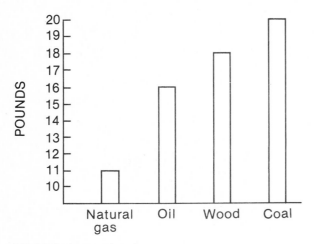

*British thermal units.

The problem is even more complex. The hotter it gets, the more energy we will need to run fans and air conditioners. In order to slow down this dangerous warming trend, scientists need to develop safer ways to produce energy.

7. The slow warming of the earth is called the greenhouse effect because
   (1) CO_2 is found in the air inside greenhouses
   (2) gases in the atmosphere act like the glass in a greenhouse
   (3) it is usually warmer inside a green house than it is outside

8. Which gas is the major cause of the greenhouse effect? _____

9. How are the details organized in the second paragraph?
   (1) cause and effect
   (2) comparison
   (3) list structure
   (4) time order

10. Which sentence in the third paragraph is irrelevant to the main idea of the paragraph?
    (1) If this global warming trend continues, life on earth may change.

(2) Summers may be longer and hotter.
(3) The heat could melt the polar ice caps, which would cause the oceans to rise.
(4) In the United States, rainfall might decrease by as much as 40%.
(5) The United States alone generates 21% of the gases causing the greenhouse effect.

11. Which one of the following conclusions is NOT supported by the information in the passage?
    (1) If the earth continues to get warmer, cities on the seacoasts may be covered with water.
    (2) If the earth continues to get warmer, the land may become too dry to grow certain crops.
    (3) If the earth continues to get warmer, the size of the population will decrease.

12. Based on information in the passage, it is possible to conclude that if we continue burning fossil fuels at the current rate, the amount of CO_2 in the atmosphere will
    (1) increase
    (2) stay the same
    (3) decrease

13. According to the bar graph, how many pounds of carbon dioxide are emitted per million Btu's of heat created by burning oil? _____

14. Which conclusion is supported by the information in both the passage and the bar graph?
    (1) Burning wood does not pollute the atmosphere.
    (2) When it is burned, coal pollutes the atmosphere more than any other fossil fuel.
    (3) Only fossil fuels produce CO_2.

LIGHT WAVES

Light is a kind of energy. Light is released by electrons, which move around an atom's nucleus, in tiny packets called **photons**. Some photons contain more energy than others.

Light travels in waves. **Waves** are motions that carry energy from one place to another. They move up and down like the waves in the ocean.

Waves are measured in **wavelengths**. A wavelength is the distance from a point on one wave to the same point on the wave that follows it.

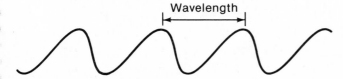
Wavelength

Waves are also measured by **wave frequency**: how many waves occur per second. Long waves have a low frequency because there are very few waves per second.

Short waves have a high frequency because there are several waves per second.

The amount of energy in a photon determines the kind of light wave it produces. The higher the frequency, the more energy a light wave gives out.

The total range of wavelengths of light and other forms of radiant energy is

> RADIANT ENERGY: all energy that travels in waves

called the **electromagnetic spectrum**. Wave lengths range from the longest to the shortest in this spectrum.

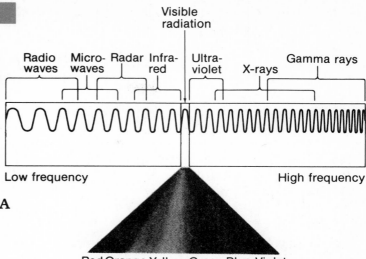

Visible radiation

Radio waves | Micro-waves | Radar | Infrared | Ultra-violet | X-rays | Gamma rays

Low frequency — High frequency

Red Orange Yellow Green Blue Violet

Our eyes can see very few light waves. The light waves that we can see are called **visible light**. Visible light is made up of the colors red, orange, yellow, green, blue, indigo, and violet. Together these colors form "white light," or sunlight. The eye sees different wavelengths of light as different colors. Red light waves are the longest; they also have the lowest frequency. Violet light waves are the shortest; they also have the highest frequency.

Infrared light waves are below the color red in the visible spectrum. They are longer waves with a lower frequency than that of visible light rays. We cannot see infrared light waves, but we can feel them. They give off a lot of heat. Some electrical appliances, such as toasters and electric broilers, cook food with infrared light waves.

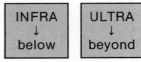

INFRA
↓
below

ULTRA
↓
beyond

Ultraviolet light (UV light) is also invisible. UV light waves are above the color violet in the visible spectrum. UV waves are shorter than visible light waves. They also have a higher frequency. UV rays are given off by the sun. They cause sunburn. UV lamps are often used in hospitals to kill germs.

15. Match each item in Group A with its definition in Group B.

Group A
____ A. light
____ B. wave
____ C. photon
____ D. wavelength
____ E. wave frequency
____ F. electro-magnetic spectrum
____ G. infrared light
____ H. ultraviolet light

Group B
(1) the total range of wavelengths of radiant energy
(2) the distance from a point on one wave to the same point on the next wave
(3) a packet of light released by an electron
(4) the type of wave below red in the visible spectrum
(5) a measure of the number of waves that occur per second
(6) a type of energy that travels in waves
(7) the type of wave above violet in the visible spectrum
(8) the type of motion that carries energy

16. Which of the following colors has the highest frequency?
   (1) blue
   (2) green
   (3) indigo
   (4) orange
   (5) yellow

17. Which of the following gives out the least energy?
   (1) X-rays
   (2) radio waves
   (3) gamma rays
   (4) infrared waves
   (5) ultraviolet waves

ELECTRICITY

Like light, electricity is a form of energy created by an atom's electrons. An object develops an electric charge either by gaining or losing electrons. The energy created when electrons move from place to place is called **electricity**.

Static electricity is produced by rubbing two objects together. The friction created by rubbing moves electrons from one object to another.

> STATIC: not moving; at rest.
>
> STAT
> ↓
> stand

"Fly-away" hair is caused by static electricity. Both hair and a comb contain neutral atoms. When you comb your hair, the comb removes some electrons from your hair. The comb gains those electrons and becomes negatively charged. Because your hair loses electrons, it becomes positively charged. Since things with the same charge repel each other, the positively charged hairs move away from each other. Because things with opposite charges attract each other, the positively charged hairs move toward the negatively charged comb. Eventually, the hair and the comb lose their electric charges, and the fly-away hair settles down.

Unlike static electricity, which loses its electric charge after it moves from one object to another, **current electricity** moves constantly. When electrons flow through a wire in one direction, the current is called **direct current**, or **DC**. Batteries supply direct current. When electrons reverse their direction regularly, the current is called **alternating current**, or **AC**. A generator in a power plant supplies your home with alternating current.

An electric current travels along a path called a circuit. A **circuit** includes a source, wires, and an object that uses electricity. The **source** begins the flow of electrons. The **wires** carry the electricity to an appliance that uses the power, such as a hair dryer. The appliance converts the electric energy into one or more forms of energy—heat, light, or mechanical.

Electricity cannot flow through an open circuit. It can flow only through a closed circuit. A switch opens and closes a circuit. For example, when a light switch is on, the circuit is closed and electricity flows to the light bulb. In contrast, when a light switch is off, the circuit is open and electricity cannot flow to the light bulb.

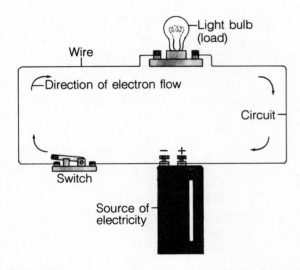

When a wire in a circuit breaks, electricity can leak. The electric current produces heat and may cause a fire. A break of this kind is called a **short circuit**.

Fuses are safety devices used to prevent fires caused by too much electricity. A fuse can be added to a circuit. When many appliances on the circuit are used at the same time, a lot of heat can build up. The high temperature causes the conductor in the fuse to melt. When the fuse melts, the circuit opens. This process is known as "blowing a fuse."

18. What is electricity a form of? _____

19. Which one of the following appliances runs on direct electric current?
    (1) refrigerator
    (2) portable radio
    (3) dishwasher

20. When a fuse blows in a circuit, what happens to the flow of electricity?

_____

21. Sometimes the clothes in a dryer stick to each other. This "static cling" occurs because
    (1) the clothes are all positively charged
    (2) the clothes are all negatively charged
    (3) some of the clothes are positively charged and some are negatively charged

22. The diagram shows
    (1) an open circuit
    (2) a closed circuit
    (3) a short circuit

23. The diagram shows electricity changed into
    (1) mechanical energy
    (2) light energy
    (3) solar energy

LIGHTNING

When electrons move from one object to another, static electricity results. In time, these electrons leave the second object, and the object loses its electrical charge. The loss of static electricity as electric charges move off an object is called **electric discharge**. Sometimes the

DISCHARGE: release

discharge of electricity is slow and quiet. Other times it is very quick and accompanied by a shock, a spark of light, or a crackle of noise.

Lightning is the best example of a powerful discharge of static electricity. During thunderstorms, opposite electrical charges build up in storm clouds. Lightning is the sudden discharge of electricity between these clouds or between a cloud and the ground. As electrons jump through the air, intense light and heat are produced. The light is the bolt of lightning that you see. The heat, which ranges from 27,000°F to 54,000°F, causes the air to expand suddenly. The rapid expansion of the air produces the thunder you hear after you see the light.

Lightning contains great amounts of electric energy. An average lightning bolt transfers billions of electrons between a cloud and the earth. A single lightning bolt may measure more that 15,000,000 volts. Heat lightning is often seen on the

> VOLT: a unit of measure of voltage, which is the energy, or "push," that moves electrons

evening of a hot day. One bolt of lightning may generate more power than every electric power plant in the country.

Lightning rods protect buildings from being hit by lightning. A lightning rod is a metal rod, usually attached to the top of a building so that it is the highest thing on the building. A wire connects the rod to the ground. The rod and the wire make a path for the lightning to travel on. Because lightning follows the shortest path to the ground, it hits the tallest object around. For that reason, it will hit a lightning rod instead of a building.

Each year, lightning kills about 100 people in the United States. It starts thousands of forest fires. In addition, it damages buildings, aircraft, and power equipment.

The most dangerous places to be during a thunderstorm are near a tree, on high ground, or in an open field. One of the safest places to be is in a car. When lightning hits a car, the energy spreads over the metal body and drains into the air or passes into the ground.

24. What is lightning a form of? _____

25. Why is it dangerous for a person to be in an open field during a thunderstorm? _____

26. Which of the following would be the safest activity during a thunderstorm?
    (1) lying on a beach
    (2) climbing a mountain
    (3) walking in a forest
    (4) sitting in an airplane waiting to take off

27. Which of the following sentences from the third paragraph is irrelevant to the main idea of the paragraph?
    (1) Lightning contains great amounts of electric energy.
    (2) An average lightning bolt transfers billions of electrons between a cloud and the earth.
    (3) A single lightning bolt may measure more that 15,000,000 volts.
    (4) Heat lightning is often seen on the evening of a hot day.
    (5) One bolt of lightning may generate more power than every electric power plant in the country.

28. Which of the following conclusions is supported by the information in the passage?
    (1) Lightning never strikes the same place twice.
    (2) Lightning travels easily through metal.
    (3) Lightning never strikes buildings.

Check your answers on page 219.

SCIENCE READINGS 4 SKILLS CHART

To review the reading skills covered by the questions in Science Readings 4, study the following parts of this book.

		Question Number
Unit 1		
Chapter 3	Details in Passages	2, 3, 4, 8, 15, 18, 24
Chapter 5	Patterns of Organization	9
Chapter 6	Tables and Graphs	13
Unit 2		
Chapter 1	Inferences	5, 7, 20
Unit 3	Applying Information You Read	1, 6, 16, 17, 19, 21, 22, 23, 25, 26
Unit 4		
Chapter 1	Relevant and Irrelevant Information	10, 27
Chapter 3	Conclusions and Supporting Information	11, 12, 14, 28

This section will give you practice in answering questions like those on the GED. The Science Test of the GED has 66 multiple-choice questions. Each question has 5 choices. The 10 questions in this section are all multiple choice, like the ones on the GED.

As you do this practice, use the reading skills you've studied in this book.

Directions: Choose the one best answer to each item.

Item 1 is based on the following circle graph.

ENERGY USE IN U.S. HOUSES AND APARTMENTS

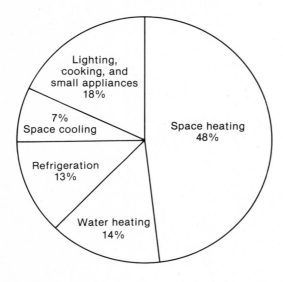

1. According to the circle graph, what percent of the energy used in residences is for heat and hot water?

    (1) 14%
    (2) 18%
    (3) 48%
    (4) 55%
    (5) 62%

Item 2 is based on the following table.

ELECTRICAL POWER USED BY COMMON HOUSEHOLD APPLIANCES

Appliance	Power used (in watts)
Clock	3
Clothes dryer	4000
Color television	300
Dishwasher	2300
Hair dryer	1000
Microwave oven	1450
Radio	100
Range/oven	2600
Refrigerator/freezer	600
Toaster	700

2. The appliance for which of the following activities uses the most electrical power?

    (1) cooling food
    (2) cooking food
    (3) drying laundry
    (4) watching the evening news
    (5) washing dishes

Item 3 is based on the following passage.

Energy always changes its form during chemical reactions. When energy takes the form of heat or light, it can be either released or absorbed. A chemical reaction in which heat or light energy is released is an exothermic reaction. A chemical reaction in which heat or light energy is absorbed is an endothermic reaction.

3. Which of the following is an exothermic chemical reaction?

    (1) exploding a firecracker
    (2) baking a cake
    (3) putting out a fire
    (4) freezing a cake
    (5) mixing cake batter

Item 4 is based on the following passage.

Electric charges move through matter. Conductors are substances that allow electric charges to move easily through them. Silver, copper, and aluminum are excellent conductors. The flow of electric charges through a conductor is called an electric current.

Insulators are substances that do not allow electric charges to move easily through them. Rubber, plastic, glass, and wood are the best insulators. They stop electric charges from flowing out of conductors to other objects.

4. Which of the following conclusions is supported by the information in the passage?

    (1) Rubber is used for a variety of things.
    (2) Silver is a better conductor than aluminum.
    (3) Plastic can serve as either an insulator or a conductor.
    (4) Metals are good insulators.
    (5) Metals are good conductors.

Item 5 is based on the following passage.

It is important for everyone to know about acid rain. When fossil fuels are burned, some released gases combine with water vapor in the air and form weak acids. These acids fall to the earth's surface when it rains or snows. This precipitation is called acid rain.

Although acid rain is created in the air, it causes a variety of problems for living things on land and in water. Acid rain destroys many kinds of plants. Many fish and other forms of aquatic life cannot survive in lakes, rivers, and streams because the acid content of the water is too high. In addition, the acid in the rain picks up toxic metals in the soil and carries them to water supplies.

5. Which of the following sentences from the passage expresses an opinion?

    (1) It is important for everyone to know about acid rain.
    (2) When fossil fuels are burned, some released gases combine with water vapor in the air and form weak acids.
    (3) Acid rain destroys many kinds of plants.
    (4) Many fish and other forms of aquatic life cannot survive in lakes, rivers, and streams because the acid content of the water is too high.
    (5) In addition, the acid in the rain picks up toxic metals in the soil and carries them to water supplies.

Item 6 is based on the following passage.

In 1666, Isaac Newton discovered that sunlight, or white light, is a mixture of all colors. Newton held a three-sided piece of glass, called a prism, in a beam of sunlight. When the sunlight passed through the prism, it was divided into seven colored rays: red, orange, yellow, green, blue, indigo, and violet. These seven colors make up the visible spectrum of light. The same thing happens when a sunbeam passes through a raindrop. The beam of sunlight becomes a rainbow, an arc displaying the seven colors of the spectrum.

Newton found that each color in a beam of sunlight bends at a different angle when it goes through a prism. This is because each color has a different wavelength.

6. Which of the following does NOT contain the colors red, orange, yellow, green, blue, indigo, and violet?

    (1) sunlight
    (2) white light
    (3) a prism
    (4) the visible spectrum
    (5) a rainbow

Item 7 is based on the following passage.

Deep inside a star, the force of gravity is very strong. In fact, the gravity is strong enough to cause atoms of hydrogen gas inside the star to fuse together. Two hydrogen atoms join together to form one helium atom. This process is called nuclear fusion.

Nuclear fusion in the sun, an average-sized star, changes about 600 billion kilograms of hydrogen into 595.8 billion kilograms of helium every second! The remaining 4.2 billion kilograms of hydrogen are changed to heat and light energy. Some of this energy heats and lights the earth.

7. The information in the passage explains why
   (1) the sky is blue
   (2) stars shine
   (3) hydrogen is the lightest element
   (4) helium balloons rise
   (5) matter is made of atoms

Items 8 and 9 are based on the following passage.

In some elements, protons and neutrons are bound together by very strong forces. Their nuclei are said to be stable. The forces that hold the nuclei of other elements together are weak. These elements have unstable nuclei. Elements with unstable nuclei are radioactive. All elements with atomic numbers greater than 83 are radioactive.

The nucleus of a radioactive element breaks down in a natural process called radioactive decay. When a radioactive atom decays, it releases both energy and particles of matter known as nuclear radiation. The atom eventually changes into a new element. For instance, uranium is a radioactive element. Its atomic number is 92. When it decays, it loses 2 protons and 2 neutrons and changes into the element thorium. The atomic number of thorium is 90. Thorium in turn breaks down and changes into radium. The process continues until an unstable uranium atom has changed into a stable lead atom.

8. Five elements are listed with their atomic numbers. Which one of them is radioactive?
   (1) bismuth: 83
   (2) gallium: 31
   (3) iron: 26
   (4) potassium:19
   (5) radon: 86

9. According to the information in the passage, only one of the following could be the atomic number of lead. Which one is that?
   (1) 82
   (2) 84
   (3) 86
   (4) 94
   (5) 99

Item 10 is based on the following passage.

Radiation released naturally or during nuclear fission is deadly to all forms of life. It can kill cells. It can also destroy some of the chemicals needed for chemical reactions that take place inside cells.

Exposure to a large amount of radiation results in death within days, or even hours. A lower dose of radiation destroys the bone marrow that produces the body's blood cells. The symptoms of such exposure are infection, nausea, and sterility. Without a bone marrow transplant, death can occur within 6 weeks. A low dose of radiation may not cause immediate symptoms but may lead to birth defects and cancer of the bone marrow, breast, or thyroid.

10. Which of the following conclusions is supported by the information in the passage?
   (1) All doses of radiation result in death.
   (2) Radiation sickness is common.
   (3) Scientists are working on a cure for radiation sickness.
   (4) All doses of radiation cause noticeable changes in the body.
   (5) Different doses of radiation have different effects on the body.

Check your answers on page 220.

GED PRACTICE 4 SKILLS CHART

To review the reading skills covered by the items in GED Practice 4, study the following parts of this book.

	Item Number
Unit 1	
Chapter 6 Tables and Graphs	1, 2
Unit 2	
Chapter 1 Inferences	6
Unit 3 Applying Information You Read	3, 8, 9
Unit 4	
Chapter 2 Facts and Opinions	5
Chapter 3 Conclusions and Supporting Information	4, 7, 10

Posttest

The following Posttest is similar to the Science Test of the GED. Taking it will help you find out how your skills have improved by using this book. It can also help you find out what you need to review or learn more about.

The Posttest has 33 multiple-choice items—half as many as there are on the GED. About half of the items are based on readings in biology. The rest are based on readings in the physical sciences—earth science, chemistry, and physics. The questions test your understanding of the readings and your ability to apply information and to think critically.

When glass or other solid waste is recycled, it is used over again.

SCIENCE POSTTEST

Directions: Choose the <u>one best answer</u> to each item.

<u>Items 1 to 3</u> are based on the following passage.

Once you have had certain diseases, you are immune to them. You can never get them again because your body produces antibodies against them. Antibodies are disease-fighting proteins. Different antibodies are produced for different diseases.

You can also become immune to some diseases without getting them. A vaccine—a preparation that contains a weak form of a virus—creates immunity to a disease. Usually injected, a vaccine is not strong enough to cause the disease, but it makes the body produce the antibodies that fight the disease.

Edward Jenner was a brilliant British doctor. He developed the first vaccine, a vaccine against smallpox, in 1796. Smallpox is a contagious, disfiguring, and often fatal disease. The only people Jenner found immune to it were people who had had cowpox, a cattle disease caused by a similar virus that could also infect humans. Jenner discovered that after infecting a person with a small amount of cowpox virus, the person became immune to smallpox.

1. What is the topic of the passage?
   (1) antibodies
   (2) Edward Jenner
   (3) fatal diseases
   (4) vaccines
   (5) viruses

2. Which of the following statements is NOT true?
   (1) Antibodies are proteins that fight diseases.
   (2) A vaccine contains a weak form of a virus.
   (3) A vaccine causes the body to produce antibodies.
   (4) Edward Jenner developed the first vaccine.
   (5) An injection of cowpox virus prevents all diseases.

3. Which of the following sentences from the passage states an opinion rather than a fact?
   (1) Once you have had certain diseases, you are immune to them.
   (2) Different antibodies are produced for different diseases.
   (3) A vaccine—a preparation that conains a weak form of a virus—creates immunity to a disease.
   (4) Edward Jenner was a brilliant British doctor.
   (5) Smallpox is a contagious, disfiguring, and often fatal disease.

<u>Item 4</u> is based on the following paragraph.

Aerobic exercise strengthens the heart so that it pumps more blood with each heartbeat. In addition to making the heart stronger, aerobic exercise expands the lungs, which enables them to take in more oxygen. The more oxygen there is in the lungs, the more oxygen there is for the blood to carry to all the cells in the body. Finally, aerobic exercise increases the number of capillaries, the blood vessels that connect veins and arteries.

4. The main idea of the passage is that aerobic exercise
   (1) must be performed for at least 20 minutes to be effective
   (2) takes many forms
   (3) benefits the heart
   (4) is the best form of exercise
   (5) improves the circulatory and respiratory systems

<u>Items 5 and 6</u> are based on the following passage.

To explore the depths of the seas, oceanographers need to use SCUBA devices. SCUBA stands for <u>S</u>elf-Contained <u>U</u>nderwater <u>B</u>reathing <u>A</u>pparatus.

SCUBA devices were used as long ago as 2000 years. Divers looking for sponges knew that the more air they could take under water with them, the longer they could stay down. At first, they could take air down only in their lungs. Then someone thought of making a water bladder to carry extra air.

Water bladders were made from the skins of goats, sheep, or pigs. First, the skin was peeled off the dead animal. Then, to make it waterproof, the skin was oiled and sewn up tightly. Like a balloon, it had an opening with a neck. A sponge diver could blow the skin full of air. Holding a heavy stone to stay under water, the diver could take air from the inflated skin as needed.

5. For early divers, having a water bladder was like having an extra

    (1) balloon
    (2) bladder
    (3) layer of skin
    (4) lung
    (5) neck

6. Water bladders helped sponge divers

    (1) stay under water longer
    (2) find sponges more easily
    (3) carry heavy stones
    (4) stay dry
    (5) skin animals

Items 7 and 8 are based on the following passage.

Some bacteria are essential for plant and animal growth. Nitrogen-fixing bacteria are found on the roots of legumes, including peas and beans. These bacteria take nitrogen from the air, change it into a different form that plants can use, and return it to the soil. Plants take this nitrogen from the soil and use it to make essential proteins. Animals then take in these proteins when they eat the plants.

Other kinds of bacteria are responsible for much human misery. Some venereal diseases, strep and staph infections, meningitis, and hepatitis are all caused by bacteria. Many deadly kinds of food poisoning, such as salmonella and botulism, are also caused by bacteria.

7. The main idea of the passage is that bacteria

    (1) aid growth
    (2) are helpful to human beings
    (3) are both helpful and harmful
    (4) are dangerous to living things
    (5) cause diseases

8. Meningitis is a type of

    (1) bacteria
    (2) disease
    (3) food poisoning
    (4) plant
    (5) protein

Items 9 to 11 are based on the following passage.

Osteoporosis is a condition in which bones become weakened. It usually afflicts older people. Women are more likely to develop osteoporosis than men.

Osteoporosis is characterized by a loss of bone mass. The bones become more porous. One cause for this loss of bone mass is a shortage of calcium. Another cause is a low level of the hormone estrogen. Estrogen levels decline during menopause, which can cause bone mass loss for a period of 3 to 7 years.

Osteoporosis causes bone fractures, usually of the hip, wrist, or spine. In the United States, some 1.3 million fractures a year are the result of this condition. Diseased bones grow so weak that the smallest fall or bump breaks them. The spinal bones can literally collapse, causing a hunched back called a "dowager's hump."

A fracture is often the first sign of osteoporosis, but it may not cause pain or even become apparent until a doctor takes an X-ray. In time, though, osteoporosis becomes very painful.

9. In the the second and third paragraphs, the details are organized to

    (1) show the order of the stages of osteoporosis
    (2) compare osteoporosis to other bone diseases
    (3) explain the causes and effects of osteoporosis
    (4) describe treatments for osteoporosis
    (5) list the bones affected by osteoporosis

10. Which of the following sentences from the passage is irrelevant to the main idea of its paragraph?

   (1) Women are more likely to develop osteoporosis than men.
   (2) One cause for this loss of bone mass is a shortage of calcium.
   (3) In the United States, some 1.3 million fractures a year are the result of this condition.
   (4) Diseased bones grow so weak that the smallest fall or bump breaks them.
   (5) In time, though, osteoporosis becomes very painful.

11. The word osteoporosis has three parts. The suffix, -osis, means "condition." One of the roots, por, means "porous." The other root, osteo, most likely means

   (1) fracture
   (2) estrogen
   (3) calcium
   (4) bone
   (5) hump

Item 12 is based on the following paragraph.

   A major problem with organ transplants is that human organs do not keep for a long time outside the body. A heart or lung must be transplanted into another person's body within 4 hours. A liver must be transplanted within 6 to 8 hours. Kidneys are the strongest. They can last for up to 48 hours outside the body. If an organ is not used within its time limit, it must be discarded. Research is being done to find ways to preserve organs outside the body for longer periods of time.

12. Which of the following conclusions is supported by the information in the paragraph?

   (1) All human organs can be transplanted.
   (2) More kidneys are transplanted than any other human organ.
   (3) Brains do not keep at all outside the body.
   (4) Some human organs last longer than others outside the body.
   (5) Organ transplant operations are long and risky.

Items 13 and 14 are based on the following table.

ALCOHOL'S EFFECTS ON THE BRAIN

BAC*	Part of Brain Affected	Behavior
0.05%		Lack of judgment, lack of inhibition
0.1%		Reduced reaction time, difficulty walking and driving
0.2%		Sadness, weeping, abnormal behavior
0.3%		Double vision, inadequate hearing
0.45%		Unconsciousness
0.65%		Death

*Blood alcohol concentration, or BAC, is a measure of the amount of alcohol in the bloodstream per 100 milliliters of blood.

13. At what BAC is a person's coordination first affected?

   (1) 0.05%   (3) 0.2%   (5) 0.45%
   (2) 0.1%   (4) 0.3%

14. When a person's blood alcohol concentration is 0.3%, which of the following is probably NOT true of that person?

   (1) The person has passed out.
   (2) The person can't see clearly.
   (3) The person staggers.
   (4) The person has more nerve than usual.
   (5) The person cries more easily than usual.

Items 15 and 16 are based on the following passage.

Lead poisoning occurs when too much lead, a toxic metal, is ingested. A high level of lead in drinking water contributes to lead poisoning. Most victims of lead poisoning are children under seven.

The symptoms of lead poisoning include severe stomach cramps, nausea, vomiting, weakness, and confusion. Lead poisoning can cause mental retardation in children. It can also cause kidney damage, anemia, and hearing loss in both children and adults.

The most common cause of lead in drinking water is corrosion, a chemical reaction between water and the lead pipes or solder in a plumbing system. Pipes installed before 1930 most likely contain lead. After 1930, most new home plumbing systems had copper pipes, which are safer, but lead solder was often used to seal their joints.

You cannot see, taste, or smell lead in water. Therefore, to find out if your water contains a harmful amount of lead, you need to have it tested. Your local water company or health department may test your water for you or refer you to a qualified lab.

The longer water sits in pipes, the more lead it may contain. Because of this, you can take precautions to help reduce the amount of lead in the water you ingest. Whenever your water has not been used for 6 hours or more, flush your cold-water pipes. Do this by running the water until it becomes as cold as it will get. Use only water from the cold-water tap for drinking, cooking, and especially for making baby formula.

15. Which of the following is NOT an effect of lead poisoning mentioned in the passage?

    (1) anemia
    (2) blindness
    (3) hearing loss
    (4) kidney damage
    (5) mental retardation

16. It is not necessary to flush hot-water pipes to reduce the amount of lead in your drinking and cooking water if

    (1) your plumbing was installed before 1930
    (2) your plumbing was installed after 1930
    (3) you ingest only water from the cold-water tap
    (4) your children are older than seven
    (5) you and your family have no symptoms of lead poisoning

Item 17 is based on the following graph.

HUMAN POPULATION OF THE EARTH

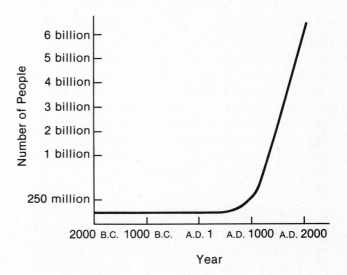

17. Which of the following conclusions is supported by the data in the line graph?

    (1) The population of the earth will continue to increase.
    (2) Before A.D. 500, most people died in childhood.
    (3) By A.D. 3000 there will be over 12 billion people on the earth.
    (4) In the past, birth control was more widely practiced than it is now.
    (5) Modern medicine has prolonged the lives of many people.

Items 18 to 21 are based on the following passage.

To form clear images of the things we see, the eye must focus light rays on the retina. The retina is the area at the back of the eyeball. If light rays do not focus on the retina, a blurred image results. Nearsightedness (myopia) and farsightedness (hyperopia) are common focusing problems.

Myopia occurs when light rays from distant objects are focused in front of the retina instead of on it. In most cases, this happens because the eyeball is too long. Nearsighted people can see nearby objects clearly, but distant objects are blurred.

In contrast, hyperopia occurs when light rays from nearby objects are focused behind the retina instead of on it. It occurs when the eyeball is too short from front to back. Farsighted people can see distant objects clearly, but nearby objects are blurred.

Both conditions can be corrected by glasses. Concave lenses correct myopia. They are thinner in the middle than at the edges. Convex lenses correct hyperopia. They are thicker in the middle than at the edges. Both types of lenses help to focus the light rays on the retina.

18. Farsighted people
    (1) have long eyeballs
    (2) can wear concave lenses to correct their vision
    (3) see clear images of nearby objects
    (4) see clear images of distant objects
    (5) see blurred images of distant objects

19. Which of the following sentences from the passage states the main idea of the passage?
    (1) The retina is the area at the back of the eyeball.
    (2) Nearsightedness (myopia) and farsightedness (hyperopia) are common focusing problems.
    (3) Myopia occurs when light rays from distant objects are focused in front of the retina instead of on it.
    (4) Both conditions can be corrected by glasses.
    (5) Convex lenses correct hyperopia.

20. Which of the following shows the eye of a farsighted person?

(1)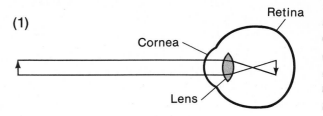

(2)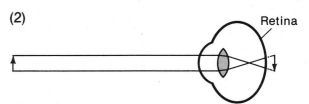

(3)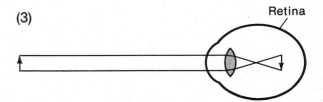

(4)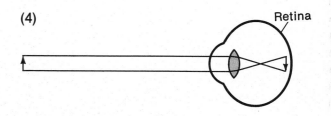

(5)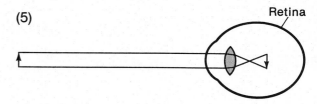

21. Which of the following lenses would correct nearsightedness?

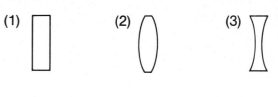

Items 22 and 23 are based on the following passage.

Solutions consist of two parts, the solvent and the solute. The solvent dissolves another substance. The solute is the substance that is dissolved. For example, a cup of instant coffee is a solution. Coffee crystals are dissolved in hot water. Thus, the water is the solvent, and the crystals are the solute.

Water is called the universal solvent because more substances will dissolve in it than in any other solvent. Sugar, salt, and gelatin all dissolve easily in water, for example.

Other solvents are useful for dissolving certain substances. For example, the acetone in nail polish remover dissolves nail polish, which will not dissolve in water.

22. To make a cup of hot chocolate, Matthew heated milk and poured it into a cup containing powdered chocolate. Which of the following is the solute Matthew used?

   (1) heat   (4) powdered chocolate
   (2) milk   (5) hot chocolate
   (3) water

23. Ben cleaned his paint brushes in turpentine because turpentine is

   (1) acetone
   (2) a solute
   (3) a solution
   (4) a solvent
   (5) a universal solvent

Items 24 and 25 are based on the following passage.

Solid waste has become a pressing problem, both in the United States and elsewhere. Manufacturers and consumers can take steps to decrease the amount of trash they create.

Manufacturers can design products that produce less waste. They can also make products more durable so that more time passes before the products have to be thrown away.

Consumers can repair broken items instead of throwing them away and replacing them. They can also use fewer disposable paper products, such as diapers, plates, and cups.

By recycling, both manufacturers and consumers can help alleviate the solid waste problem somewhat. When solid waste is recycled, it is used over again, not discarded. Glass, metal, paper, and some plastic can be recycled. Even gardening waste, such as leaves and grass clippings, can be recycled: it can be used as fertilizer for the garden. Presently in the United States, about 11% of all solid waste is recycled. Experts hope that in the future it will be possible to recycle as much as half of all solid waste.

24. The word disposable in the third paragraph means

   (1) used outdoors
   (2) used by children
   (3) used over again
   (4) used on picnics
   (5) used and thrown away

25. The word alleviate at the beginning of the last paragraph means

   (1) create   (4) solve
   (2) increase   (5) study
   (3) reduce

Items 26 and 27 are based on the following passage.

A glacier is a large, heavy, moving body of ice and snow. About 10% of the land area of the earth is covered by these moving "rivers of ice." Glaciers that cover large regions, like those that cover 90% of Antarctica, are called ice caps.

Some glaciers move toward the ocean and push forward into the water. Parts of the ice break off and drift into the sea. These heavy, floating chunks of glacial ice are known as icebergs. Only the tip of an iceberg, which is about 10% of the iceberg's mass, can be seen above the water.

26. What do you think the temperature is like most of the time in Antarctica?

   (1) very cold   (4) hot
   (2) cool   (5) very hot
   (3) warm

27. Ninety percent of an iceberg

    (1) covers Antarctica
    (2) covers 10% of the earth
    (3) floats above water
    (4) floats under water
    (5) moves toward the ocean

Items 28 to 31 are based on the following passage and table.

Sound travels to the ear from a vibrating object through a medium, or sound carrier. Although most sounds we hear come through the air, sound can travel through any medium—solid, liquid, or gas.

The speed at which sound travels is determined by two factors, the temperature and the elasticity of the medium. Sound travels faster at higher temperatures. Sound also travels faster through more elastic materials—those that quickly resume their original shape. Solids are the most elastic mediums. Gases are the least elastic.

SOUND: RATE OF TRAVEL
THROUGH VARIOUS MATERIALS

Medium	Speed (meters per second)
Carbon dioxide	277
Air (0°C)	331
Air (25°C)	346
Water (25°C)	1498
Seawater (25°C)	1531
Silver	2680
Copper	3100
Brick	3650
Wood (oak)	3850
Glass	4540
Nickel	4900
Aluminum	5000
Iron	5103
Steel	5200
Stone	5971

28. Which of the following sentences from the second paragraph states its main idea?

    (1) The speed at which sound travels is determined by two factors, the temperature and the elasticity of the medium.
    (2) Sound travels faster at higher temperatures.
    (3) Sound also travels faster through more elastic materials—those that quickly resume their original shape.
    (4) Solids are the most elastic mediums.
    (5) Gases are the least elastic.

29. The rate sound travels through seawater at 25°C is

    (1) 1210 meters per second
    (2) 1498 meters per second
    (3) 1531 meters per second
    (4) 2680 meters per second
    (5) 3100 meters per second

30. Through which of the following mediums does sound travel slowest?

    (1) air at 25°C
    (2) brick
    (3) carbon dioxide
    (4) water at 25°C
    (5) seawater at 25°C

31. Which of the following solids is the most elastic?

    (1) aluminum   (4) nickel
    (2) glass   (5) stone
    (3) iron

Items 32 and 33 are based on the following passage.

Atoms decay naturally, but they can also be split artificially by nuclear fission. During nuclear fission, an atom's nucleus is split into two smaller nuclei. In other words, a radioactive element is divided into one or more stable elements. Heavy elements with atomic numbers greater than 90 can be made to undergo fission.

In a typical fission reaction, a uranium nucleus is hit by a neutron. The products of the reaction are a barium nucleus, a krypton nucleus, and three neutrons. These neutrons may then split other uranium nuclei. Such a series of fission reactions is called a nuclear chain reaction.

In a nuclear chain reaction, billions of fission reactions may take place each second. A huge amount of energy is released. An uncontrolled chain reaction produces a nuclear explosion. Scientists have learned to control fission reactions to produce energy for human needs. For example, in nuclear reactors, the heat energy released during a chain reaction can convert water into steam for making electricity.

32. Nuclear fission cannot be used to produce

    (1) an explosion
    (2) electricity
    (3) natural radioactive decay
    (4) a nuclear chain reaction
    (5) heat energy

33. Which of the following elements can be divided by fission?

    (1) plutonium—atomic number 94
    (2) radium—atomic number 88
    (3) barium—atomic number 56
    (4) krypton—atomic number 36
    (5) cobalt—atomic number 27

Check your answers on page 221.

SCIENCE POSTTEST SKILLS CHART

To review the reading skills covered by the items in the Science Posttest, study the following parts of this book.

Unit 1	Comprehending What You Read	Item Number
Chapter 1	Prereading Strategies	1
Chapter 2	Word Parts	11
Chapter 3	Details in Passages	2, 15, 18, 32
Chapter 4	The Stated Main Idea	19, 28
Chapter 5	Patterns of Organization	9
Chapter 6	Tables and Graphs	13, 14, 29, 30
Unit 2	Inferring as You Read	
Chapter 1	Inferences	5, 6, 8, 16, 24, 25, 26, 27
Chapter 2	The Implied Main Idea	4, 7
Unit 3	Applying Information You Read	20, 21, 22, 23, 31, 33
Unit 4	Analyzing and Evaluating What You Read	
Chapter 1	Relevant and Irrelevant Information	10
Chapter 2	Facts and Opinions	3
Chapter 3	Conclusions and Supporting Information	12, 17

SCIENCE POSTTEST CONTENT CHART

The following chart shows the type of content each item in the Science Posttest is based on.

Content	Item Number
Biology	1, 2, 3, 4, 7, 8, 9, 10, 11, 12, 13, 14, 17, 18, 19, 20, 21
Earth science	5, 6, 24, 25, 26, 27
Chemistry	15, 16, 22, 23
Physics	28, 29, 30, 31, 32, 33

Answers and Explanations

In this section are the answers—with explanations—for the questions asked in the Pretest, the Exercises, the Science Readings, the GED Practices, and the Posttest in this book. The reading skill and the science content area tested are indicated for all questions except those in Exercises.

PRETEST (page 1)

1. **(4)** The earth is mentioned in the first sentence. It is mentioned and referred to several other times in the paragraph. (Comprehending What You Read/Prereading Strategies/Earth Science)

2. **(2)** This detail is in the first sentence. The other choices do not agree with the information in the paragraph. (Comprehending What You Read/Details in Passages/Earth Science)

3. **(3)** All the other sentences in the paragraph tell about mammals and what they have in common. (Comprehending What You Read/The Stated Main Idea/Biology)

4. **(5)** The paragraph lists the five things mammals have in common. (Comprehending What You Read/Patterns of Organization/Biology)

5. **(5)** In the paragraph the words *return*, *move*, and *fly south* are the strongest clues to the meaning of *migrate*. (Inferring as You Read/Inferences/Biology)

6. **(1)** As an example of migration when food supplies diminish, the paragraph says that *birds fly south to look for food*. If birds move to find food, their food supplies must have decreased. (Inferring as You Read/Inferences/Biology)

7. **(3)** The point on the line above −100°C is at about 175 units on the vertical scale. (Comprehending What You Read/Tables and Graphs/Physics)

8. **(4)** The paragraph says that light enters the eye through the pupil and that the pupil enlarges when light conditions are dim. You can infer that the pupil gets bigger to let in as much light as possible. (Inferring as You Read/Inferences/Biology)

9. **(2)** The passage has one paragraph about each of the three states of water. It does not mention living things, so Choice (1) is not correct. Choices (3), (4), and (5) each mention only one of the states of water. (Inferring as You Read/The Implied Main Idea/Chemistry)

10. **(1)** The passage says that at 32°F and below, water is a solid. It also says that when its temperature is 212°F or above, it becomes a gas. These two facts support the correct conclusion. Choices (2), (4), and (5) are not supported by information in the passage. Choice (3) is contradicted in the passage: liquid water becomes a gas both when it evaporates and when it boils. (Analyzing and Evaluating What You Read/Conclusions and Supporting Information/Chemistry)

11. **(4)** Ultrasonic sound is mentioned in the first sentence and two other times in the paragraph. (Comprehending What You Read/Prereading Strategies/Physics)

12. (1) All the other sentences in the paragraph give examples of the uses of ultrasonic sound in medicine. (Comprehending What You Read/The Stated Main Idea/Physics)

13. (3) This detail is in the last sentence of the paragraph. (Comprehending What You Read/Details in Passages/Biology)

14. (2) The foods are listed alphabetically in the table. The answer is in the last column—under *Fat*—in the *Peanut butter* row. (Comprehending What You Read/Tables and Graphs/Biology)

15. (5) The foods are listed alphabetically in the table. The answer is in the *Calories* column in the *Potato chips* row. (Comprehending What You Read/Tables and Graphs/Biology)

16. (3) According to the table, ½ cup of peanuts contains 35 grams of fat. The other choices have only between 1 and 18 grams of fat each. (Comprehending What You Read/Tables and Graphs/Biology)

17. (4) All the foods in the table contain fat. They come from both plants and animals, so Choices (2) and (3) are wrong. Choice (1) is not right because peanuts contain more fat than turkey, for example. Since the table does not list all foods, it is not possible to draw the conclusion in Choice (5). (Analyzing and Evaluating What You Read/Conclusions and Supporting Information/Biology)

18. (4) The prefix indicates that the epidermis is the upper, or outer, layer of skin. (Comprehending What You Read/Word Parts/Biology)

19. (4) This detail is in the fourth sentence. (Comprehending What You Read/Details in Passages/Biology)

20. (1) The paragraph describes and compares the two layers of the skin, the dermis and the epidermis. Choices (2) and (5) make statements that are not supported by information in the paragraph. Choices (3) and (4) are incorrect because each tells something about only one layer of the skin. (Inferring as You Read/The Implied Main Idea/Biology)

21. (3) The other choices do not explain why a test is needed in order to find out whether or not radon is in your home. (Inferring as You Read/Inferences/Chemistry)

22. (4) All the other choices are facts: They can be proved. Choice (4) expresses an opinion with which you can agree or disagree. (Analyzing and Evaluating What You Read/Facts and Opinions/Chemistry)

23. (4) In the paragraph the words *often do not appear* are the strongest clue to the meaning of *latent*. (Inferring as You Read/Inferences/Chemistry)

24. (4) Since asbestos fibers do not burn or conduct heat, they would have made good protection for fire fighters. (Applying Information You Read/Chemistry)

25. (3) Following the examples in the second paragraph, you can figure that if the relative humidity is 50%, the air is holding 50%, or half, of the water that it can hold. (Applying Information You Read/Earth Science)

26. (5) The last sentence says that warm air can hold more moisture than cold air. When the relative humidity of cold air is 80%, there is little moisture in the air since cold air—especially air at 0°F or lower—can't hold much moisture. (Applying Information You Read/Earth Science)

27. (1) As the second paragraph says, an object appears white if it reflects all the colors of the spectrum. (Applying Information You Read/Physics)

28. (3) According to the information in the first sentence, a blue object reflects blue. (Applying Information You Read/Physics)

29. (5) All the other choices are facts: they can be proved. Choice (5) expresses an opinion with which you can agree or disagree. (Analyzing and Evaluating What You Read/Facts and Opinions/Biology)

30. (3) In the second paragraph, the first sentence is the main idea. A sentence about Red Dye No. 40 does not support this main idea. (Analyzing and Evaluating What You Read/Relevant and Irrelevant Information/Biology)

31. (5) Miami is located two time zones east of Denver. Therefore, as the passage explains, it is 2 hours later there than in Denver. (Applying Information You Read/Earth Science)

32. **(3)** Los Angeles and San Francisco are in the same time zone. According to the passage, local time throughout each time zone is the same. (Applying Information You Read/Earth Science)

33. **(2)** Because Hawaii is four time zones to the west of Dallas, it is 4 hours earlier in Hawaii than in Dallas. (Applying Information You Read/Earth Science)

UNIT 1 COMPREHENDING WHAT YOU READ

EXERCISE 1 (PAGE 15)

1. **Bones.** The first sentence is about bones. The word *bones* is used 8 times in the passage.

2. **Fish.** The first sentence is about fish. The word *fish* is used 6 times in the passage.

3. **Vitamins.** The words *vitamin* and *vitamins* are used 11 times in the passage.

EXERCISE 2 (PAGE 18)

1. Sample answers: can break; are hard; give the body shape

2. Sample answers: live in water; swim; good to eat; many kinds

3. Sample answers: pills; in food; important for health

EXERCISE 3 (PAGE 19)

1. **Calcium** and **phosphorus** are stored in bones. The answer is in the last sentence.

2. **(2)** The answer is in the last two sentences of the first paragraph.

3. **(1)** The answer is in the last two sentences of the second paragraph.

EXERCISE 4 (PAGE 22)

Part A
Your answers should be the same, or nearly the same, as the following.

1. **test before**
2. **produce again**
3. **small wave(s)**
4. **against war**
5. **not honest**
6. **one rail**
7. **not sane**
8. **not violent**
9. **having many colors**
10. **having three angles**

Part B

1. **cannot control**
2. **without backbones**
3. **one cell**
4. **Two-shelled**
5. **two**
6. **high**

Part C

1. **(e)** *Tri-* means "three," so *3* is part of the definition.

2. **(b)** *Poly-* means "many," so *more than one* is part of the definition.

3. **(d)** *Auto-* means "by itself," so *its own* is part of the definition.

4. **(a)** *Hypo-* means "below," so *abnormally low*, which means "below normal," is part of the definition.

5. **(c)** *Mono-* means "one," so *one* is part of the definition.

EXERCISE 5a (PAGE 24)

1. **(e)** *Chlor* means "green," so *green* is part of the definition.

2. **(c)** *Neur* means "nerve," so *nerve* is part of the definition.

3. **(b)** *Hydr* means "water," so *water* is part of the definition.

4. **(a)** *Cardi* means "heart," and *gram* means "record." Therefore, *heart* and *record* are parts of the definition.

5. **(d)** *Path* means "disease," so *disease* is part of the definition.

EXERCISE 5b (PAGE 26)

Note: Your answers for Steps 1 to 3 should be close to the ones here. Your answers for Step 4 will depend on the dictionary you use.

1. Step 1: **epi + derm(is)**
   Step 2: **outer + skin**
   Step 3: **outer skin**
   Step 4: **the outer, protective layer of skin**

2. Step 1: **hypo + derm(ic)**
   Step 2: **under + skin**
   Step 3: **under (the) skin**
   Step 4: **relating to parts under the skin**

3. Step 1: **anti + tox(in)**
   Step 2: **against + poison**
   Step 3: **against poison**
   Step 4: **a substance that acts against a poison**

4. Step 1: **poly + graph**
   Step 2: **many + record**
   Step 3: **record many (things)**
   Step 4: **an instrument that records changes in body processes (such as the heartbeat, blood pressure, and breathing) that is used to detect when a person is lying**

5. Step 1: **psych(o) + path**
   Step 2: **mind + disease**
   Step 3: **disease (of the) mind**
   Step 4: **a person with a mental disorder**

EXERCISE 6 (PAGE 27)

Part A

1. **(d)** -*phobia* means "abnormal fear of," so *abnormal fear of* is part of the definition.

2. **(a)** -*itis* means "inflammation," so *inflammation* is part of the definition.

3. **(e)** -*ist* means "a person who," so *a person who* is part of the definition.

4. **(b)** -*ology* means "study of," so *study of* is part of the definition.

5. **(c)** -*ize* means "to make," so *to make* is part of the definition.

Part B

Note: Your answers for Steps 1 to 3 should b[e] close to the ones here. Your answers for Ste[p] 4 will depend on the dictionary you use.

1. Step 1: **auto + bio + graph + er**
   Step 2: **self + life + writes + a person who**
   Step 3: **a person who writes (about the) life (of the) self**
   Step 4: **a person who writes the story [of] his or her own life**

2. Step 1: **card + itis**
   Step 2: **heart + inflammation**
   Step 3: **(an) inflammation (of the) hear[t]**
   Step 4: **an inflammation of the heart**

3. Step 1: **path + ology**
   Step 2: **disease + study of**
   Step 3: **(the) study of disease**
   Step 4: **the study of disease**

4. Step 1: **psych + ologist**
   Step 2: **mind + a person who studies**
   Step 3: **a person who studies (the) min[d]**
   Step 4: **a person who studies the mind**

5. Step 1: **hydr(o) + phobia**
   Step 2: **water + abnormal fear of**
   Step 3: **(an) abnormal fear of water**
   Step 4: **a fear of water**

EXERCISE 7 (PAGE 30)

1. The **nucleus** is in charge of the whole cell. This detail is in the second and thi[rd] sentences of the paragraph.

2. Cytoplasm is **a clear, jellylike fluid**. T[his] detail is in the fifth sentence of the par[a]graph.

3. Mitochondria provide a cell with energ[y] **by breaking down sugar**. This detail i[s in] the eighth sentence of the paragraph.

4. The **cell membrane** separates cells fro[m] each other. This detail is in the last se[n]tence of the paragraph.

5. The **cell wall** also protects a plant cell. This detail is in the third sentence of t[he] paragraph.

6. The **cell wall** gives a plant support. Th[is] detail is in the fifth sentence of the par[a]graph.

7. **Chlorophyll** makes plants green. This [de]tail is in the next-to-last sentence of th[e] paragraph.

8. **Chloroplasts** contain a plant's chlorophyll. This detail is in the sixth sentence of the paragraph.

9. Plants make their own food by **photosynthesis**. This detail is in the first sentence of the paragraph.

10. A plant uses **carbon dioxide**, **water**, **chlorophyll**, and **sunlight** to make its own food. This detail is in the second sentence of the paragraph.

11. Carbon dioxide comes from **the air**. This detail is in the third sentence of the paragraph.

12. Water enters a plant through its **roots**. This detail is in the fourth sentence of the paragraph.

13. **Chlorophyll** absorbs energy from the sun. This detail is in the fifth sentence of the paragraph.

14. Plants make **glucose**. This detail is in the last sentence of the paragraph.

EXERCISE 8a (PAGE 34)

1. **(1)** *All living things* in Sentence 1 means the same thing as *plants and animals* in the restated sentence. The words *need food to stay alive* in Sentence 1 mean about the same thing as *would die without food* in the restated sentence.

2. **(1)** The words *stay alive by eating* in Choice (1) mean about the same thing as *eat . . . to survive* in the original sentence. Likewise, *other living things* means the same thing as *plants and other animals*.

3. **(2)** Only Sentence 2 is about letting out, or releasing, the energy in food.

4. **(2)** Both sentences are about mixing, or combining, food and oxygen to get energy.

5. **(3)** Since *some foods contain more calories than others*, as the original sentence says, Choice (3) is the only choice that restates this idea.

6. **(3)** Both sentences are about losing weight by using the energy in stored fat.

EXERCISE 8b (PAGE 35)

1. **(1)** The sentence restates the information in the middle of the second paragraph: *they cause a sudden rise in the amount of sugar in the blood.*

2. **(2)** The last paragraph says that *simple sugar foods are often high in calories*. Therefore, it would not be true to say that simple sugar foods deprive the body of calories. The last paragraph also says that simple sugars cause tooth decay, or cavities, and obesity, which means weight gain. Therefore, Choices (1) and (3) are true statements.

3. **(2)** The first paragraph says that *experts* think that *50% to 60%* of one's calories should come from complex carbohydrates. In the field of nutrition, the *experts* are *nutritionists*; *50% to 60%* is about the same as *half or more*.

4. **(3)** The last two paragraphs say that processing, or refining, complex carbohydrates removes *nutrients*, which are *vitamins and minerals*. The second paragraph says that *processed carbohydrates are "simpler,"* which means they are no longer in their natural state. It also says they give *a surge of energy*. Therefore, Choices (1) and (2) are wrong.

EXERCISE 9 (PAGE 39)

Part A

1. **plants**
2. **insects**
3. **flowers**
4. **mammals**

Part B

1. Sample answers: kidneys; lungs
2. Sample answers: bass; flounder; tuna

Part C

1. Sample answers: blue jays; cardinals; crows; robins
2. Sample answers: dogwoods; elms; maples; oaks

Part D

Answers will vary for the two lists in this part. Be sure that the headings for your lists are broad enough to cover all the words in each of the lists.

EXERCISE 10 (PAGE 43)

1. The topic is **living things**.
2. The **first sentence** states the main idea.
3. The topic is **plants**.
4. The **first sentence** states the main idea.
5. The topic is **trees**.
6. The **third sentence** states the main idea.
7. The topic is **vertebrates and inverte-brates**.
8. The **last sentence** states the main idea.
9. The topic is **frogs**.
10. The **first sentence** states the main idea.
11. The topic is **plants**.
12. The **last sentence** states the main idea.

EXERCISE 11 (PAGE 48)

1. The topic is **the immune system**.

2. Paragraph 1: **The immune system is a network of special cells and organs that defend the body against old and new enemies.**
   Paragraph 2: **The immune system knows the difference between what belongs in the body and what does not.**
   Paragraph 3: **The immune system also remembers past invaders.**

3. The main idea of **the first paragraph** is the main idea of the passage.

4. The topic is **AIDS**.

5. Paragraph 1: **AIDS is one of the most serious worldwide health problems that has ever existed.**
   Paragraph 2: **AIDS is caused by a virus, called HIV, that attacks the body's main weapon against disease.**
   Paragraph 3: **Without a healthy immune system, people with AIDS are defenseless against many diseases.**
   Paragraph 4: **AIDS is contagious.**
   Paragraph 5: **There is no cure for AIDS, but drugs called AZT and ddI have been approved for its treatment.**

6. The main idea of **the first paragraph** is the main idea of the passage.

EXERCISE 12 (PAGE 53)

1. The main idea of the paragraph is the first sentence: **Heart attack risk factors are traits and habits that increase a person's chances of having a heart attack.**

2. The nine items are **age**, **sex**, **family history**, **cigarette smoking**, **high blood pressure**, **high blood cholesterol**, **obesity**, **diabetes**, and **lack of exercise**.

3. The two signal words are **another** and **in addition**.

4. The main idea of the paragraph is the first sentence: **Blood has four main parts.**

5. The four items are **plasma**, **red blood cells**, **white blood cells**, and **platelets**.

6. The four signal words are **one**, **two**, **three**, and **four**.

EXERCISE 13 (PAGE 56)

1. You should have numbered the steps in this order:
   2 Look at a clock.
   1 Find your pulse.
   4 Add a zero to the number you get.
   3 Count your pulse rate for 6 seconds.

2. The first human heart was transplanted in **1967**. The answer is stated in the first sentence.

3. Washkansky died **18 days** after the transplant.

EXERCISE 14 (PAGE 59)

Part A

1. Cause: **heart disease**; Effect: **death**

2. Cause: **exercise**; Effect: **tiny new blood vessels develop**

3. Cause: **cigarette smoking**; Effects: **shrinks arteries**; **releases carbon monoxide into the blood**; **reduces lung capacity**

4. **Eat a large meal** → **Intestines take more oxygen from the blood** → Less oxygen reaches the brain → **You feel tired**

Part B

1. The blood puts pressure on **artery walls**. This detail is in the second sentence of the paragraph.

2. **Strokes**, **heart attacks**, and **kidney failure** are the three possible effects. They are mentioned in the last sentence of the paragraph.

3. **Fibrin** stops a cut from bleeding, as the second through fifth sentences of the paragraph explain.

4. **When a blood clot is on the surface of the skin**, a scab develops. The answer is in the last sentence of the paragraph.

EXERCISE 15 (PAGE 62)

Part A

1. Things compared: **high blood pressure** and **high blood cholesterol**
   Likeness: Both: **can often be controlled by reducing dietary fat**

2. Things compared: **plant products and animal products**
   Difference: Plant products: **low in fat**; Animal products: **high in fat**

3. Things compared: **stroke** and **heart attack**
   Likeness: Both: **occur when major arteries are clogged**
   Difference: Stroke: **occurs when the brain does not get enough blood**; Heart attack: **occurs when the heart does not get enough blood**

4. Things compared: **running** and **swimming**
   Likeness: Both: **aerobic exercise**
   Difference: Running: **puts pressure on the joints**; Swimming: **does not put pressure on the joints**

Part B

1. **The blood in veins and the blood in arteries** are compared.

2. The **difference in color** is explained.

3. The **atria and the ventricles** are compared.

4. **Both the atria and the ventricles are chambers of the heart.**

5. **The atria are the upper chambers of the heart; they receive blood from the veins. The ventricles are the lower chambers of the heart; they force blood out of the heart into the arteries.**

EXERCISE 16 (PAGE 64)

1. **(1)** A chain of causes and effects is explained in the first three sentences.

2. **(4)** The steps in an operation are described.

3. **(3)** Six dietary changes are listed.

4. **(2)** Red and white blood cells are compared.

5. **(4)** Events are described in the order in which they happened.

EXERCISE 17 (PAGE 69)

1. There are **3.1** grams of fiber in 1/4 cup of raisins.

2. There are **155** calories in 1 cup of whole wheat pasta.

3. There are **2.9** grams of fiber in 1/2 cup of corn.

4. Of the foods listed in the table, **1/2 cup of kidney beans** contains the most fiber—7.3 grams.

5. **(2)** Of the choices, 1/2 cup of lima beans has the fewest calories, 65, and the most fiber, 4.5 grams.

6. **Desirable Weights for Men Aged 25 and Over**.

7. **Desirable Weights for Women Aged 25 and Over**.

8. **Height, Small Frame, Medium Frame,** and **Large Frame**.

9. **116 to 130 pounds**

10. **164 to 184 pounds**

11. **136 pounds**

12. **113 pounds**

EXERCISE 18 (PAGE 72)

1. **Gases That Humans Inhale**

2. **Gases That Humans Exhale**

3. Humans inhale and exhale **nitrogen, oxygen**, and **carbon dioxide**.

4. **79.01%** of the gases that humans inhale is nitrogen.

5. **4.1%** of the gases that humans exhale is carbon dioxide.

6. **(3)** Gases that humans exhale contain 16.4% oxygen, which is less than the 20.96% oxygen in the gases they inhale.

1. **Average Heights of Children and Adolescents**

2. The horizontal axis shows the **ages** of children and adolescents.

3. The vertical axis shows **average heights**.

4. The black bars stand for **females**.

5. The white bars stand for **males**.

6. **(2)** The bar stops between the lines for 115 centimeters and 120 centimeters.

7. **(3)** The bar stops between the lines for 170 centimeters and 175 centimeters.

8. At ages **8 and 10**, the average heights for boys and girls are the same.

9. Girls are taller than boys at age **12**.

10. There is no change in the average height of girls between the ages of **16 and 18**.

1. **Infant Mortality Rate**

2. The vertical axis shows the **number of deaths**.

3. The horizontal axis shows the **year**.

4. **(1)** The point above 1910 on the horizontal scale is at about 90 on the vertical scale.

5. **(2)** The line shows a downward trend as it moves from the past toward the present.

6. **Life Expectancy**

7. The vertical axis shows **ages**.

8. The horizontal axis shows **years**.

9. **(2)** The point above 1940 on the horizontal scale is at about 60 on the vertical scale.

10. **(2)** The line shows an upward trend as it moves from the past toward the present.

SCIENCE READINGS 1 (page 79)

1. The four branches of earth science are **geology, meteorology, oceanography**, and **astronomy**. These details are in the third paragraph. (Details in Passages/Science)

2. The **last sentence** of the first paragraph states the main idea of the passage: *Science is divided into four main branches: biology, earth science, chemistry, and physics.* (The Stated Main Idea/Science)

3. **(3)** The second paragraph lists and describes the divisions of biology. (Patterns of Organization/Science)

4. A. **(6)**; B. **(1)**; C. **(5)**; D. **(2)**; E. **(4)**; F. **(3)**. (Details in Passages/Science)

5. **(1)** This detail is in the first paragraph. The table also shows it. (Details in Passages/Biology)

6. **(3)** Walking on two legs is a trait of primates, as the fifth paragraph says, not of mammals. The traits of mammals are in the fourth paragraph. (Details in Passages/Biology)

7. **(2)** This detail is in the third paragraph. (Details in Passages/Biology)

8. **(2)** This detail is in the fifth row, third column, of the table. (Tables and Graphs/Biology)

9. **(1)** The first sentence of the passage states the main idea. The whole passage is about cells, tissues, organs, and systems. (The Stated Main Idea/Biology)

10. **(1)** This detail is in the second paragraph, where red blood cells are mentioned. (Details in Passages/Biology)

11. **(3)** This detail is in the last paragraph. (Details in Passages/Biology)

12. **(2)** Skin, which covers the body, is epithelial tissue, as the third paragraph says. (Details in Passages/Biology)

13. **(4)** This detail is at the end of the fourth paragraph. (Details in Passages/Biology)

14. **(1)** This detail is in the fifth row, first and second columns, of the table. (Tables and Graphs/Biology)

15. **(3)** This detail is in the eighth row, second column, of the table. (Tables and Graphs/Biology)

16. **(2)** This detail is in the tenth row, third column, of the table. (Tables and Graphs/Biology)

17. **(1)** This detail is in the fourth row, first and second columns, of the table. (Tables and Graphs/Biology)

18. **(1)** This detail is in the first row, third column, of the table. (Tables and Graphs/Biology)

19. **The digestive system** is the topic. It is mentioned in the first paragraph. The words *digested, digestion, digestive,* and *undigested* are used in the passage. (Prereading Strategies/Biology)

20. Digestion starts **in the mouth.** This detail is at the beginning of the second paragraph. (Details in Passages/Biology)

21. The small intestine is about **25 feet** long. This detail is in the fourth paragraph. (Details in Passages/Biology)

22. **Bile** breaks down fat by separating it into tiny balls. This detail is in the fourth paragraph. (Details in Passages/Biology)

23. **(2)** This detail is in the fourth paragraph. (Details in Passages/Biology)

24. **(4)** The passage describes digestion in the order in which it occurs. (Patterns of Organization/Biology)

25. **(3)** All the other sentences in the passage are supporting details that explain how the digestive system breaks nutrients down. (The Stated Main Idea/Biology)

26. **The atmosphere** is the topic. It is mentioned in the first sentence and throughout the passage. (Prereading Strategies/Earth Science)

27. **(a), (d), (e)** These details are in the second paragraph. (Details in Passages/Earth Science)

28. The troposphere is **11 miles thick** at the equator. This detail is in the third paragraph. (Details in Passages/Earth Science)

29. The ozone layer is in **the stratosphere.** This detail is in the fourth paragraph. (Details in Passages/Earth Science)

30. **The thermosphere** is the outside layer of the atmosphere. This detail is in the last paragraph. (Details in Passages/Earth Science)

31. *Therm* means **heat.** Paragraph 6 says that *thermosphere* means "heat sphere," therefore, the word part *therm* means "heat." (Word Parts/Earth Science)

32. There is **nothing** in empty space. This detail is in the first paragraph. (Details in Passages/Chemistry)

33. Matter is **everything that has weight and takes up space.** This detail is at the beginning of the second paragraph. (Details in Passages/Chemistry)

34. All matter is made of **atoms.** This detail is near the beginning of the second paragraph. (Details in Passages/Chemistry)

35. **(2)** The rest of the sentences in the second paragraph describe the atoms matter is made of. (The Stated Main Idea/Chemistry)

36. The topic of the passage is **energy.** The word *energy* is used in the first sentence of the passage and is repeated throughout the passage. (Prereading Strategies/Physics)

37. Energy is **the ability to do work,** as the second sentence of the passage says. (Details in Passages/Physics)

38. **(1)** The whole paragraph describes kinetic energy and potential energy. (The Stated Main Idea/Physics)

39. **(2)** Potential energy and kinetic energy are compared throughout the paragraph. (Patterns of Organization/Physics)

GED PRACTICE 1 (page 85)

1. **(1)** All the other sentences in the passage give supporting details about the two kinds of immunity. (The Stated Main Idea/Biology)

2. **(3)** The passage mentions all the topics listed in the choices, but it explains only the difference between the two kinds of immunity. (Patterns of Organization/Biology)

3. **(2)** This detail is in the second and third sentences. (Details in Passages/Biology)

4. **(1)** This detail is in the third sentence. (Details in Passages/Biology)

5. **(4)** The answer comes from the fifth and sixth sentences. (Patterns of Organization/Biology)

6. **(1)** All the other sentences in the passage explain the steps in or the purpose of the procedure. (The Stated Main Idea/Biology)

7. **(3)** The answer comes from the fourth and fifth sentences. (Details in Passages/Biology)

8. **(4)** The answer comes from the third and fifth sentences. (Details in Passages/Biology)

9. **(5)** As the top part of the table shows, normal systolic blood pressure is *Lower than 140.* (Tables and Graphs/Biology)

10. **(4)** As the bottom part of the table shows, a diastolic blood pressure reading between 105 and 114 is described as moderate hypertension. (Tables and Graphs/Biology)

UNIT 2 INFERRING AS YOU READ

EXERCISE 21 (PAGE 91)

1. **(3)** Renewable resources and nonrenewable resources are opposites. Therefore, if renewable resources *can't be used up,* nonrenewable resources can be used up.

2. **(2)** The first sentence in the second paragraph states that *some minerals are made of a single element.* The second sentence says that *others are compounds.* Therefore, compounds are not made of one element. The rest of the paragraph is about compounds, which are made of two or more elements.

3. **(1)** The first paragraph states that metals *conduct heat and electricity.* The second paragraph says that the properties of nonmetals are opposite those of metals and that *nonmetals cannot carry heat or electricity.* Therefore, metals can carry electricity.

4. **(2)** The third sentence states that *metals can be extracted from* ores. The last sentence gives an example. It uses the word *separated,* which can mean *removed.*

5. **(1)** The paragraph contrasts aluminum and gold. Aluminum is *abundant* and *not expensive,* while gold is *rare* and *expensive.* Since something rare is hard to find, something abundant is easy to find, or plentiful.

6. **(3)** Conservationists protect resources. Since nonrenewable resources cannot be replaced, it is logical that conservationists would want to make sure that people do not use them up.

7. **(2)** If ash, soot, and gas are added to the air when coal and oil are burned for fuel, then they must be released when coal and oil are burned.

8. **(3)** The use of the word *most* with the word *detrimental* tells you that the third sentence compares the effect it mentions to the effects mentioned in the first two sentences of the paragraph, which are both harmful.

9. **(1)** An existing respiratory problem can get either better or worse. Since air pollution *causes* health problems, it must make existing respiratory problems worse.

10. **(1)** In the first paragraph, *toxic* is used in a description of *harmful substances.* The second paragraph says that *toxic chemicals* are *used to kill.* A harmful substance that kills must be poisonous.

11. **(2)** These context clues lead to the conclusion that when chemicals contaminate water, they make it impure. The second paragraph says, *Pesticides also contaminate water.* The last paragraph says that contaminated water *cannot be used for drinking, bathing, or recreation* and that things that live in it *become diseased or die.*

12. **(1)** The third paragraph mentions *medical waste.* When it gives examples of this waste, it calls it *refuse from hospitals.*

13. **(3)** The beginning of the first paragraph talks about throwing away garbage. The second sentence mentions *milk cartons* and *cereal boxes* as examples of garbage that is thrown away, but it uses the word *discarded.*

14. **(3)** The second paragraph says that some communities without landfill space, where garbage is dumped, ship their garbage to disposal sites in other states. These out-of-state sites must be for dumping.

15. **(2)** The beginning of the fourth paragraph tells about the EPA's *new protective standards for landfills.* The second sentence gives examples of ways to *diminish risks.* If protective standards diminish risks, they must reduce risks.

1. **(2)** The first sentence in the paragraph states that the atmosphere is a mixture of gases. The second sentence says that nitrogen and oxygen make up most of the atmosphere. Therefore, nitrogen and oxygen must be gases.

2. **(1)** The answer is stated in the fourth sentence of the paragraph.

3. **(1)** The largest section of the graph shows that nitrogen makes up 78% of the air.

4. **(2)** The graph shows that carbon dioxide is only one of several gases that make up 1% of the atmosphere. Therefore, you can infer that carbon dioxide alone makes up less than 1%.

5. **(2)** You know that people need to breathe oxygen. The third sentence says that at higher altitudes there is less oxygen in the air. Therefore, at higher altitudes, it is harder to breathe.

6. **(1)** The answer is stated in the second sentence of the paragraph.

7. **(1)** The answer is stated in the third sentence of the paragraph.

8. **(2)** You know that the higher the altitude is, the less air there is above a place. The last sentence of the paragraph says that the more air there is above a place, the greater the air pressure is. The opposite must also be true.

EXERCISE 23 (PAGE 101)

1. The ocean's temperature is warmest in the **surface zone**. The line on the graph extends farthest to the right, where the highest temperatures are on the horizontal axis, in the surface zone.

2. As the line on the graph shows, the temperature in the thermocline zone ranges **from about 5°C to 21°C**.

3. **(2)** The warmest part of the ocean is the part closest to the sun, the surface. The oceans get colder the deeper you go, or the farther from the sun you go. Therefore, you can infer that the sun warms the oceans.

4. **Nearly three-fourths** of the earth is covered by water. This detail is in the first sentence of the paragraph.

5. Most of the water on earth—97% of it—is found **in the oceans**. This detail is in the second sentence of the paragraph.

6. **About 15%** of the earth's fresh water can be used by living things on land. The passage states that 85% of all fresh water is trapped in polar ice caps and glaciers. You can infer that the remaining 15% is available for use.

7. The tide changes **every 6 hours**. This detail is in the fourth sentence of the passage.

8. Tides are caused by **the pull of the moon's gravity**. This detail is at the beginning of the second paragraph.

9. It is high tide **twice a day** in the same place. Since the tide changes every 6 hours, you can infer that there are four tides in a 24-hour day. Because high and low tides alternate, two of the four daily tides are high.

10. A year on Pluto is **247.7 earth-years** long. The second sentence of the paragraph says that a year on a planet is the time it takes the planet to make one revolution around the sun. Since it takes Pluto 247.7 earth-years to revolve around the sun, you can infer that a year on Pluto equals 247.7 earth-years.

11. It takes the earth **365 days** to revolve around the sun. Since you know that a year on earth is 365 days long, you can make this inference based on the information in the second sentence of the paragraph.

12. **Mercury** is the closest planet to the sun. You can infer this because it takes Mercury less time to revolve around the sun than it takes Venus.

13. The Southern Hemisphere leans **toward the sun** when it is summer there. The fourth sentence says that it is summer in the Northern Hemisphere when this hemisphere tilts toward the sun. You can infer that the same must be true for the Southern Hemisphere.

14. During autumn in the Southern Hemisphere, it is **spring** in the Northern Hemisphere. The last two sentences show that at the same time of year the seasons are opposite in opposite hemispheres. You can infer that when it is autumn in the Southern Hemisphere, it must be the opposite season in the Northern Hemisphere: spring.

15. It takes Earth **24 hours** to rotate on its axis. The second sentence says that the time it takes a planet to make one rotation is a day on that planet. You know that a day on Earth is 24 hours long. Therefore, you can infer that the earth's rotation takes 24 hours.

16. A day on Mercury is **as long as 59 earth-days.** You can infer this from the information in the second and the last sentences in the paragraph.

17. **(4)** Of the four planets, it takes Saturn the least time to rotate on its axis—only 10.5 hours. This, together with the information in the second sentence of the paragraph, lets you infer that Saturn has the shortest day of the four planets.

EXERCISE 24 (PAGE 107)

1. **Colors**
2. **Bodies of water**
3. **Gases**
4. **Branches of science**
5. **Continents**

EXERCISE 25 (PAGE 109)

1. The topic is **trees**.

2. **(1)** Every sentence demonstrates that trees prevent erosion.

3. The topic is **erosion**.

4. **(3)** The sentences in the paragraph tell about the four kinds of erosion.

5. The topic is **rocks**.

6. Sample answers: Rocks are formed in three different ways; or, There are three kinds of rocks.

7. The topic is **maximum life spans**.

8. Sample answers: The maximum life spans of living things vary; or, Maximum life spans are different.

9. The topic is **Mercury and Earth**.

10. Sample answers: Mercury and Earth are different in many ways. Mercury is very different from Earth.

EXERCISE 26 (PAGE 113)

1. The topic of the passage is **the water cycle**.

2. Paragraph 1: **In the first step of the water cycle, called evaporation, water on the earth's surface changes to a vapor, or gas.**
Paragraph 2: **During the second step of the water cycle, called condensation, vapor changes back into a liquid.**
Paragraph 3: **The third step of the water cycle, called precipitation, occurs when water returns to the earth as rain, snow, sleet, or hail.**

3. Sample answers: The three stages of the water cycle—evaporation, condensation, and precipitation—renew the earth's supply of water; or, There are three stages in the water cycle.

4. The topic of the passage is **endangered animal species**.

5. Paragraph 1: **An endangered species is one that will probably disappear unless it is given special protection.**
Paragraph 2: **Many species of animals are endangered because their habitats are being destroyed.**
Paragraph 3: **Unfortunately, many animals are endangered by hunting.**
Paragraph 4: **Chemical pollution also endangers many animals.**

6. Sample answers: Many species of animals are endangered because of the actions of humans; or, Many animal species are endangered for various reasons.

SCIENCE READINGS 2 (page 116)

1. **Protons, neutrons,** and **electrons** are the three parts of an atom. These details are in the first paragraph. (Details in Passages/Chemistry)

2. A compound is made of **two or more different kinds of atoms.** This detail is in the fourth paragraph. (Details in Passages/Chemistry)

3. The smallest part of a compound is **a molecule.** This detail is in the last sentence of the passage. (Details in Passages/Chemistry)

4. The main idea of the third paragraph is stated in **the first sentence**: *Substances that are made up of only one kind of atom are called elements.* (The Stated Main Idea/Chemistry)

5. There are **11 protons** in the nucleus of a sodium atom. The second paragraph says that the atomic number of an atom is the same as the number of protons in its nucleus. The last sentence of this paragraph says that the atomic number of sodium is 11. By putting both those pieces of information together, you can infer the answer. (Inferences/Chemistry)

6. **(3)** The context clues are these: All the matter and energy that was in a small space shot out in all directions, which caused the universe to expand. The universe must have spread out. (Inferences/Earth Science)

7. The big-bang theory may explain **how the universe was formed**. This detail is in the first sentence of the passage. (Details in Passages/Earth Science)

8. A galaxy is **a huge group of stars**. This detail is at the beginning of the third paragraph. (Details in Passages/Earth Science)

9. At the speed of light, it would take **30,000 years** to travel from the sun to the Milky Way's center. The fourth paragraph shows that it would take 100,000 years for light to travel a distance of 100,000 light years. Since the sun is located 30,000 light-years from the center of the Milky Way, it would take 30,000 years to travel from the sun to the center of the Milky Way. (Inferences/Earth Science)

10. There are **nine** planets in our solar system. The beginning of the second paragraph says that our solar system includes Earth and eight other planets. (Details in Passages/Earth Science)

11. **(1)** All the other sentences in the third paragraph describe moons, meteoroids, asteroids, and comets. (The Stated Main Idea/Earth Science)

12. **(3)** Most of the sentences in the passage give details about the parts of our solar system. (The Stated Main Idea/Earth Science)

13. **(3)** The second paragraph says that the inner planets are closest to the sun. They include Venus and Mercury, Choices (1) and (2). Since Uranus is an outer planet, it must be the farthest of the three from the sun. (Inferences/Earth Science)

14. **(1)** The first sentence of the passage says that when a smaller object gets close enough to a star, it gets caught in the star's field of gravity. The sun is the star around which all the smaller bodies in our solar system revolve. Therefore, the sun is the largest body in our solar system. (Inferences/Earth Science)

15. Sample answers: The earth has four layers—the crust, the mantle, the outer core, and the inner core; or, Four layers make up the earth. (The Implied Main Idea/Earth Science)

16. The earth's crust is most likely the thinnest **under the ocean**. The first paragraph says that the crust is thinner in some places than in others. The second paragraph says that scientists drilled through the crust under the ocean. They probably drilled where the crust was the thinnest. (Inferences/Earth Science)

17. The **mantle**, which is 2900 kilometers thick, is the thickest layer of the earth. The passage gives the thickness of each of the other layers: None is as thick as the mantle. (Details in Passages/Earth Science)

18. The temperature of the mantle ranges from **870°C to 2200°C**. This detail is near the end of the second paragraph. (Details in Passages/Earth Science)

19. A. **(2)**; B. **(4)**; C. **(1)**; D. **(5)**; E. **(3)**. (Details in Passages/Biology)

20. **(1)** The other sentences in the paragraph support the main idea by describing what a habitat provides and by giving examples. (The Stated Main Idea/Biology)

21. **(2)** This detail is near the end of the fourth paragraph. (Details in Passages/Biology)

22. **Breathing** is the name of the process by which air moves in and out of the lungs. This detail is near the beginning of the second paragraph. (Details in Passages/Biology)

23. **Food** is combined with oxygen to give the body energy. This detail is in the first paragraph. (Details in Passages/Biology)

24. Carbon dioxide and oxygen are exchanged **in the alveoli**. This detail is in the last three sentences of the passage. (Details in Passages/Biology)

25. Dust and bacteria are trapped by **the nose and the trachea**. These details are in the third and fourth paragraphs. (Details in Passages/Biology)

26. **(2)** Most of the passage explains how the respiratory system works so that it can exchange oxygen and carbon dioxide. (The Stated Main Idea/Biology)

GED PRACTICE 2 (page 122)

1. **(5)** The circle represents the earth's crust. One segment of the graph represents the portion of the crust that is aluminum. It shows that aluminum makes up 8.1% of the crust. (Details in Passages/Earth Science)

2. **(3)** The graph shows that 46.6% (nearly 50%, or half) of the earth's crust is made up of oxygen, which, as you know, is a gas. (Inferences/Earth Science)

3. **(4)** The majority of the passage is made up of examples of how plastic waste kills animals. (The Implied Main Idea/Biology)

4. **(3)** The last sentence of the passage says that pelicans starve when their bills get stuck in six-pack rings. The plastic must keep them from opening their bills to eat. (Inferences/Biology)

5. **(2)** Both paragraphs support the main idea. The first tells how the bald eagle was saved from extinction, and the second, how the American alligator was saved from extinction. (The Implied Main Idea/Earth Science)

6. **(1)** The passage says that after the alligator was declared endangered—which meant that it could not be hunted— it made a comeback. People must have stopped killing it after it became a protected species. (Inferences/Earth Science)

7. **(2)** This detail is in the middle of the second paragraph. (Details in Passages/Earth Science)

8. **(2)** The first paragraph says that at first there seemed to be signs of life in soil from Mars. Then, the word *however* signals that a contrasting idea will follow. This idea is that the soil was sterile. Therefore, the soil showed no signs of life. It must have been without organisms, or living things. (Inferences/Earth Science)

9. **(4)** All the other choices are details stated in the passage. (Details in Passages/Earth Science)

10. **(4)** This detail is in the middle of the first paragraph. (Details in Passages/Earth Science)

UNIT 3   APPLYING INFORMATION YOU READ

EXERCISE 27 (PAGE 127)

1. LSD is an **hallucinogen**. It distorted Sandy's sense of reality. Instead of seeing the cars as they were, she saw them as happy, harmless rubber things that would greet her.

2. Seconal is a **depressant**. At first it helped Richard relax because it slowed down all of bodily functions. When he needed the drug just to function, he had built up a tolerance to it.

3. Amphetamines are **stimulants**. They gave Suzanne extra energy and helped her stay thin because they speeded her bodily functions up and suppressed her appetite.

4. Percodan is an **opiate**. It relieved Charlie's pain and created a sense of euphoria. His withdrawal symptoms indicate that he became addicted to it.

5. Alcohol is a **depressant**. It relieved Carrie's anxiety so that she felt more at ease in social situations. However, her nervous system slowed down to the point that she eventually could not speak clearly or walk without stumbling. She finally fell asleep.

6. A seesaw is **a lever**. It is made of a bar that moves up and down on a fixed point at the middle. When Kathy and Alan are using it, they lift each other's weight.

7. An ax is a **wedge**. It has one thick end and one thin, sharp end. It can be used to chop or split wood.

8. The simple machine called **a wheel and axle** allows a wagon to move and carry loads.

9. A ramp is an **inclined plane**. Dominick and his friend wheeled the motorcycle up the ramp—a slanted surface—into the truck.

10. Aunt Nellie's clothesline is **a pulley**. There are wheels with grooved rims at each end that allow her to pull the rope easily.

11. This illustrates **Newton's first law**. The planets continue to move around the sun because no outside force stops them.

12. This illustrates **Newton's second law**. The 8-pound bowling ball moved down the alley faster than the 16-pound ball because it has less mass. According to the law, *the greater the mass of the object, the smaller the acceleration*. Therefore, the smaller the mass, the greater the acceleration.

13. This illustrates **Newton's third law**. The action of the bullet moving forward creates an equal and opposite reaction: The rifle kicks backward against Tom's shoulder.

14. This illustrates **Newton's third law**. When the burning gases shoot downward, the force creates an equal and opposite reaction: The rocket lifts off.

15. This illustrates **Newton's first law**. The motion of the car was stopped by an outside force, the truck. The passengers continued moving forward, because they had been moving forward, until their safety belts stopped them.

EXERCISE 28 (PAGE 132)

1. **(a)**, **(b)**, and **(e)** apply the principle of thermal expansion. (a) The liquid in a thermometer expands when it is heated. (b) Like other solids, wood expands when the temperature rises. (e) The air in tires expands in warm weather.

2. **(a)**, **(b)**, **(d)**, and **(e)** apply the principles about water that are explained in the passage. (a) Frozen water takes up more space than liquid water, so when ice melts in a glass, there is less liquid water. (b) When water freezes in a pipe during cold weather, it expands and puts pressure on the pipe, which can cause it to crack. (d) The ice on a pond floats on top of the water because it is less dense than the liquid water. (e) Without anti-freeze, the water in a car's cooling system can freeze, expand, and crack the radiator.

3. (a) **gas**; (b) **solid**; (c) **liquid**. Gas particles are the farthest apart; particles in solids are the closest together. Therefore, the particles in liquids are closer than those in a gas and farther apart than those in a solid.

4. **(3)** A gas, such as oxygen, will completely fill its container. Therefore, the oxygen will completely fill the 2-quart jar. Two cups of beans will fill a quarter of the jar, and one quart of water will fill half the jar.

5. **(3)** Alcohol boils at a temperature far below the boiling point of water, so it boils faster than water. Salt water has a higher boiling point than water, and the boiling point is higher at sea level than at higher altitudes. Both these factors indicate that salt water at sea level will take longer to boil than water above sea level.

6. **(1)** The second paragraph implies that the higher the melting point of a solid, the stronger the force of attraction between its molecules. Of the three choices, the melting point of gold is the highest, so the bond between gold molecules is the strongest.

7. (a) **mixture**; (b) **solution**; (c) **solution**; (d) **mixture**; (e) **solution**. Each of the substances in a tossed salad and in garlic salt can be seen, so they are not chemically combined. Coffee, pudding, and sterling silver, however, are solutions, because the particles that make them up are dissolved and cannot be seen.

1. **(2)** The passage says that a harder mineral scratches a softer mineral. Since stibnite scratches talc, it is harder than talc; since it is scratched by calcite, it is softer than calcite. Stabite's hardness must be between 1 and 3, therefore.

2. **(3)** Since orthoclase scratches apatite and is scratched by quartz, its hardness must be between 5 and 7.

3. **(1)** Since galena scratches gypsum and is scratched by calcite, its hardness must be between 2 and 3. Therefore, the hardness of galena is about 2½.

4. A cork will **float** in water. According to the second paragraph, a substance will float in a fluid that has greater density. According to the table, water has greater density than cork.

5. **(b)** and **(c)** Since a substance will float in a fluid with greater density, copper and aluminum will float in mercury, but gold will not.

6. Helium balloons rise **because helium is less dense than air**. The second paragraph states that less dense substances float on more dense substances.

7. **(a)** and **(b)** Because a substance will float on a fluid with greater density, both oil and solid water (ice) will float on liquid water.

8. **(1)** The passage explains the number values on the pH scale. Substances with a pH value of 7 or above are bases. An egg has a pH of about 7¾, so it is a base. A banana and vinegar each have a pH lower than 7, so they are acids.

9. **(2)** Substances with pH values lower than 7 are acids. The strongest acids have the lowest numbers. Of the choices, a lemon, with a pH of 2½, contains the most acid. The pH of an apple is about 3½. Lye, with a pH of 15, is a very strong base.

10. Milk of magnesia is **a base**. According to the sixth paragraph of the passage, when an acid and a base are combined, they neutralize each other. Since milk of magnesia neutralizes stomach acid, it is a base.

11. Limestone is **a base**. Since limestone neutralizes the acid in lakes, it must be a base.

12. **The drain cleaner most likely burned a hole through Tony's pajamas.** Lye is a very strong base with a pH of 15. The second paragraph says that strong bases are highly corrosive and can burn through material.

SCIENCE READINGS 3 (page 143)

1. *Converted* means **changed**. The second paragraph says that *matter can be converted to energy, and energy can be converted to matter*. Then, as part of an example, it says that *matter is changed into energy*, which is another way of saying *converted to energy*. These are the clues to the meaning of *converted*. (Inferences/Physics)

2. **(3)** This detail is in the fourth paragraph as part of the explanation of Einstein's formula. (Details in Passages/Physics)

3. **(1)** The second paragraph says that matter can be changed into energy. Choice (1) is an example of this. The second paragraph also says that the total amount of matter and energy remains the same. Therefore, the other choices are incorrect because they say that the amount of matter and energy changes. (Applying Information You Read/Physics)

4. **(2)** The rest of the passage is about both physical and chemical properties. (The Stated Main Idea/Chemistry)

5. **(2)** This detail is at the end of the third paragraph. (Details in Passages/Chemistry)

6. **(5)** The first sentence of the last paragraph says that *chemical properties determine how a substance reacts with other substances*. Only Choice (5) describes a reaction between two substances. All the other choices describe physical properties. (Applying Information You Read/Chemistry)

7. **(1)** The third paragraph says that during a physical change, matter changes its shape, size, or state, but that it is still made of the same molecules. When a liquid changes to a gas, it changes its state. Choices (2) and (3) are examples of chemical changes that create new kinds of molecules. (Applying Information You Read/Chemistry)

8. **(1)** When wood burns, it combines with oxygen in the air and produces ashes, gases, and smoke. Therefore, both the physical and chemical properties of the wood change, which means that a chemical change takes place. The other two choices are examples of physical changes. Chopped or painted wood is still wood: Its physical and chemical properties don't change. Only its size or color changes. (Applying Information You Read/Chemistry)

9. Table salt is made of **sodium and chlorine**. This detail is at the end of the passage. (Details in Passages/Chemistry)

10. **The sun** is the main source of energy for all living things. This detail is in the second sentence of the passage. (Details in Passages/Biology)

11. **(3)** The grass is a producer. The cow eats the grass, so it is a primary consumer. The human eats the cow, so it is a secondary consumer. (Applying Information You Read/Biology)

12. **(2)** The brown rice and vegetables are producers. The Kim family eats these plants, so the family is a primary consumer. (Applying Information You Read/Biology)

13. The frog eats the **cricket**. (Tables and Graphs/Biology)

14. The **snake** is the tertiary consumer. A tertiary consumer is an animal that eats a secondary consumer. The frog is the secondary consumer because it eats the cricket, the primary consumer. (Applying Information You Read/Biology)

15. The atomic number of tin is **50**. The number at the top of the square in the Periodic Table is the element's atomic number. Tin is the fourth element in Column 14. (Applying Information You Read/Chemistry)

16. The atomic mass of barium is **137.33**. The number at the bottom of the square in the Periodic Table is the element's atomic mass. Barium is the fifth element in Column 2. (Applying Information You Read/Chemistry)

17. **(1)** Al is the symbol for aluminum, which is the second element in Column 13 of the Periodic Table. Of the symbols listed, it is the only one made up of letters from the English name for the element. Pb is the symbol for lead, the fifth element in Column 14. Cu is the symbol for copper, the first element in Column 11. Pb is from the Latin word for lead, *plumbum.* Cu is from the Latin word for copper, *cuprum.* (Applying Information You Read/Chemistry)

18. The chemical symbol for potassium, which is the fourth element in Column 1, most likely comes from **its Latin name**. Since *potassium*, the English name, does not contain the letter K, its symbol cannot come from the English name. In fact, the *K* comes from the Latin *kalium*. (Applying Information You Read/Chemistry)

19. **(1)** The fourth paragraph says that the elements in the first column of the Periodic Table are all highly reactive metals. Of the choices, only lithium is in Column 1. Krypton and neon are in the last column. (Applying Information You Read/Chemistry)

20. Radon **does not** react easily with other elements. The fourth paragraph says that the elements in Column 18 of the table, which includes radon, are gases that rarely take part in chemical reactions. The elements in Column 1 are the ones that are highly reactive. (Applying Information You Read/Chemistry)

21. **(b) and (c)** are true. The first paragraph says that the crust is made of blocks of rock—Choice (b). The second paragraph says that a new crust is constantly being created — Choice (c). Choice (a) is wrong because the first sentence of the passage says that the earth's crust is not solid. (Details in Passages/Earth Science)

22. **(a)** and **(c)** are explained by plate tectonics. The third paragraph says that plate tectonics explains how surface features of the land, including mountains, are formed—Choice (a). The fourth and fifth paragraphs say that plate tectonics explains where earthquakes occur—at the edges of plates—Choice (c). The passage says nothing about when earthquakes occur—Choice (b). (Details in Passages/Earth Science)

23. An earthquake is **any trembling or shaking of the earth's crust**. The answer is stated in the fourth paragraph. (Details in Passages/Earth Science)

24. Earthquakes are caused by **sudden movements along faults**. The answer is stated in the fifth paragraph. (Details in Passages/Earth Science)

25. During an earthquake, the most violent shaking occurs **at the epicenter**. The answer in stated in the sixth paragraph. (Details in Passages/Earth Science)

26. **(2)** The clues you need to answer this question are in the fifth and sixth paragraphs. The fifth paragraph says that about 95 percent of earthquakes occur at the edges of plates, so Choice (1) is incorrect. The fifth and sixth paragraphs say that faults are cracks in the earth's crust and that an earthquake always begins along a fault. Therefore, Choice (3) is incorrect. It makes sense, then, that the earth's crust is most stable above the middle of plates. (Inferences/Earth Science)

GED PRACTICE 3 (page 150)

1. **(3)** According to the passage, friction works against the motion of an object. A waxed floor is more slippery than an unwaxed floor, so waxing decreases friction. All the other choices describe ways to increase the friction between objects. (Applying Information You Read/Physics)

2. **(2)** Work is performed when a force moves an object in the direction of the force. When a woman carries a box of books <u>downstairs</u>, she holds the books <u>up</u>. Therefore, the books move in the direction opposite the direction of the force. Because the books do not move in the same direction as the force, work is not performed. Choices (1), (3), (4), and (5) give examples of work. In each case, a person applies force to an object and moves the object in the direction of the force. (Applying Information You Read/Physics)

3. **(3)** According to the table, C is the symbol for carbon, and H is the symbol for hydrogen. Therefore, the chemical formula CH shows that carbon and hydrogen make up methane. (Applying Information You Read/Chemistry)

4. **(2)** The passage says that there are two hydrogen atoms in a molecule of water—H_2O. You can infer that in a chemical formula, a number after the symbol for an element shows how many atoms of that element are in a molecule of a compound. Therefore, in Freon there are two atoms of chlorine. (Applying Information You Read/Chemistry)

5. **(2)** Most of the passage is about the dangers to health posed by ground-level ozone. (The Stated Main Idea/Chemistry)

6. **(3)** The passage states that the ozone level is dangerous when it is higher than 120 parts per billion, and that time outdoors should be limited when the level is that high. According to the line graph, the ozone level in Anaheim on a typical day is highest, and exceeds 120 parts per billion, between 11:00 A.M. and 4:00 P.M. Therefore, the worst time to exercise outdoors is between these hours. (Applying Information You Read/Chemistry)

7. **(1)** The second paragraph says that the hotter the weather, the higher the ozone level. The last paragraph says that exercising outside when the ozone level is high can cause a decrease in lung function. Therefore, of the choices, jogging in a park is the least healthy way to exercise because it is an outdoor activity. (Applying Information You Read/Chemistry)

8. **(4)** The first paragraph says that the ozone layer protects the earth from UV rays but that it has a hole in it caused by human use of CFCs. The fourth paragraph says that UV rays harm living things. Therefore, if the ozone layer is not protected, UV rays will probably cause increasing harm to living things. (Details in Passages/Chemistry)

9. **(2)** The third paragraph says that ozone is made up of three atoms of oxygen. It also says that when a chlorine atom pulls one of the three oxygen atoms away from ozone, the kind of oxygen we breathe is left. Therefore, the oxygen we breathe is made up of two atoms. (Inferences/Chemistry)

10. **(3)** The fourth paragraph says that it takes a CFC molecule as long as 10 years to travel to the ozone layer. It also says that a CFC atom is active in destroying ozone for as long as 130 years. Therefore, CFCs that began floating toward the ozone layer yesterday will still be active as long as 140 years from now. (Inferences/Chemistry)

UNIT 4 ANALYZING AND EVALUATING WHAT YOU READ

EXERCISE 30 (PAGE 155)

Part A

1. **apple**
2. **sink**
3. **aluminum**

Part B

1. The irrelevant word on the list is **lungs** because it names part of the respiratory system. A possible replacement word is **veins**.

2. The irrelevant word on the list is **galaxies** because it is the name for groups of solar systems, not parts of one solar system. Possible replacement words are **planets** and **comets**.

3. The irrelevant word on the list is **ozone** because it names a gas. Possible replacement words are **aluminum**, **lead**, **steel**, or the name of any other metal.

EXERCISE 31 (PAGE 156)

Part A

1. **Sentence 3** is irrelevant to the main idea. All the other sentences in the paragraph support the main idea by giving examples of ways energy changes forms. Sentence 3 introduces a new idea about the amount of gas different cars use.

2. **Sentence 4** is irrelevant to the main idea. All the other sentences explain how electricity is produced in an electric generator. Sentence 4 is about cars.

3. **Sentence 5** is irrelevant to the main idea. All the other sentences support the main idea by telling how power plants get the energy they need to make electricity. Sentence 5, however, is about air pollution caused by burning coal.

4. **Sentence 5** is irrelevant to the main idea. All the other sentences in the paragraph are about nuclear energy and how it is used to generate electricity. Sentence 5, however, is about the Nuclear Regulatory Commission.

Part B

1. **Sentence 1**

2. **Sentence 5** is irrelevant to the main idea. All the other sentences support the main idea by describing fossil fuels. Sentence 5 is irrelevant to the main idea because it is about carbon monoxide.

3. **Sentence 1**

4. **Sentence 3** is irrelevant to the main idea. All the other sentences support the main idea by telling how fossil fuels were formed. Sentence 3 is not about how fossil fuels were formed. It's about bones found in sediments.

5. **Sentence 5**

6. **Sentence 2** is irrelevant to the main idea. All the other sentences explain why fossil fuels are useful as energy sources because of their chemical composition. Sentence 2, however, is about carbon, not fossil fuels.

7. **Sentence 2**

8. **Sentence 1** is irrelevant to the main idea. All the other sentences describe the four kinds of coal and how they are formed. Since Sentence 1 is about the use of coal as a fuel, it does not belong in this paragraph.

EXERCISE 32 (PAGE 162)

1. **Fact**
2. **Fact**
3. **Opinion**
4. **Fact**
5. **Opinion**
6. **Fact**
7. **Fact**
8. **Fact**
9. **Fact**
10. **Opinion**
11. **Opinion**
12. **Fact**
13. **Fact**
14. **Fact**
15. **Fact**
16. **Fact**
17. **Opinion**
18. **Opinion**
19. **Opinion**
20. **Fact**

EXERCISE 33 (PAGE 165)

1. **Sentences 2** and **5** state facts.
2. **Sentences 1, 3, 4, 6, 7, 8, 9,** and **10** express opinions.
3. **Sentence 6** expresses an opinion.
4. The passage is made up mainly of **facts**.
5. **Sentences 1, 6,** and **7** state facts.
6. **Sentences 2, 3, 4, 5, 8,** and **9** express opinions.

EXERCISE 34 (PAGE 169)

1. **(2)** Although there are many reasons why water would make an excellent major energy source, as Choice (3) suggests, there are not many places in the world where dams can be built. Choice (1) is not supported by the passage, which does not discuss the cost of building power plants.

2. **(3)** Coal, natural gas, and oil are all fossil fuels. Together they provide 90%—nearly all—of the energy used in the United States.

3. **(3)** The passage states that solar collectors are painted black. If the purpose of solar collectors is to collect the sun's energy, then the black paint must help them absorb energy. Choice (1) is not supported because passive solar energy is available only when the sun is shining. Choice (2) is not supported by the passage, which does not discuss costs.

4. **(1)** According to the table, gasoline, jet fuel, and asphalt and road oil account for the use of 58.9% of all oil. Therefore, more than half of the crude oil in a barrel is used for transportation. Choice (2) is not supported by the table, since it doesn't show how much fuel oil is used in homes for heating. The table shows several useful crude oil products, so Choice (3) is not supported.

5. **(2)** The second paragraph states that fusion reactions take place only at temperatures of at least 100,000,000°C. It implies that fusion reactions take place on the sun. These two pieces of information combined support Choice (2). Choice (1) is not supported because the passage implies that fusion reactions take place on the stars where matter must exist as plasma, not liquid, at such high temperatures. Choice (3) is also not supported because the passage does not compare the amount of energy produced by fission and fusion.

EXERCISE 35 (PAGE 173)

1. **(a)** The sun heats the earth unevenly and indirectly causes wind. Choices (b) and (c) do not support a statement about the source of wind power.

2. **(a)** and **(b)** The fact that solar energy is free, as Choice (a) says, is a benefit. Another benefit is the great quantity of energy from the sun that reaches the earth, as described in Choice (b). Choice (c) does not mention a benefit; rather, it mentions a problem with solar energy.

3. **(b)** and **(c)** That fusion reactions don't cause explosions—Choice (b)—or produce radioactive waste— Choice (c)—makes them safer than fission reactions, which do. That fusion reactions must take place at high temperatures does not make them more or less safe than fission reactions—Choice (a).

4. **(c)** Geothermal energy is not a major source of energy mainly because it can't be reached. Because geothermal energy is limitless—Choice (a)—it could be a major source of energy if it could be reached. That it is used in some places—Choice (b)—does not make it a <u>major</u> source of energy.

5. **(b)** and **(c)** Owning electrical appliances and having more than one car per family certainly make life more comfortable. However, these comforts require energy, which increases the demand. Recycling—Choice (a)—doesn't increase the demand for more energy.

SCIENCE READINGS 4 (page 175)

1. A. **(3)**; B. **(1)**; C. **(4)**; D. **(2)**. (Applying Information You Read/Science)

2. The three kinds of muscles are **smooth**, **cardiac**, and **skeletal**. These details are in the fourth paragraph. (Details in Passages/Biology)

3. Skeletal muscles **move all the parts of the body**. This detail is in the sixth paragraph. (Details in Passages/Biology)

4. **Voluntary muscles move only when you want them to, but involuntary muscles move on their own.** Involuntary muscles are defined in the fourth paragraph, voluntary muscles, in the sixth paragraph. (Details in Passages/Biology)

5. When the triceps contracts, **the biceps relaxes**. The next-to-last paragraph says that the triceps and biceps work as a pair: When the biceps contracts, the triceps relaxes. You can infer that the opposite is also true. (Inferences/Biology)

6. **(2)** The last sentence says that muscles that are not used shrink. Sara did not use the muscles in her broken leg for 6 weeks. (Applying Information You Read/Biology)

7. **(2)** The second paragraph compares the gases in the atmosphere to a greenhouse. It implies that the gases act the same way glass does in a greenhouse. (Inferences/Earth Science)

8. **Carbon dioxide (CO_2)** is the major cause of the greenhouse effect. This detail is in the fourth paragraph. (Details in Passages/Earth Science)

9. **(1)** The paragraph explains the chain of causes and effects that produce the greenhouse effect. (Patterns of Organization/Earth Science)

10. **(5)** The main idea of the paragraph is in the first sentence. The other sentences support it by giving examples of how life on Earth may change. The last sentence, however, does not. It is about the amounts of greenhouse gases generated in the United States. (Relevant and Irrelevant Information/Earth Science)

11. **(3)** The third paragraph says that the oceans could rise and that there could be a sharp decrease in rainfall. These details support Choices (1) and (2). There is nothing in the passage that ties global warming to a change in the size of the population. (Conclusions and Supporting Information/Earth Science)

12. **(1)** The second paragraph says that the gases that cause the greenhouse effect *accumulate* in the atmosphere. The fifth paragraph says that the amount of <u>extra</u> CO_2 in the atmosphere could be <u>reduced</u> (not cut down to none) if we stopped burning fossil fuels. It is logical to conclude from this information that continued burning <u>at the current rate</u> will cause an increase in CO_2. (Conclusions and Supporting Information/Earth Science)

13. **Sixteen pounds.** The bar for oil reaches up to *16* on the vertical axis of the graph. (Tables and Graphs/Earth Science)

14. **(2)** According to the passage, carbon dioxide is the major cause of the greenhouse effect. Of the fuels shown on the bar graph, coal releases the most CO_2. Therefore, when coal is burned, it pollutes the atmosphere more than any other fossil fuel. Choices (1) and (3) are both wrong because the graph shows that wood, which is not a fossil fuel, produces CO_2, which pollutes the atmosphere. (Conclusions and Supporting Information/Earth Science)

15. A. **(6)**; B. **(8)**; C. **(3)**; D. **(2)**; E. **(5)**; F. **(1)**; G. **(4)**; H. **(7)**. The definitions of the terms, which are printed in dark type in the passage, are scattered throughout the passage. (Details in Passages/Physics)

16. **(3)** On the visible light spectrum, indigo is the farthest to the right of all the colors listed in the choices. A wavy line near the top of the figure shows that frequencies are higher toward the right end of the scale. Therefore, indigo is at the end of the scale with the highest frequency (Applying Information You Read/Physics)

17. **(2)** On the electromagnetic spectrum, radio waves are the farthest waves to the left. The fifth paragraph of the passage says that the energy level is higher for high-frequency waves—the waves toward the right end of the electromagnetic spectrum. Therefore, radio waves are at the end of the scale with the least amount of energy. (Applying Information You Read/Physics)

18. Electricity is a form of **energy**. This detail is in the first sentence. (Details in Passages/Physics)

19. **(2)** The fourth paragraph says that batteries supply direct current. A portable radio uses batteries. (Applying Information You Read/Physics)

20. When a fuse blows in a circuit, **the flow of electricity stops**. The sixth paragraph says that electricity cannot flow through an open circuit. The last paragraph says that when a fuse melts, the circuit opens. With these two pieces of information, you can infer the answer. (Inferences/Physics)

21. **(3)** The third paragraph says that things with opposite charges attract each other. Therefore, for the clothes to stick together, some must have positive charges and some must have negative charges. They move toward each other just a hair moves toward a comb. (Applying Information You Read/Physics)

22. **(2)** The light bulb in the figure is giving off light, so electricity is flowing to it. The sixth paragraph says that electricity can flow only through a closed circuit. (Applying Information You Read/Physics)

23. **(3)** The fifth paragraph says that appliances change electrical energy to another form of energy. The diagram shows electrical energy changed to light energy. (Applying Information You Read/Physics)

24. Lightning is a form of **static electricity**. This detail is at the beginning of the second paragraph. (Details in Passages/Physics)

25. In an open field, **the person would be the tallest object around, so lightning might strike the person on its way to the ground**. The fourth paragraph says that lightning follows the shortest path to the ground by striking the tallest thing around. (Applying Information You Read/Physics)

26. **(4)** The last paragraph explains why one of the safest places to be during a thunderstorm is in a car. Of the choices, sitting in an airplane waiting to take off is most similar to being inside a car. In all the other choices, a person could be a target for lightning. (Applying Information You Read/Physics)

27. **(4)** The main idea of the paragraph is in the first sentence. All the sentences except the fourth support this idea by describing how much electric energy lightning contains. (Relevant and Irrelevant Information/Physics)

28. **(2)** Since lightning rods are made of metal and provide a path to the ground for lightning, as the fourth paragraph says, it makes sense to conclude that lightning travels easily through metal. There is nothing in the passage to support Choice (1). Choice (3) is an invalid conclusion. If lightning did not strike buildings, there would be no need for lightning rods. (Conclusions and Supporting Information/Physics)

GED PRACTICE 4 (page 184)

1. **(5)** The heating of residences, or space heating, accounts for 48% of the energy used. Heating water accounts for 14%. The total of the two is 62%. (Tables and Graphs/Physics)

2. **(3)** Of all the appliances shown in the table, a clothes dryer uses the most electrical power—4000 watts. (Tables and Graphs/Physics)

3. **(1)** Exploding a firecracker is the only choice that involves a chemical reaction in which heat or light energy is released. Choice (2) is an example of an endothermic reaction because heat is absorbed. Choices (3), (4), and (5) are not chemical reactions. (Applying Information You Read/Chemistry and Physics)

4. **(5)** Since the metals silver, copper, and aluminum are excellent conductors, it is logical to conclude that metals are good conductors. There is not enough information in the passage to support Choices (1) and (2). Choices (3) and (4) do not make sense based on the information in the passage. Plastic cannot both allow and prevent the flow of electricity. Metals, since they are are excellent conductors, cannot be good insulators. (Conclusions and Supporting Information/Physics)

5. **(1)** All the other choices state facts that can be proved. Choice (1) expresses an opinion with which you may or may not agree. It cannot be proved (Facts and Opinions/Earth Science)

6. **(3)** As the first paragraph says, white light, or sunlight, is made up of the seven colors of the visible spectrum—Choices (1), (2), and (4). These colors are seen in a rainbow—Choice (5). A prism does not <u>contain</u> the colors. Rather, it breaks sunlight into the seven colors. (Inferences/Physics)

7. **(2)** The passage explains that when hydrogen atoms fuse to create helium atoms, the matter lost in the fusion reaction changes into heat and light energy. This explains why stars shine. None of the other choices are discussed in the passage. (Conclusions and Supporting Information/Physics)

8. **(5)** According to the first paragraph, all elements with atomic numbers greater than 83 are radioactive. Of the choices, the only element with an atomic number greater than 83 is radon. (Applying Information You Read/Chemistry and Physics)

9. **(1)** A stable element must have an atomic number lower than 83. The second paragraph explains that uranium breaks down until it becomes lead, which is stable, or not radioactive. Of the choices, only the first could be the atomic number of lead, because it is the only number lower than 83. (Applying Information You Read/Chemistry and Physics)

10. **(5)** The second paragraph explains that the effects of different doses of radiation on the human body are different. Choices (1) and (4) are not supported because low doses do not necessarily result in death or produce noticeable symptoms. The passage says nothing about Choices (2) and (3). (Conclusions and Supporting Information/Physics)

POSTTEST (page 189)

1. **(4)** The second paragraph explains what vaccines are and how they produce antibodies and immunity—concepts introduced in the first paragraph. The last paragraph tells about the first use of a vaccine. (Comprehending What You Read/Prereading Strategies/Biology)

2. **(5)** The last sentence says that a person infected with cowpox virus develops immunity to smallpox, not to all diseases. (Comprehending What You Read/Details in Passages/Biology)

3. **(4)** All the other choices are facts: They can be proved. You can agree or disagree that Jenner was brilliant. (Analyzing and Evaluating What You Read/Facts and Opinions/Biology)

4. **(5)** The paragraph describes the benefits of aerobic exercise for the the heart, the capillaries (parts of the circulatory system), and the lungs (part of the respiratory system). Choice (3) is too narrow to be the main idea. The paragraph doesn't include any of the ideas mentioned in the other choices. (Inferring As You Read/The Implied Main Idea/Biology)

5. **(4)** Early divers used water bladders to carry air under water just as they used their lungs. (Inferring As You Read/Inferences/Earth Science)

6. **(1)** The second paragraph says that sponge divers knew that the more air they could take under water, the longer they could stay down. Since water bladders enabled them to take more air under water, the bladders helped divers stay down longer. (Inferring As You Read/Inferences/Earth Science)

7. **(3)** The first paragraph talks about one way bacteria benefit plants and animals, and the second paragraph talks about how bacteria harm people. (Inferring As You Read/The Implied Main Idea/Biology)

8. **(2)** Meningitis is mentioned in a sentence that lists diseases, so you can infer that it is a disease. (Inferring As You Read/Inferences/Biology)

9. **(3)** The second paragraph tells about the causes of osteoporosis, and the third paragraph tells about its effects. (Comprehending What You Read/Patterns of Organization/Biology)

10. **(3)** The third paragraph is about the effects of osteoporosis, not about U.S. bone fracture statistics. (Analyzing and Evaluating What You Read/Relevant and Irrelevant Information/Biology)

11. **(4)** The word *osteoporosis* describes a "condition" in which "bone" becomes overly "porous." (Comprehending What You Read/Word Parts/Biology)

12. **(4)** The examples in the paragraph show how soon certain organs must be transplanted. Each organ mentioned has a different time limit, so it is reasonable to conclude that some organs last outside the body longer than others. (Analyzing and Evaluating What You Read/Conclusions and Supporting Information/Biology)

13. **(2)** At 0.1% BAC a person has difficulty walking and driving, which require coordination. Before that, only judgment is affected. (Comprehending What You Read/Tables and Graphs/Biology)

14. **(1)** According to the table, a person does not lose consciousness until the BAC level is 0.45%. All the other choices are associated with BACs of 0.3% or lower. (Comprehending What You Read/Tables and Graphs/Biology)

15. **(2)** The second paragraph lists the effects of lead poisoning, but it doesn't mention blindness. (Comprehending What You Read/Details in Passages/Chemistry)

16. **(3)** If you ingest water only from the cold-water tap, you do not drink or cook with water from the hot-water pipes. Therefore, there is no reason to flush them. (Inferring As You Read/Inferences/Chemistry)

17. **(1)** The line graph shows that the human population has grown quickly in the last 1000 years. This suggests that it will continue to grow. The information in the graph does not support Choice (3) or suggest the reasons for population sizes offered in Choices (2), (4), and (5). (Analyzing and Evaluating What You Read/Conclusions and Supporting Information/Biology)

18. **(4)** This detail is at the end of the third paragraph. (Comprehending What You Read/Details in Passages/Biology)

19. **(2)** The whole passage is about the causes and effects of nearsightedness and farsightedness and the means to correct both. The other choices are all too narrow to be the main idea. (Comprehending What You Read/The Stated Main Idea/Biology)

20. **(2)** The third paragraph says farsightedness *occurs when light rays from nearby objects are focused behind the retina* because *the eyeball is too short*. The diagram in Choice (2) shows these aspects of hyperopia. (Applying Information You Read/Biology)

21. **(3)** The last paragraph says that concave lenses, which are thinner in the middle than at the edges, correct myopia. Choice 3 shows such a lens. (Applying Information You Read/Biology)

22. **(4)** The first paragraph says that the solute is what is dissolved. In a solution of hot chocolate, the powdered chocolate is dissolved. (Applying Information You Read/Chemistry)

23. **(4)** Because turpentine cleans paint brushes by dissolving the paint, it is a solvent. (Applying Information You Read/Chemistry)

24. **(5)** The third paragraph is about ways consumers can create less solid waste, such as paper products which are used and discarded. That is the clue to the meaning of *disposable*. (Inferring As You Read/Inferences/Earth Science)

25. **(3)** The passage, including the last paragraph, is about ways to decrease the amount of solid waste. Therefore, Choices (1), (2), and (5) are incorrect. Recycling can take care of only part of the problem, as the last two sentences say, therefore Choice (4) is not right. This leaves *reduce* as the best answer. (Inferring As You Read/Inferences/Earth Science)

26. **(1)** The first paragraph says that glaciers, which are made of ice and snow, cover 90% of Antarctica. You can infer that the weather there must be very cold most of the time. (Inferring As You Read/Inferences/Earth Science)

27. **(4)** The last sentence says that only 10% of an iceberg is above water, therefore, 90% is below water. (Inferring As You Read/Inferences/Earth Science)

28. **(1)** All the details in the second paragraph are about the two factors, temperature and elasticity, that affect the rate at which sound travels. The other choices are too narrow to be the main main idea. (Comprehending What You Read/The Stated Main Idea/Physics)

29. **(3)** The *Seawater* row of the table shows that sound travels at 1531 meters per second through this medium. (Comprehending What You Read/Tables and Graphs/Physics)

30. **(3)** The table is organized with the slowest sound travel in the first row and the fastest in the last row. The first row is *Carbon dioxide*. (Comprehending What You Read/Tables and Graphs/Physics)

31. **(5)** The last paragraph says that sound *travels faster through more-elastic materials*. Of the choices given, sound travels fastest through stone. Therefore, stone is the most elastic solid among the choices. (Applying Information You Read/Physics)

32. **(3)** During nuclear fission atoms are split artificially. Since the process is artificial, it cannot produce a natural result. The passage mentions all the other choices as products of fission. (Comprehending What You Read/Details in Passages/Physics)

33. **(1)** The end of the first paragraph says that elements with an atomic number over 90 can be made to undergo fission. Of the choices, only plutonium has an atomic number greater than 90. (Applying Information You Read/Physics)

PHOTO AND ILLUSTRATION CREDITS